THE IRISH AT CHELTENHAM

THE IRISH AT CHELTENHAM

EOGHAN CORRY ~

Gill & Macmillan

Gill & Macmillan Ltd
Hume Avenue, Park West, Dublin 12
with associated companies throughout the world
www.gillmacmillan.ie

© Eoghan Corry 2009
978 07171 4666 6

Index compiled by Cover to Cover
Type design by Make Communication
Print origination by Carole Lynch
Printed and bound in Great Britain by MPG Books Ltd,
Bodmin, Cornwall

This book is typeset in Linotype Minion.

The paper used in this book comes from the wood
pulp of managed forests. For every tree felled, at least
one tree is planted, thereby renewing natural
resources.

A CIP catalogue record for this book is available from
the British Library.

5 4 3 2 1

To Sheila Milne,
racegoer, friend and mother-in-law

And to the memory of Colm Maguire (1962–2008)
with whom I stood at the rails of many a national
hunt meeting and who has gone prematurely to the
winner's enclosure in the sky

CONTENTS

PREFACE

Where best to begin our story of the Irish love affair with Cheltenham?

Shall we start at the end, after the first decade of the twenty-first century has brought national hunt silverware to newly prosperous Ireland on a scale never seen before, silverware carried home to Adare and Alasty?

Or shall we start where the records bring us, to the days of civil war when Algy Anthony came home, after taking a gamble at Cheltenham, two chances for the price of one, and winning his second with Ireland's alleged first success at Cheltenham, only to die within eighteen months like an archaeologist who opened Tutankhamen's tomb and perished under its curse?

Or with Frank Morris, the first to nab a Gold Cup, when the Gold Cup was noted for its outlandishly pretentious name rather than its status on the calendar?

Or further back again into the mists of prehistory before there was a festival in Cheltenham or even organised steeplechasing, when James Knaresborough rode over the course against Captain Becher (of the Brook) on his feted Irish champion hunter, appropriately called in the heady days midway between Emancipation and Repeal, Dan O'Connell? Ireland's great equine battle against England was won by England, and the nation mourned.

Or should it begin with the greatest Anglo-Irish contest of all, between Arkle and Mill House, the sporting event that ushered two nations into the television age?

Or perhaps with the great horses that turned Cheltenham into an event in itself, not just a preliminary for the Aintree Grand National, Easter Hero and Golden Miller?

Or their modern counterparts in four-legged folklore, L'Escargot, Best Mate, Dawn Run and Istabraq?

Maybe we should start with all of them. Maybe we should find out what happens when a Cheltenham champion is born.

Is there a portent? Is there a star? Are there wise men making their way to the stable? Is there frankincense and myrrh?

Because we surely know now there is gold.

Chapter 1 ~

'WILL HE MAKE IT TO CHELTENHAM?'

It is easy enough to breed a horse that will get across the
country with a light weight on his back, and many
thoroughbred horses of no great value as hunters make
very good steeplechase horses, but to carry a man above 12
stone across all sorts of ground and over all kinds of fences
safely and pleasantly, a horse must have good shape and
good size, both height and substance, and must be capable
of going for a long time at a fast, though not a racing,
pace. Thoroughbred horses seldom answer this description,
or if they do, they are commonly too valuable for racing
purposes to be attainable for hunting purposes. Though a
good hunter should have a thoroughbred sire, the dam
should have more size and substance. And this is one of the
great difficulties of hunter breeding. It is scarcely possible
to tell beforehand whether a mare, herself large and
powerful, will throw colts equal to herself in power.
The Economist, 12 May 1866

The birth of a foal on an Irish farmstead is an enchanting and spiritual event. The drop to the ground with an undignified thump is a precursor for all the life experiences that lie ahead of the newborn.

It is an event where you find speculation and jubilation in equal amounts. The stable hands around often make an assessment of the prospects of the young horse in the minutes after he is born. When Arkle arrived at 3.30 am on 19 April 1957 in Ballymacoll Stud, between Maynooth and Dunboyne in Co. Meath, his prospects of ever making the big time were written off with one look.

One of the greatest stallions ever, The Tetrarch, won fame in his first hours for surviving a frosty night alone when he arrived unexpectedly early in a field rather than the stable, an indication that he was something special.

Birdcatcher's birth was accompanied by a thunderstorm, if folk memory from the early nineteenth century is to be believed. Even earlier, John Archibald's 1745 champion mare Irish Lass was said to have had a pair of wings attached to her heart when her body was cut open after her death.

There are legends told about the birth of other great champions that suggest their greatness was apparent as they were born. Trainers, riders and stable hands have a long list of superstitions and traditions which they feel will indicate if fame and fortune lies ahead for them. Cork All Star was nominated by his owner Cathal Ryan as a future Cheltenham champion before he had walked, never mind run.

We know an extraordinary amount about every newborn horse as soon as it arrives. The tracking of the genealogy of horses is much more extensive and sophisticated than that accorded to mere humans. You can find the same champions back in the bloodlines of the champions, Nearco, Birdcatcher, Eclipse and the official four thoroughbred horses from which every champion is descended, including The Byerley Turk which was ridden at the Battle of the Boyne.

Newborn horses don't know whether they are going to race on the flat or over jumps. Many are tried on the flat first and only after a few failures are they sent to hurdles or fences. A good horseman can tell whether it is worth rushing the horse off to compete in the sprints as a 2 and 3-year old and retire, or to wait for five, six, seven or even eight years before sending the horse off on the winter circuit of hurdles and jumps.

If that is the case, there is only one question on everyone's lips. Will he make it to Cheltenham?

Cheltenham represents the irresistible qualities of a game which, at its best, is one of the most natural and attractive metaphors for life that sport has to offer.

HUGH McILVANNEY

What makes Cheltenham so special for everyone to want their horse to run there?

At first glance it seems to be the one event on the racing calendar when the top horses over all distances can be guaranteed to be in action. If a horse doesn't run at Cheltenham, it is either injured or it doesn't have any ambitions.

The racecourse has special characteristics of its own, not least the availability of three courses, the old, the new and the cross-country course. By switching from one course to the other, the organisers can avoid excessive wear on any of them. The range of terrain on offer helps the organisers prepare the ground in ways that one-course venues cannot.

Cheltenham's trump card was not the decision to award it the 'National Hunt Steeplechase' in 1904, although that was important, but two decisions in the 1920s to stage the Gold Cup and the Champion Hurdle.

At the time weight-for-age races for jumpers were relatively rare. The only significant non-handicap races at the time were the National Hunt Steeplechase at Cheltenham and the Champion Steeplechase at Aintree.

The Gold Cup and, a few years later, the Champion Hurdle, were both outstanding successes. Within a short period of time they became recognised as the principal races at the national hunt festival.

The Champion Hurdle has always been what its name implies, while the Gold Cup is acknowledged as the greatest test of jumping, stamina and courage for staying steeplechasers. By the 1950s it was no longer considered simply as a warm-up race for the Aintree Grand National but as a pinnacle event in its own right. Gold Cup winners have nowhere to go but the following year's Gold Cup, for which a surprising number of them are already installed as favourites by the ante-post market within minutes of winning the race.

Despite the impressive list of sponsored races that have been added to the growing list of richly endowed contests, the Gold Cup and Champion Hurdle, along with the unique Aintree Grand National, stand out as the three most important races of the national hunt season.

Cheltenham provides an important gateway into the ritual of the sport. While Gaelic games have a straightforward county system, rugby a provincial system and soccer a club system to catch the attention of the curious, those entering the world of racing have to negotiate a bewildering array of grade 1 and grade 2 races, classics, races on the flat, over hurdles and fences, ages, handicaps, SPs, ante-post odds, weights, ages and distances.

Aintree's Grand National is a lure, one thundering rollicking endurance test over fences with a clear first, second and third place that comes around every year, equally accessible and comprehensible. For the punter or the follower, Cheltenham is the gateway into a wider racing world. It provides a climax and a focus that the flat season so badly lacks.

For the horseman there is another dimension. It is a nostalgic place. Walking around Cheltenham racecourse during the festival is like stepping into a time warp in which tweed is a compulsory uniform and no head can be seen uncovered by a trilby or a flat cap.

Cheltenham is a course that simulates traditional hunting terrain. Unlike Aintree, Sandown, Kempton and the rest, Prestbury Park is not an enclosed racehorse forum built at a convenient location for an urban audience. Its stands and ancillaries were designed around eighteenth-century hunting gallops. That has the effect of bringing national hunt racing back to its roots, still a long way from the horns and hounds, but with enough of a hint of it to count.

It would not be easy to prove that this endears Cheltenham even more to Irish horsemen, but it is worth noticing that Punchestown was the original national hunt course built on hunting terrain, rather than the other way round, as with Leopardstown and Fairyhouse.

It is also worth noticing that since the addition of the cross-country course at Cheltenham in 2005, Irish-trained horses won the first cross-country chases and just three English-trained horses were among the fifteen placed horses over those five years.

> Cheltenham has its place in the slipstream of eternal questions, where people ask: Has anybody seen my hat? What's for dinner? Who'll win the Gold Cup?
>
> BILL BARICH, *A Fine Place to Daydream* (2005)

And that is it, despite what racing fans will tell you.

They will try to convince you that Cheltenham is a gateway to the gods, the greatest connect between sporting culture and real life that you will come across. They may be right, but we have to go beyond the meeting itself to reach that metaphysical state.

When you get beyond the unique selling point of Cheltenham, you meet the astonishing amount of four-legged folklore that has been accumulated by the event as a cultural showpiece in its own right.

Owners, trainers, jockeys and punters will happily forgo more lucrative successes elsewhere for the experience of winning just one event at Cheltenham. Racing fans will tell you, at length, how special it is. The two furlong finish up the killing hill makes for great finishes to otherwise forgettable races. The length of the key race, the Gold Cup, and its 22 stout birch fences leave little room for error. Even Arkle crashed through a fence at Cheltenham, the eleventh, in 1966.

But these trials are peripheral and even a threat to Cheltenham. Tough courses kill horses and have long gone out of fashion.

They will tell you it is the Mecca of jump racing, except for the 18,000 bottles of Champagne and the 214,000 pints of Guinness which presumably are not consumed during the Haj, and the array of Catholic priests, led at one stage by the iconic Father Breen.

One of RTÉ's favourite racing recordings is a comment by aviation magnate Michael O'Leary, in the flush of his horse's Gold Cup victory in 2005, that 'Cheltenham is the Olympics of national hunt racing.'

He has a point. All the best are there, except the same place gets awarded it every year, and as Jack Houghton of Betfair.com says: 'There's no synchronised swimming.'

Trilby-hatted English television personality John McCririck describes the lure of Cheltenham as 'the natural amphitheatre, the hype, the anticipation, and the Irish. Much as we hate the Irish, they do make Cheltenham.' (He was being ironic, we hope.)

> The owners and the trainers, the stable boys and jockeys
> With silk around their arses getting up on rich men's horses
> The convention wives and daughters and marriages and divorces.
> Hey Ruby hold her back, give her the crack and up she'll go.
> 'The Ballad of Ruby Walsh', CHRISTY MOORE

McCririck touched on an important point, that only three countries compete in the so-called Olympics of national hunt.

Wherever horses race, either with a jockey bouncing around uncomfortably on their backs or a man sitting in a sulky, there are just three main disciplines: flat racing, jumping over hurdles and fences, and trotting.

Ireland has no high grade trotting; Northern Europe, the United States and Australia stage little steeplechasing; just France has a presence in all three.

France and Britain still regard jumping over fences or hurdles (or 'national hunt' as it has been known since the 1860s) as a poor relation, often racing the cast-offs of flat racing. In Ireland, where suspicion of the wealth and snobbery of flat racing has always been highest, racing over jumps is still regarded as the more natural and purer form of the sport.

So while runners from Eastern Europe (particularly in the Cross-Country Chase) and Germany are becoming more common, the fact remains that only three countries compete in the Olympics of horse racing, and it is naturally going to be Ireland where the impact of national hunt is going to be greatest. Hence the emergence of the great Anglo-Irish battles of the second half of the twentieth century, headlined by Arkle v Mill House in 1964, and an unofficial festival scorecard since the heyday of Vincent O'Brien in the 1950s.

The scorecard was once delineated by birthplace, scoring which country had bred the most winners, before Irish trainers began to compete successfully against English trainers. In the TV age, when the riders themselves became the celebrities of the sport, it extended to jockeys as well.

Ireland supplies one-sixth of the 350-odd runners at the festival and they win about a third of the races. Most years Ireland can expect to win between four and six races.

In 1958 Irish-trained horses won 8 of the 18 races, 7 out of 18 in 1977, 6 out of 18 in 1979 and 1982, 10 out of 26 in 2007, 9 out of 24 in 2005 (when Irish jockeys rode 18 winners) and 9 out of 26 in 2009 (when Irish jockeys rode 21 winners and the English 5: just one of the British winning jockeys was a professional).

The worst year for the Irish was 1989 with no winners. It is often pointed out that there were no Irish winners in 1947, but that year's festival was devastated by the harshest winter on record and when it was reconvened the six main races were run off in one day with just three Irish contestants, Cool Customer and Happy Home in the Gold Cup and Mill Boy in the Grand Annual Steeplechase.

Legend tells of an Irishman who won enough on Istabraq in the Champion Hurdle of 1998 to pay off his mortgage and then lost his house on Dorans Pride in the Gold Cup. It was only a small house anyway, he is reputed to have said.

WWW.CHELTENHAMRACES.COM

Each Irish success sets the mood for the festival. Ireland's supporters, having been treated with whimsical tolerance in the early days, are now lauded as central to Cheltenham's pageantry.

Of the festival's daily attendance (capped at 55,000 on Tuesday, Wednesday and Thursday and 65,000 on Friday, Gold Cup day), a third come from Gloucestershire and the local hinterland, another third from London and the South East, a quarter from Wales and north England, and around 5,000 from Ireland.

'People speculate about 10,000 and 15,000 Irish,' Cheltenham managing director Edward Gillespie said, 'but all we can track is about 5,000. It seems that a lot of Irish in Britain come to the meeting and a lot of people emerge from elsewhere claiming to be Irish.'

Joe Tully, the tour operator who transports most of the Irish, says the figure has always been overstated and has hovered between 3,000 and 5,000 since the early 1970s when they first started travelling in numbers. Joe's father landed the first Boeing 747 at Birmingham Airport filled with Irish racegoers in 1979, when an airport strike threatened to prevent the exodus. They were unable to use a 747 for the return journey because of the runway length at Birmingham. Another strike by Aer Lingus in 1978 also disrupted travel to the festival.

Paddy Dignam, a veteran travel journalist who was once a Stena sales manager, says that in the heyday of the coach trips before the advent of low-cost airlines, Stena transported 1,500 to Cheltenham by ferry.

'People from the Home Counties will come here and behave as if they are Irish for a week,' Gillespie explained to *The Guardian* in 2009, 'in a way that they couldn't if they went to Sandown Park.'

Those that come every March are a hardy group of travellers. 'Cheltenham is the coldest place on the planet,' says EU Social Affairs Commissioner Charlie McCreevy, the man who once scheduled his budget speech to the Dáil as Minister for Finance to avoid missing a big race at Cheltenham. 'When you stand at the rails at the bottom of that hill with the wind coming down from the Cotswolds, it could be Vladivostok or Antarctica.'

Hence the fact that the attendance is almost exclusively male. Society women don't show up with flowers and bananas in their hats like they do on Derby Day at the Curragh or at Galway or Ascot. Welsh-born PR executive Carly Reed, who won the best-dressed award on ladies' day at Cheltenham in 2008, reckoned it may have been because she was the only lady there. 'There we were, my best friend and I, at Cheltenham racecourse on a cold and rainy ladies' day, her in red and me in orange. We stood out like sore thumbs, dressed up to the nines in a sea of grey men in the Guinness village. After that you had to do some serious searching.'

Cheltenham has become a sporting event which is much more important than the track, the races or the personalities who go there. It has developed its own multi-theistic theology with about 1,300 stable births, one for each of the winners that has graced the festival since 1924.

> I come to the House this evening after two successful days at Cheltenham, which should give me some authority on this matter. However, I was successful because I did not go.
>
> SENATOR SAM McAUGHTRY speaking in Seanad Éireann,
> 12 March 1997

Agreeing rules for this tri-nation contest proves problematic. The British, French and Irish handicapping systems are separate and their ratings are not interchangeable. Irish horses running in Britain almost invariably compete from a rating which is a much higher number than their Irish rating, and a core belief among Irish punters is that Irish horses are handicapped too highly when they run in Britain.

The English argue that there is no indication that the handicaps have been raised by a dramatic amount. The Irish say that without coping with 'unfair' English handicapping they would have won more than their 30 per cent share of recent meetings.

Often a horse's performance depended on factors other than weight. Punters claim it is easy to overstate the importance of a few pounds in a race where jumping judgment and pacing count for more than the weight carried. Dawn Run's victory in 1986 was questioned by those who felt she was given a too generous 5 lb mare's allowance.

If a horse is fit, in form and has conditions to suit, it is likely to run well regardless of its mark. If it is not fit, is out of form or unsuited by the conditions, it is very unlikely to make the frame whether it has a handy weight or not.

Cheltenham has this intoxicating effect, unlike anything else I have experienced in sport, and it lends itself to words and books.

ALAN LEE, *London Times*, 11 March 2006

The emotional clichés are fuel for that wispy, overblown, bombastic style beloved of sportswriters on both sides of the Atlantic, popularised, though not invented, by Grantland Rice.

'The tweed-and-Barbour set is prominent at Cheltenham but subsidiary to the other descending force, known simply as The Irish,' Alan Lee wrote in the *London Times* of 11 March 2006. 'They comprise a third of the total crowd but make the noise of double that number. For most who fly across the Irish Sea, it is a pilgrimage that shapes their view of a year. The Irish come to carouse and they do it in style, turning this elegant town and its surrounds into a bacchanalian stage-set. The Queen's Hotel used to take down its paintings and replace the period furniture with garden chairs and tables for festival week. But they also come in the same guise as national football supporters, their gambling focused almost exclusively on horses trained in their homeland.'

'When they bet on an Irish horse at Cheltenham, Irish fans are betting on national property, investing emotional as well as tangible currency,' John Scally wrote in *Them and Us*, an account of the Anglo-Irish rivalry at Cheltenham. 'When an Irish horse loses, the loss is more than just monetary. Any Irish win precipitates a show of national identity. The eyes have it, grown men blubbering like babies as they come back from the winner's enclosure. Cheltenham torments them in their waking hours and haunts them in their dreams.

'The traditional roar at the start of the first race is an outpouring of emotions, from the relief of the racing community that Cheltenham has finally come around again, to the exhilaration of the crowd at the thought of what lies ahead—four days of high drama, effort and excess that will test both wallets and livers.'

'Cheltenham always produces its fair share of basket cases,' Californian Cheltenham convert Bill Barich wrote in 2004, 'but every owner, trainer and jockey longs to be there in March, if only once in a lifetime. For the Irish the festival has an extra dimension, a metaphorical value. In their familiar role as underdogs, they accept the disadvantage of shipping their horses to Cheltenham, glad for an opportunity to take on their colonisers on English ground. The contest is friendly, but every patriot in Ireland prays that the Hourigans and Meades will stick it to the Brits. The Irish have an extraordinary way with horses after all.'

Master wordsmith Hugh McIlvanney has an excuse for his hamming of Cheltenham. He was a veteran visitor of more than twenty years when he was present for Dawn Run's victory in 1986: 'The rest of humanity had better be wary from now on of the 42,000 of us who were at Cheltenham racecourse on Thursday. We cannot begin to guarantee that our babblings of what we saw will not be sufficiently relentless to clear bars, cause communication cords to be grabbed on trains or tempt fellow passengers on aeroplanes to head for the exit at 35,000 ft. People who witness miracles, even small ones of the sporting kind, are liable to carry around forever afterwards a deadly parcel of reminiscence. In three decades of watching supreme performers in a wide range of contests, there have been few experiences that have precipitated a greater flood of excitement and pleasure than the sight of Jonjo and that incomparable mare battling out of what seemed the hopeless finality of third place at the last fence.'

Quite.

One of the victims wondered aloud in the hotel bar if the humane killer might not be used on punters who have broken down.

HUGH McILVANNEY, 16 March 1975

Cheltenham is important to the punter for another reason: it is often where shifts are first noticed in the accepted way of assessing form for big races. Cheltenham has an agreed trigonometry of indicators, guide races, ages, weights and other indications. Favourites win less than 10 per cent of the races. Only two favourites won in 2008 and three in 2007.

In the 1930s speed was first regarded as an issue and has remained so. Slow horses win the Grand National and other races at Aintree. But even the endurance races at Cheltenham were being won by faster horses. Cheltenham Festival races were run at a pace generally well above most other jump races, particularly in the early stages.

In the 1990s betting models placed a great deal of emphasis on recent form: the known potential ability of a horse and a consideration of its chances of re-attaining that level in the upcoming race. Over the next decade it was felt that punters were over-emphasising recent form at the expense of other factors. When in 2009 both Voy Por Ustedes and Cape Tribulation went into the meeting with impeccable credentials, and both were beaten, there were calls to revise the established way of assessing Cheltenham prospects.

Tipster Nick Fox suggested a straightforward, if crude, speed check: that punters should look at the best speed rating returned by a horse lining up at Cheltenham and question those yet to post a figure at least 90 per cent as good as the best in the race.

Where races attract large fields, experience in competing amid similar conditions is often of paramount importance. As always, the ground is crucial. If the going is on the quick side, then the flat-bred runners often hold the key. Hard ground is bad news for Cheltenham, hence the practice of watering the ground well in advance of the opening day.

> I couldn't believe how big the car park was, never mind the size of the fences.
>
> ADRIAN MAGUIRE recalls his first ride at Cheltenham, riding
> Omerta to win when he was still an amateur

The scale of the event is what will most impress a Cheltenham first-timer. Since 1831 the venue has grown from a canter over three fields into a 500 acre site that has become a metropolis dedicated to national hunt racing, hopelessly out of place in the bucolic landscape behind.

The expansion began in 1958 with the addition of a second course which had two fences in a longer home straight than the Old Course, but only one fence on the downhill run. It was facilitated by acquiring Jack Anthony's farm next door under what was for all intents and purposes a compulsory purchase order. Until then the National Hunt Steeplechase course ran behind the back of the stands.

Amid rumours that a developer was interested in acquiring the course, Racecourse Holdings Trust (later Jockey Club Racecourses) was formed in 1964 to secure the future of Cheltenham. The Group now owns thirteen other racecourses—a combination of jumps, flat, dual-purpose and all-weather racecourses. A new stables complex was opened in 1990 adjacent to Hunters Lodge. A stable staff hostel was built three years earlier to sleep 124. The pre-parade ring was used for the first time in 1992 and a Hall of Fame entrance officially added in 1993.

The Cross-Country Course was introduced in 1995 and is now raced three times each season over a selection of natural and man-made obstacles incorporating banks, ditches, hedges, water and timber rails. The race weaves around the centre of the course. Chase fences are constructed from 'dead' materials, whereas the fences on the cross-country course are living, growing trees, shrubs and bushes, which are regularly trimmed.

Following a controversial running of the Glenfarclas Cross-Country Chase in November 2008, where jockey Davy Russell got one over his colleagues by taking a 'legal' shortcut that didn't follow the normal racing line, the racecourse imposed more rigorous conditions to the cross-country course.

The festival uses all three of Cheltenham's courses. The Old Course stages racing on the first two days of the meeting, with the New Course taking over on the third and fourth days. Since the festival changed to a four-day meeting in 2005, the amount of ground available to race on has been increased.

> At this month's Cheltenham Festival, the new stands at the head-quarters of British steeplechasing will be packed with enthusiasts, flushed with drink and derring-do, betting like heroes and losing like gentlemen: a world class sporting occasion.
>
> *The Economist,* 12 March 1994

Off the sward, the development has been even more dramatic. A second Tattersalls Grandstand was completed in 1960 to cope with the growing crowds. A new weighing room was constructed underneath the Festival Restaurant and the winner's enclosure above the parade ring, and opened in 1965.

The main grandstand was completed in 1979 and extended twice in the 1980s. The top two levels were dedicated entirely to private hospitality, and in 1982 the parade ring, weighing room and Hurdlers Hall were built behind the stands with terraced viewing for 4,000.

In 1997 the original Tattersalls Grandstand was knocked down and replaced with tiered viewing, a betting hall, bars and food outlets. The Panoramic Restaurant on the top floor of the grandstand overlooking the winning line offers spectacular views of the racing through vast windows. The restaurant accommodates 300 diners and offers first-class cuisine. There's a television on every table and tote representatives will come to you to take your bets. Racegoers in Tattersalls have access to the Centaur, paddock, unsaddling enclosure, the Hall of Fame, the Gold Cup and Festival restaurants, the trade stands in the tented village and all bookmakers in the betting ring. At the festival the Guinness Village, opposite the last fence, extends the Tattersalls enclosure with extra viewing steps, bars, bands and other entertainment.

Club, as its name suggests, is the most exclusive enclosure with the best viewing, refreshment outlets and betting areas. The purchase of a Club day badge for the festival also entitles racegoers to use all the facilities within Tattersalls. At the festival the chalets and boxes in the tented village are in the Club enclosure.

During 2003–2004 the Best Mate Enclosure was constructed in the centre of the racecourse, giving a new grandstand and new views of the action. The enclosure is directly opposite the main stands and the festival entertainment often includes leading cover bands. During the same period £17 m was invested in providing additional raceday facilities with the Centaur, a new conference and events centre with a capacity of 4,000.

The fences on the New Course were widened by five metres, which gives the racecourse the flexibility to use the outside portion of them during the early part of the season, saving around twelve metres of entirely fresh ground (and fence) on the inside of the New Course specifically for the festival.

Planned redevelopment includes the weighing room and media centre beside the parade ring, more paddock viewing and new 'A & R' boxes to provide improved and new facilities for racegoers, 8,500 members, box holders and sponsors.

The racecourse employs 60 permanent staff, which rises to approximately 1,000 for a race meeting and over 5,000 at the festival when trade stands are located around the paddock, with the majority in the tented village. After the festival there are 3,960,000 hoofprints on the racecourse.

While the English are fond of their racing, I soon discovered the Irish can't live without it.

BILL BARICH, *A Fine Place to Daydream* (2005)

Irish-bred horses had won 38 Aintree Grand Nationals before the Gold Cup was initiated in 1924, and the Irish began to achieve an affinity with the new races almost straightaway.

The 'Sligo mare' Ballinode, trained by Frank Morgan on the Curragh and the appropriately named jockey Ted Leader beat the odds-on favourite Alcazar in a canter by five lengths in the second race in 1925 to start a great Irish tradition.

Koko, trained by Frank Barbour in Meath, won the third race in 1926. Barbour had moved his stable to England where he trained the remarkable Easter Hero, who won the 1929 and 1930 Gold Cups. After spreadeagling the Gold Cup field by twenty lengths in 1929, he came out a fortnight later to finish second in the Aintree Grand National in a field of 66, carrying the impossible burden of 12 st 7 lb. The next year Easter Hero again won the Gold Cup by twenty lengths, but was unable to run in the Grand National through lameness. In 1931 he was robbed of the chance to become the first three-time winner when bad weather caused the race to be abandoned. He retired at the end of the season, but the public did not have to wait long for a new hero, Meath-bred Golden Miller, which won the Gold Cup five years in succession and won the Gold Cup and Grand National just seventeen days apart in 1934, the only horse to win both in the same year.

It was Tom Dreaper's Prince Regent in 1946 and Vincent O'Brien's three-time winner Cottage Rake (1948–50) that sealed the connection between Ireland and Cheltenham. Prince Regent won the first post-war running at the age of 11. Trained by Tom Dreaper and ridden by Tim Hyde, he came to Cheltenham with a huge reputation and a special guard.

Cottage Rake, with a flat racer's speed and looks, became the first celebrity trained by the master of Ballydoyle, Vincent O'Brien. Ridden by Aubrey Brabazon in each of his three victories, he inspired the ballad:

Aubrey's up, the money's down;
the frightened bookies quake.
Come on my lads and give a cheer
Begod, 'tis Cottage Rake!

O'Brien also sent out Hatton's Grace to win the Champion Hurdle in successive years, 1949–51.

When you've won, you've always done right.

AIDAN O'BRIEN

Cheltenham moved away from the racing pages and into the heart of Irish popular culture in the 1960s when several great personalities, equine and human, won new followers. Press coverage increased and television brought the sport to a new audience. By 1970 steeplechasing was rivalling flat racing in public support.

Arkle's success was the most mythologised of all, an Eden of steeplechasing, against whom new horses' prospects are measured. Most modern Cheltenham racegoers were not born then, but it doesn't stop the mythologising about Arkle's Gold Cup victory in 1964, when he left the highly rated cup holder Mill House an effortless five lengths behind and the 1960 winner Pas Seul 25 lengths away in third.

Arkle won again at the prohibitive odds of 100/30 on in 1965, beating Mill House by twenty lengths. For his third, he started at odds of 1/10, the shortest price in the race's history, and won by the longest distance, 30 lengths. His skeleton now resides at the National Stud museum.

L'Escargot's first win, from his compatriot French Tan, came at 33/1 in 1970 after the fall of the Willie O'Grady-trained favourite Kinloch Brae three out, for trainer Dan Moore and jockey Tommy Carberry. The following year it was another Irish one-two when L'Escargot beat Leap Frog, this time as a joint-favourite.

In 1972 a courageous performance by Glencaraig Lady, a faller three fences out the previous year, won the cup for Francis Flood, but it was close. She battled home under Frank Berry to beat Royal Toss and The Dikler in a photo-finish and then survived a stewards' inquiry and an objection.

An emotional day followed in 1974 as Bobby Beasley guided novice Captain Christy to a five-length beating of The Dikler. Beasley had made a comeback after beating alcoholism. The trainer was Arkle's jockey, Pat Taaffe, the biggest success for his Alasty Stud.

More emotion followed in 1986 as Charmian Hill's Dawn Run, the Champion Hurdler two years previously, battled back up the hill to beat Wayward Lad and Forgive n Forget for Gowran-based Paddy

Mullins. Jockey Jonjo O'Neill was returning to the saddle after recovering from a serious leg injury and chaired his predecessor Tony Mullins into the winner's enclosure. Dawn Run was put down within a year, her place in mythology secure.

There followed a barren decade until Imperial Call's victory in 1996. The scenes afterwards prompted Edward Gillespie, Cheltenham's managing director, to query the safety of the winner's enclosure. New security measures were consequently introduced. Gillespie himself contributed to Cheltenham folklore when he zealously rugby tackled an intruder after Istabraq's first Champion Hurdle victory. The intruder turned out to be none other than Aidan O'Brien, destined to become the most successful trainer in Irish racing history.

Chapter 2 ᢗ

OUT OF THE MIST

Cad a dhéanfaimid feasta gan adhmad?
Ta deireadh na coillte thar lear
                    A Munster poet mourns the passing of his
                    native country's woodlands. *Cill Chais c.*1740

The destruction of the forests on both sides of the Irish Sea, mourned by an unknown Irish poet, also brought an end to the traditional stag hunt, beloved of horsemen in the sixteenth and seventeenth centuries.

With cleared forests, pasturage and tree lined hedges, from the 1730s the construction of drains and the development of arterial drainage changed the nature of hunting. The horseman's attention switched from the stag to the fox and the skills required in riding jumping horses changed too.

It became clear that slower horses who were not required to jump much, or show much speed, were inadequate to keep up with faster prey that could race across open country.

Initially, fox hunts were a matter of running down the fox in a battle of attrition through heavy country, but the notion of chasing foxes at speed across open grazing country enclosed by hedges and stone walls, and irrigated by ditches, caught on. The lightly wooded landscape with ever bigger enclosures offering good open runs became a fashionable location, and horses that could run fast and jump handily became the mounts of choice.

The cry of the hounds and the noise of the men
Disturbed poor Reynard quite out of his den
                    Folk song, 1750s

The racing of horses over obstacles developed naturally out of fox hunting. Gentlemen who rode to hounds settled their arguments with a race over a set distance. Races took place over natural hunting country with natural obstacles.

Steeple hunting, or as it later became known, steeplechasing, has its roots in 'pounding matches' held in Ireland in the late seventeenth century. Matches between two horses were held across haphazardly chosen country until the loser was pounded into the ground by being outlasted by the winner, or fell. The horses were, typically, heavy animals that could handle rough ground, stay and jump.

By the mid-eighteenth century chosen courses with a terminating winning post of a pre-agreed upon landmark, often a church steeple or tower, were more typical than not. Thus, the word 'steeplechase', although the term 'steeple hunt' was the original term used.

Landed gentlemen began to maintain their own packs of hounds and hunted with their guests or with other gentlemen's packs. By the mid-eighteenth century there were several packs in Meath. The Ffrenches of French Park in Roscommon had a pack of foxhounds. Hares were hunted every morning at Ballinasloe. Thomas Matthew kept a pack in Thomastown, and Thomas Browne, Earl of Kenmare, organised stag hunts in Killarney for the entertainment of visitors, and there were diversions such as the doe hunt at Loughmore near Limerick or the buck hunt at Portarlington. In 1744 the hunt of Chaworth Brabazon, Earl of Meath, was celebrated in a typical broadsheet ballad, 'The Kilruddery Hunt'. Brabazon's own progeny was to ride Ireland's first three-time Gold Cup winner to victory at Cheltenham 200 years later.

Ireland's relationship with Cheltenham Festival is a recent development. To understand it we need to look at the parallel but subtly different history of horse racing on the two islands over the past 300 years, and in particular how jump racing for mature horses was subjugated by flat racing for younger horses.

By the end of the seventeenth century mixtures of dog and horse races were staged at pre-appointed venues at which large crowds gathered to watch, and the tradition of jockeys in distinctive colours, handicapping and odds of up to 5/1 had evolved. In 1717 the duties of the ranger of the Curragh extended to 'supervising the proper conduct of the King's Plate'. The *Dublin Gazette* and the *Weekly Courier* advertised races on the Hill of Crockafotha in Co. Meath in 1726, where Bellewstown races are still held today. In 1731 the *Dublin Intelligentser* noted that 'horse-racing has become a great diversion in the country'. Ten years later a £40 plate was reported in Galway and a King's Plate was run at the Curragh. An Act passed in 1739 made it illegal to run for plates less than £120 in value, but it was largely ignored and 71 race meetings took place in Ireland in 1750—an impressive figure which compares with 300 today.

We know very little about the form of these races. The results of the races at Celbridge in September 1753 list Charles Lambert's bay gelding Trifle as the winner of Tuesday's plate and John St Leger's bay gelding as the winner of Wednesday's, suggesting that hunters or steeplechasers were in competition. We don't know whether the course was over jumps or even its location, although Daingean or Lyons common is a possibility—a report a month later on 4 October 1763 recounts how the Grand Canal overflowed at Lyons and flooded the course.

We do know that things were about to change dramatically in the rules of racing.

Dasher was soon to outmanoeuvre Prancer in the organisation of horse racing, to borrow some characters from Clement Clarke Moore's 1822 poem about Santa's reindeer, when a series of one mile dashes was established. These races, restricted to 3-year olds, superseded the old King's Plates and dictate the flat racing calendar to this day: England's St Leger in 1776 (named after 'handsome Jack' St Leger from Grangemellon, Co. Kildare, the man whose gelding had won at Celbridge), the Epsom Oaks in 1779, the Epsom Derby in 1780, the Two Thousand Guineas in 1809 and the One Thousand Guineas in 1814.

Ireland followed the trend, if unsteadily. To feed the new appetite for flat racing, Pat Connolly became Ireland's first registered racehorse trainer in 1812 when he took over Waterford Lodge, now the racecourse stables at the Curragh.

The Northumberland Gold Cup was inaugurated at the Curragh in 1781 over two miles, to run until 1933, after the Curragh 'new course' was made equidistant with Newmarket in 1811. It was followed in 1815 by the short-lived 1500 Guineas over a mile, which lasted just three years, and in 1821 by the O'Darby Stakes over a mile and a half, which lasted just seven.

Older horses and hunters were effectively forced off the racing calendar.

This does not make athletic sense. Athletically, racehorses peak at 5 years old rather than 3. But it suited the emerging breeding industry and enriched flat racing in a way that jump racing never could be.

Races over jumps were completely ignored by the Turf Club, which came into being in 1790 to regulate wagers and ensure fair play on the racecourse. This was traditionally held to have happened 'in a coffee house in Kildare' but it is more likely to have originated in Patrick Daly's club in Dame Street. Dublin's gambling scene revolved around Daly's club when it moved to its new premises in College Green on 15 February 1791.

Away from this regulated world, the notion of matching the ever faster hunters, often mixed with thoroughbred blood, against each other, without the fox, proved irresistible. It led to the famous pounding matches, where groups of riders jumped their way across country until only the winner remained and the losers were 'pounded' into the ground by being outlasted by the winner, or fell. Races took place over natural hunting country with natural obstacles. The horses were typically heavy animals who could handle rough ground, stay, and jump. The races were popular in Munster and Connacht,

One of them became the first steeplechase: a four and a half mile gallop from Buttevant church to the spire of Doneraile church across St Leger estate lands in 1752.

> Happily for the world at large Dashing Dick broke his neck in a steeple chase, on a stolen horse, which he would have been hanged for purloining, had he lived a day longer.
>
> MRS S. C. HALL, *Sketches of Irish Character*, 1828

As the poor cousin of the racing industry, steeplechasing needed inspiration to survive. Part of that inspiration was a foundation myth of the type which was so popular in the immediate post-industrial age.

Edmond O'Brien's library in Dromoland Castle carries the only evidence of the foundation myth of steeplechasing. O'Brien was one of the racing enthusiasts of the 1830s who laid the basis of the Irish stud industry, going so far as to name his model village near Ennis 'Newmarket on Fergus' as a potential racing centre of excellence (the tradition continued long after O'Brien's home became one of Ireland's leading luxury hotels). The Thinker, Cool Dawn, Cool Ground, Imperial Call, Midnight Court, Best Mate and Florida Pearl were all bred here or passed through the locality.

O'Brien's document is not contemporary and is scant on detail. It records that Cornelius O'Callaghan raced Edmund Blake. No winner is recorded, whether the bet was paid out or whether the winner and loser were satisfied. Hopefully they were. Blake's son is listed by raconteur barrister Jonah Barrington in a memoir from his student days in the 1780s as one of Ireland's leading duellists. By the 1890s Buttevant and the carefully manipulated mythology of Irish steeplechasing had been widely accepted.

For the 250th anniversary of the original steeplechase in 2003, writer Anne Holland retraced the route of the four and a half miles from Buttevant to Doneraile. The place was overgrown and unkempt, and a small plaque was the only indication that this major episode of sporting history took place there.

The yellowing archives of contemporary newspapers give us lots of evidence of the popularity of steeple hunting within years of this mythologised foundation.

> A sweepstake with added money of a hogshead of claret, a pipe of port and a quarter-cask of rum.
>
> > Draft of conditions for a Mayo steeplechase race held in 1803

In Ireland the Prancers continued to prove as popular as anything the Dashers could offer. The use of the word 'steeplechase' in the *Irish Racing Calendar* of 1807 to describe a six mile cross-country match race helped establish the use of the term.

There was also an Anglo-Irish dimension to these early steeplechases. The *Ipswich Journal* of 20 March 1802 advertised: 'A steeple chase is to be run from Acton common, on Wednesday next, for 100 guineas, between two English and Irish hunters. We understand that the latter, brought over for this purpose, are the property of a Roscommon Gentleman, and are reckoned amongst the best horses of the day.'

London's *Morning Chronicle* of 30 October 1807 carried a report from Co. Laois: 'On Tuesday se'en night, a steeple chase was run from Ballybrophy, in the Queen's County, for six miles across the country, between Mr White's horse Jerara, and Mr Weir's horse Cornet, for 90 guineas a side, pp Mr Evans rode Jerara, Mr Weir his own horse. At starting 5 to 4 on Mr White, who won easy, though carrying 7 lb over his weight. The race was run in 20 minutes and 11 seconds.'

As with Ballybrophy, the report in the *Freeman's Journal* of 27 February 1811 on the annual steeplechase for the Silver Cup belonging to the Newtownbreda Club Hunt, even gives a winning time: 'The ground chosen for this trial was different from that of preceding years, and was generally considered better adapted for that purpose. It was infinitely the best contested race we have yet seen for the cup. The distance, which was four miles, was run in 16 minutes and 57 seconds, through a very deep and enclosed country. An immense crowd of spectators were present at the contest, covering every eminence that commanded a view of the scene, which was rendered very pleasing from the unusual fineness of the day. Othello has held this cup for the three preceding years, and was the confident, but it appeared that Mr McCauce's horse [Harlequin] had too much foot for him.'

The *Freeman's Journal* of 4 May 1813 advertised a steeplechase of six miles in Roscommon 'including six five feet walls, with several large ditches, was run on the 17th March over the plains of Kacroghan, for a plate of 100 Guineas, and 10 Guineas stake in each horse entered; four years old, carrying 10 stone, five years old carrying 10 stone 7 lb, six years old carrying 11 stone.'

The same newspaper reported on 20 October 1814 that 'Captain Barclay of the 42nd Highlanders, has, we understand, declined accepting the challenge of a Queen's County man, noticed some time ago in this Paper, to run with him a steeple chase of ten miles for a given sum. The gallant Captain has, however, offered to run the challenge on an ordinary course race of any distance from one mile to a hundred, but how this proposal has been received we have not learned.'

The newspaper also gives us an idea of how the horses built up their reputation. A sales notice appeared in 1827 for the 'superior Styron steeple chase hunter Ruler, now eight years old, got by Fawnus, his strength, action and temper, render him a treasure to a weighty man. He won the Armagh and Ringcourt Cups in October, carrying 13 stone, three Irish miles, over a desperate country.'

> I think the Irish hunter now is a specialty, and I think in most cases it is one of the only things I see to help the farmer in his ever increasing difficulties, which I think are bound to increase as far as I can see.
>
> J. O'CONNELL MURPHY to the Commission on Horse Breeding in Ireland, 1898

Despite its unregulated state, the newly enclosed courses of Ireland continued to prefer racing over jumps. The result was that flat racing in Ireland had a poor time until the 1880s.

Fergus D'Arcy attributes this to the smallness and modesty of the middle class, citing an *Illustrated London News* report of the opening of the new Stand House in the Curragh in 1853: 'The attendance of the country people was by no means large, nor was there a tithe of the ordinary concomitants of a racecourse in England—the handsome vehicles, the vast conflux of money-spending power, in fact, the middle class substance which so largely predominates on these occasions with us.'

In the 1830s courses were laid out in Mayo, with graded obstacles and weight based on age, at Ballinrobe, Tuam, Cashir and elsewhere. Still, the actual route of travel to the final flag was left to the rider.

Ireland's most famous national hunt course was a hybrid between a new style enclosed course and traditional hunting terrain, a little like Prestbury Park was to become. It originated over the favourite hunting territory of the Kildare hounds, a course with rolling hills, pasture (not plough) and a large number of land drains from Punchestown Gorse to Eadestown and on to Arthurstown.

Punchestown races were first staged in 1844 at the beginning of April at the 'Kildare Foxhounds Annual meeting', and a second day was added at the suggestion of the Great Southern and Western Railway Company in 1854, an indication of the importance of railway companies to the development of the sport—Ireland was the first country in which a special train was run for a sporting event, the Curragh, in 1846.

It was Henry Moore of Monasterevan, Marquis of Drogheda, who redesignated the Punchestown meeting the Kildare and National Hunt Steeplechases in 1861. The Conyngham Cup was inaugurated in 1865. The three mile five furlong Irish Grand National was inaugurated in 1870 at Fairyhouse.

Punchestown transformed Irish culture. Permanent stands and enclosures were constructed; the Conyngham Cup course was opened and first used in 1862 for the National Hunt Steeplechase. The course featured the famous 'double', a 6 foot 6 inch wide and 3 foot deep first ditch, the top 6 foot 6 inches wide, the second ditch 4 foot wide.

A feature on Punchestown attributes the eclipse of flat racing due to the growth of the hunt festival there: 'The Punchestown Steeplechases seem completely to have swallowed up all the flat racing in Ireland and create as much local interest as the Derby in London.'

The visit of Albert Saxe-Corburg, the Prince of Wales, later to become Edward vii of England, and his wife Alexandra to Punchestown in 1868 swelled the crowd at the first day's racing to a reported 150,000.

It is almost certainly a wildly exaggerated figure by an enthusiastic press. Nineteenth-century estimates of attendances are notoriously unreliable. In a 1993 paper on attendance figures at Daniel O'Connell's monster meetings, historian Gary Owens quoted how in Sligo eight constables put the attendance at a meeting between 2,000 and 5,000, while the *Freeman's Journal* reported that 100,000 attended. At Castlebar the local magistrate T. Banon estimated 7,000; the *Freeman's Journal* and the *Mayo Constitution* estimated 150,000, while the *Nation* estimated 400,000. But the mythology of Punchestown had been constructed and the event had been placed at the heart of Irish sporting culture, a position it retains today, even if it remains a notch or two behind Cheltenham in that position.

> If the Irish farmer is not, according to English notions, making any rapid progress as an agriculturist, the Irish squire is doing something for his country's husbandry. It is said that many of them are now rearing shorthorns and cart-horses in preference to hunters and steeple-chase horses, not without benefit to themselves and the society of their several districts.
>
> *Economist*, 11 September 1858

These tensions between flat, hurdle and jump racing took a century to ease. Ignored by the toffs who ran racing, steeplechasing remained underground until the 1860s.

Steeplechasing was regarded as the bastard offspring of hunting and flat racing for many purists. Until the end of the nineteenth century steeplechasing was referred to by detractors as the 'illegitimate sport'. England's racing establishment and fox hunting community did not favour steeplechasing: Charles Apperley ('Nimrod'), the first influential turf writer, considered it dangerous to man and horse. Prominent members of the Jockey Club such as Admiral Rous, the 'dictator of the English Turf', opposed it.

As the number of steeplechase races increased both in England (from 300 to 700 in a seven year period 1861–68) and Ireland, so did the abuses. Out in the country, rivals would run into interference from a favourite's supporters: holes in fences would appear to ease a fancied horse's way, and other abuses were common. In this, chasing was not unlike its sister sport flat racing at this time. The *Economist* magazine of 13 April 1844 denounced efforts to legitimise what it regarded as a cruel and corrupt sport: 'These are the manly sports which the Duke of Richmond is so anxious to encourage, that he must needs carry through parliament a base measure, defying all the rules of justice and jurisprudence, to save expenses legally incurred by the "gentlemen of England" in betting on them and who take pleasure in them.'

France was the first to bring steeplechasing in from the cold when it organised the *Société des Steeplechases* in 1863. America's Jockey Club was established in 1866 and took control of steeplechasing in 1869. In 1866 a number of English Jockey Club members were persuaded that the illegitimate sport was damaging the image of all racing and established the Grand National Hunt Committee (renamed the National Hunt Committee in 1889) to control the sport and assess penalties and employed the Jockey Club secretaries Messrs Weatherby to issue a steeplechasing calendar on the lines of the *Racing Calendar*.

Three years later Henry Moore from Monasterevan, the founder of Punchestown who was also steward of the Turf Club, formed the Irish National Hunt Steeplechase Committee. The first reports of their deliberations began to appear in the Irish newspapers at the end of 1869.

The new body instigated a new focus for Irish jump racing, the 3 mile, 5 furlong Irish Grand National, which was inaugurated in 1870 at Fairyhouse.

We can get a sense of how badly some regulation was required from the reports of those early meetings. Colonel Knox proposed that no hurdle race should be a shorter distance than a mile and a half, and have no fewer than six hurdles, to get over the propensity for organising three-quarters of a mile races with one hurdle to suit flat horses.

Crucial early rules were that no horse should carry less than 10 stone in steeplechases and 9 stone 7 lb in hurdle racing, and that no 3-year old should be allowed to race before 1 September.

Nothing in the act shall apply to royal palaces, in which the king shall then actually reside.

An *Act of 18 George 2 c34, Section 6* to explain, amend and make more effectual the Laws in being to prevent Excessive and Deceitful Gaming, and to restrain and prevent the excessive increase of Horse Races. (1744)

If the Jockey Club and Turf Club had no interest in steeplechasing, another type of legislator certainly had. Parliamentarians have long been anxious to regulate the betting industry, although the enthusiasm for curtailing gambling never extended to England's royal family.

The widespread gambling that was going on throughout the three kingdoms was a concern for the gentlemen who drew up legislation both in Westminster and on College Green, notwithstanding the fact that both bodies had some of the most prominent gamblers in the two kingdoms in their midst.

More than a dozen half-hearted attempts were made to try to curtail the evil of gambling, as they were of the betting scheme on shipping at Lloyd's Coffee House that has since been elevated by revisionist historians to the birth of a great industry, insurance.

The Gaming Act of 1739 confined racing to Newmarket and Black Hambleton on the Cleveland Hills in England and the Curragh in Ireland, and restricted racing to plates of £50 (13 George 2 c19 s 3).

Another 'Act to explain, amend and make more effectual the Laws in being to prevent Excessive and Deceitful Gaming, and to restrain and prevent the excessive increase of Horse Races' of 1744 stated that a person losing £10 or £20 within 24 hours was to be liable to be indicted within six months and fined five times their losses.

There was little appetite to enforce the laws among the sheriffs and magistrates, many of whom were horse racing and gambling enthusiasts themselves. The laws were contradictory in several places. A statute of the eleventh clause of the Gaming Act of 1739, making it lawful to run for a £50 plate, or value, was contradicted by the Gaming Act of 1710 (9 Anne), which prohibited wagers exceeding £10 in amount on either side.

The new rule also contradicted the old one as to securities for money lost, or to mere bets on a race. A Horse Racing Act of 1840 repealed some sections of the 1744 Act and even rendered the entire sport of horse racing illegal, according to one reading.

It was 1844 before another select committee on Gaming in the House of Commons decreed that a steeplechase was a race within the statute, as decided by the court case Evans v Pratt in Shrewsbury in 1842. A clause in the 1849 Cruelty to Animals Bill almost outlawed racing over jumps. The proposal 'that if at any time after the passing of the Act any person shall ride, or, being the owner, shall permit any other person to ride any animal in any steeple chase, or other race in which any hedges etc. are intended to be leaped or jumped over by the animals engaged in such steeple chase or other race as aforesaid, every such person shall be deemed to have cruelly used such animal' was defeated by the uncomfortably tight margin of 58–50.

Racecourses and horse owners complained they were now at the bookmakers' mercy. Politicians also. Legend has it that the English 1960 Betting and Gaming Act was crafted when the toffs of the Jockey Club were mired in gambling debts.

Cheltenham could be the Lisdoonvarna of England with the added bonus of a mighty racetrack thrown in.

FINBARR SLATTERY, *Following the Horses* (1996)

Prancers were as popular in the Cotswolds as they were in Doneraile and Celbridge. Cheltenham was hunting country, but its first Cheltenham Gold Cup was a flat race. The reason was that horse racing was an activity for tourists, not locals. After a saline spring was discovered in 1716, Cheltenham became a spa town with holiday makers bringing all their pursuits such as theatre, gambling and equestrian sports with them. Cleeve Hill, the highest point on the Cotswolds, was the racecourse from August 1818 until a permanent course was built in Prestbury Park.

The first racing at Cheltenham in the early 1800s was on the flat. Later steeplechasing was added at three disparate tracks in the Cotswolds area. As in other spa towns, hoteliers promoted and sponsored many of these races. Racing's popularity soared over the next decade with crowds of 30,000 visiting the course for its annual two-day July meeting featuring the Gold Cup—then a three mile flat race. Cheltenham thrived too, increasing in population from 13,396 in 1821 to 35,051 in 1851.

Despite the popularity of the flat race meeting, the local allegiance to steeplechasing and hunting persevered, with early races over

Andoversford. The *New Sporting Magazine* of March 1834 gave notice that a 'steeplechase of 10 sovereigns each for horses that have been bona fide the property of subscribers since the 1st January 1834 carrying 12 st will take place over the hill country on the 31st inst, Lord Segrave umpire,' and warned that 'no innkeeper, trainer, jockey, or hired servant [was] permitted to subscribe or ride.'

The Cheltenham steeplechases advertised for 1 April 1835 included 'seventeen horses entered in one race and thirteen horses in the other', according to the *Freeman's Journal* in Dublin of 23 March 1835, the first mention of Cheltenham steeplechases in an Irish newspaper.

The *Racing Calendar* of 1836 noted the 'second year of the Cotswold stakes of 25 sovereigns each, 15 st for three year old colts, 8 st 7 lb, and fillies 8 st 3 lb, one mile and a half. Four subs. Renewal of the Gloucestershire stakes of 25 sovs each.'

The scale of the fences was left to the organisers. A reminiscence on renowned Cheltenham course builder Bill Bean recalled that his 'greatest abomination was the modern way of building a steeplechase course, lowering this, and digging that, and dodging the other thing. He liked the sport when it was a thing of nature—a steeple-chase on the hill: there's your country gentlemen, and get over it how you can.'

Like much of steeplechasing across England, those Andoversford races died out in the 1860s. The last race of the festival, the Johnny Henderson Grand Annual Chase, is a revival of one of those 1830s Andoversford races.

The present course at Prestbury Park on the outskirts of the town was first used in 1902, and in 1907 the Cheltenham Steeplechase Company was founded.

> Papists, gambling and profligacy are the essential concomitants to Cheltenham's horse racing.
>
> FRANCIS CLOSE

The greatest opponent of Cheltenham races was, by unhappy co-incidence, the local pastor. The foundation of the Cheltenham branch of the Church Missionary Society in 1824 was to create an unexpected problem for the race organisers.

Francis Close, a zealous evangelist Christian, dreamed of turning his home town into a leading evangelical centre instead of a tourist resort, and indeed Charles Simeon described Cheltenham in the 1840s as 'a heaven upon earth'. He was vehemently anti-Catholic and anti-Semitic, an instigator of the Auxiliary Society for Promoting Christianity Among the Jews. He was also the author of such bestsellers as 'The book of Genesis considered and illustrated, in a series of historical discourses, as preached in the Holy Trinity Church, Cheltenham', and a 'Course of nine sermons, intended to illustrate some leading truths contained in the Liturgy of the Church of England'.

In 1829, at the age of 34, he wrote the influential 'Evil Consequences of attending the racecourse'. In it he complained that 'the Heathen festivals of Venus and Bacchus are exceeded on the raceground'. Priced at three pence, it was a popular success and ran to six editions. Close pondered, rather rhetorically, 'whether we shall be an infidel or a believing people, a people among whom Christianity shall be established and upheld by the legislature, or whether it should be left to the unruly wills and affections of sinful men.

'I verily believe that, in the day of judgment, thousands of the vast multitude who have served the world, the flesh and the devil, will trace all the guilt and misery which has fallen on them either to the racecourse or the theatre.'

The pamphlet and accompanying sermons aroused such strong feelings among his congregation that the race meeting in 1830 was disrupted. Indeed the grandstand was burnt to the ground before the 1831 meeting.

In 1828 Close had been appointed chaplain to John Horsley-Beresford, Lord Decies. Which was ironic, for Beresford's great-nephew Henry Beresford was the leading Irish steeplechase rider of his generation and frequently raced on his own horses at Cheltenham.

To overcome this violent opposition, the course was moved to Prestbury Park in 1831. Close continued to fight and prevented the re-construction of Cheltenham's theatre after it was destroyed by fire in 1839. He went on to found the Evangelical Anglican colleges at Cheltenham in 1847 before departing to become Dean of Carlisle in 1856. A frequenter of the village, Alfred Lord Tennyson deemed him the Parish Pope of Cheltenham.

Dean Close School, which he founded, has long since given up the quest to divert the chosen faithful from the evils of horse racing. The husband and sons of Charmian Hill, owner of 1984 Champion Hurdle and 1986 Gold Cup winner Dawn Run, were all educated there. Its most famous Irish past pupil was also its shortest stayer, artist Francis Bacon, who ran away from school here and was not put off the joys of the racecourse by his being horsewhipped by a groom on the instructions of his father during his unhappy childhood in Straffan Lodge in Co. Kildare.

The training career of the artist's father, AE 'Eddy' Bacon, then based at Connycourt, Brannockstown, peaked in 1911 with ten wins from his eight horses. They included Repeater II, the winner of the Irish Grand National of 1911 and an entrant in the National Hunt Handicap in Cheltenham in 1912. As late as 1926 he was sending his own horse Turmeric to compete in steeplechases in England. But it was a testing time for the Bacon family finances. He sold off horses, cattle, traps and 'superior household furniture', about two tons of potatoes and 20 hens in September 1921. His Humber tourer car followed in July 1928, and another car, a Riley tourer, and residue household effects in a clearance sale in February 1932.

Francis Bacon was a frequenter of Cheltenham racecourse in the 1930s, when he served as racing secretary to the flamboyant *Daily Express* racing correspondent Geoffrey Gilbey.

> The Marquis of Waterford came out amazingly well, winning five times, in capital style, against the elite of our best gentlemen jockeys.
> *New Sporting* magazine, review of the racing season, December 1839

If there was an antithesis to Francis Close and his racecourse rantings, it was to be found in the episcopal palace in Armagh at the same time. John Beresford, Archbishop of Armagh from 1822 to 1862, restorer of St Patrick's and Armagh cathedrals and builder of the campanile at Trinity College, Dublin, was from one of Ireland's premier horse racing families. His nephew Henry rode his own horse in the Cheltenham steeplechase of 1837. A great-nephew Marcus Beresford became the manager of the future Edward VII's racing stables and is still regarded as the leading authority on racing at the end of the nineteenth century.

Like Francis Close, the Archbishop founded a school, St Columba's College in the Dublin mountains, whose alumni include Ireland's former politician, now bookmaker, Ivan Yates, Northern Ireland former prime minister Brian Faulkner (a keen huntsman and racegoer who died, like the Archbishop's nephew, in a fall from a horse), and one of Ireland's leading racing photographers, Billy Stickland, as well as U2 guitarist Adam Clayton, the group's unofficial Cheltenham tipster.

Not to be outdone, the Catholic bishops banned their priests from attending races, but even reforming Bishop James Warren Doyle, who normally opposed the gathering of the lower classes as scenes of drunkenness and sin, granted Naas parish priest Gerard Doyle permission to attend a race meeting in June 1825: 'I wish you with all my heart peace and good running during this week and I wish you will be present on the turf to preserve the one as I am confident you will enjoy the other.'

> Still it seems but yesterday that we had him in all his blue and black cap glories, going yards out of his way to get an extra fence in Northamptonshire, Leicestershire, and Warwickshire, and that too with Captain Becher, Jem Mason and Oliver as his opponents.
>
> HENRY BERESFORD's obituary in the *New Sporting* magazine,
> April 1859

At the Aylesbury steeplechase of 1834, *New Sporting* magazine noted: 'It was here that the Marquis of Waterford made his first appearance in England as a steeplechase rider, and fully carried out the high reputation he had earned in the sister isle.'

Henry Beresford from Curraghmore on the Waterford-Tipperary border, nephew of the Lord Bishop of Armagh, had a reputation indeed. No doubt as revenge for his sore-bottomed schooldays, he stole the headmaster's flogging block from Eton and commemorated the deed with an annual dinner.

At least one etymological dictionary credits him with inventing the phrase 'painting the town red' because of his toll gate painting incident at Melton Mowbray in Leicestershire in 1837, when he and his friends were celebrating a successful fox hunt.

He was a passionate steeplechase enthusiast, when the sport had a bad reputation, and a pioneer of the Irish horse breeding industry. A frequent and consistently successful competitor on English courses, he was elected to the board of the controlling body of English racing, the Newmarket-based Jockey Club in 1851.

'Cock Robin, The Sea and Columbine seem to conjure up a host of memories of steeple-chase fields and steeple-chase matches, all marking a golden era for that sport, when it was untainted with handicaps, which can never come back again,' the *New Sporting* magazine mourned in April 1859.

'His energy in painting the Melton toll-bar, and aniseeding the heels of a parson's horse, and running him with bloodhounds—his encounter with the Norwegian watchmen—the loss of his wig (which he had to wear after that affray) in a capital thing over Burrow Hills, his patronage of Deaf Burke, his winning of three four mile steeple-chases at Eglington Park on the same day, and his zeal at the tournament are all bits of his character that amused England in their day.'

Henry Beresford died, literally with his boots on, at the age of 48. On 31 March 1859 he was rising his favourite hunter, May Boy, that he had purchased from the master of the Meath hounds, on a narrow road through the mountain grove from Corbally towards Dowlan hill. He cleared a low fence and fell into a gripe, falling out of the saddle sideways on his head. Johnny Ryan, his friend and steeplechase rider, and George Thompson, the groom, called for help but it was too late. Ireland's first and, perhaps, most flamboyant Cheltenham raider was already dead.

> Clifton, Bath or even Cheltenham, all places to which the gay and the rich, the sportsman and he who seeks fine country and agreeable society, now wander.
>
> *New Sporting* magazine, August 1849

It is surprising how the horse racing enthusiasts who came from Ireland to Cheltenham resembled their counterparts of a century later. The first was James Fitzpatrick Knaresborough (1801–5 March 1861), unsung hero of the transformation of steeplechasing in Ireland from a rakes' pastime to a proper sport, and registrar to the Down Royal Corporation of Horse Breeders.

He provided the first favourite for the 1837 race now regarded as the second Grand National, though it did not bear the famous name. It was described as 'a sweepstake of 10 sovereigns each, with 100 sovereigns added by the town of Liverpool'. The course was described as 'over a country not exceeding five miles' and the first favourite, Dan O'Connell, the greatest Irish steeplechase horse of the age, went off at 5/4.

Captain Martin William Becher, later to win the 1837 Cheltenham steeplechase, fell at a post and rail in a deep ditch, in which he had to compose himself while the whole field were making tracks over him. The jump has ever since borne his name, Becher's Brook, although it has as much degenerated in size as the race itself since then. Allegedly it was another Irish jockey, Tom Ferguson, who upended Becher into the ditch that bears his name.

A list of celebrated Irish sportsmen in the London-based *New Sporting* magazine includes James Knaresborough alongside Abbot, Baker, Byrne, Cassidy, Ferguson, McDonough, Thompson and Yourell. In 1838 Sir William (trained by Allen McDonough) was the first Irish-trained winner of the Aintree Grand National. Valentine's Brook is where Irish jockey John Power managed to get his horse Valentine through in 1840. Willie McDonough, Denny Wynne from Cork and John Courtenay from Ballyedmond also featured on winners' lists in English steeplechases in the 1840s and 1850s.

Knaresborough created the greatest stir when he brought Dan O'Connell to England in 1837, but a reminiscence in the *Gentleman* magazine of February 1870 noted that the 'Fates were not kind. He refused a bank, and threw his rider at Liverpool, and at Cheltenham he came down at the last fence, and Vyvian won.' Knaresborough also brought two of Dan's stablemates, The Wonder, and FitzMaurice which was ridden by Allen McDonough in the precursor to the Grand National. Liverpool newspaper reports referred to the 'bank where Dan failed' in their reports from the course.

Amid confusing contradictory accounts of the three races regarded as precursors to the Grand National, it can be claimed that 1838 winner Sir William (trained and ridden by Allen McDonough) was the first Irish-trained winner of the then Liverpool Steeplechase, staged at Aintree and not Magull as official histories claim. Some sources claim the horse was ridden by Henry Potts, because Allen McDonough was injured. This is unlikely. Allen McDonough rode in the race following the National, and the report in the *Liverpool Chronicle* commends McDonough's brilliant riding in the race on board Sir William.

The victory of the 'little Irisher' Abdel Kader, trained by Joseph Osborne, at the Aintree Grand National of 1853 resumed the Anglo-Irish theme, with the *Omnibus* magazine commenting: 'The Irishman who lay on his back for joy in the enclosure, flung up his hat and his legs, rapped the ground with the heels of his boots, and screeched when he found that his £80 to £2 had come off, is only a type for what other broths of boys felt when Abdel Kader twice did the trick for them.'

> Steeple chases. The conclusion of the hunting season has as usual been marked by the occurrence of these races, though judging from the number that were advertised and did not fill, we should be inclined to think that the sport was not so highly prized as it used to be.
>
> *New Sporting* magazine, May 1831

During the century steeplechasing, kept out of the the organisational aspirations of the Jockey Club in England and the Turf Club in Ireland, embarked on a delicious underground history of its own.

Flat racing managed to extricate itself from the company of bareknuckle fighting, cockfighting, gaming and bull-baiting, inhabited by a seamy collection of characters who fraternised each of these events. The Irish Turf Club regulated bareknuckle fighting in the time of Dan Dougherty and Dan Donnelly. Henry Beresford was a patron of Deaf Burke, who used to declare, with no doubt a creative touch from *New Sporting* magazine: 'I was uncommon kind to that young mans. I took him in my gig, and taught him to fights.'

A glimpse at the Pink 'un (the *Sporting Times*) of the 1880s gives a picture of life on the racing circuit, whose eccentric staff included the Dwarf of Blood (Colonel Newnham-Davis), the Stalled Ox (Jimmy Davis), the Pitcher (Arthur Binstead) and the irrepressible Shifter (Willie Goldberg). The Pink 'un was famous for its uninhibited comment on racehorse owners, welshing bookmakers, theatrical productions and any other topic of the moment. Binstead produced two books of memoirs of the bohemian world of nineteenth-century horse racing.

The hierarchy of the Jockey Club in England and the Turf Club in Ireland refused to take upon itself the governance of racing over obstacles. There was no authority to which disputes could be referred and local stewards possessed no real powers. One contemporary writer said steeplechasing became 'the recognised refuge of all outcasts, human and equine, from the legitimate turf'. The welshing bookmaker was accorded a special status of ignominy of his own.

A dodge of these rascals is to adopt the names of some respectable bookmaker and by inserting advertisements in the sporting press, induce backers of the pigeon kind to send their golden eggs to the nests of the hawks.

CHARLES DICKENS, All the Year Round, 23 June 1868

One of the great writers of nineteenth-century English society set out to explain to his readers how horse racing worked in 1868.

Charles Dickens's summary of the racing scene is surprisingly familiar and compelling to a modern reader, down to his conclusion that betting based on illicit and secret information, rather than statistical nous and skill, was a 'thing of the past' a century and a half ago.

———

Any person visiting the racecourse at Newmarket, Epsom, Ascot, Liverpool, Chantilly or any similar place in England or France, must of late years have observed a number of regular attendants upon these events, who are seen throughout the racing season, first at one town and then another, wherever anything in the shape of steeplechase or flat race is to come off.

There is uniformity in the appearance of these individuals, which distinguishes them from all other classes. Their hats are almost invariably new, and evidently bought at fashionable shops. They are, with scarcely an exception, clean shaved, or at most only wear a thin mutton-chop whisker.

Their garments are nearly new, and, with the exception of a somewhat profuse quantity of watch-chain knick-knacks, they wear no more jewellery than well-dressed men should. When they meet on the platform at a railway, they always surname each other in the most cordial manner. 'How are you, Jones?' 'Fine day, Robinson.' 'Glad to see you, Brown.'

It is clear at a glance that these persons, though they appear to have abundant leisure, have their minds preoccupied by business. These persons are 'bookmakers'. Their trade is to attend every race of importance run in this country, in France, and even some few in Germany, and to make money by betting—by 'bookmaking'—not upon the way in which one horse beats the speed or the stamina of another horse, but by careful calculations, and making the result of betting upon one event cover that of another: to turn their money, and make an uncommon good thing out of what to the world outside the betting world, is almost invariably a snare and a loss.

There was a time when betting upon racing was confined to those who really took an interest in, or had some knowledge of horses. But times have changed. The peer bets his hundreds, the stockbroker his tens, the costermonger his half crowns. They cannot all bet with one another, for they have other occupations, and their time would be inconveniently consumed in seeking for persons to take or lay them the odds, and who would be good for payment should they lose. The consequence has been the demand for betting agents has created the supply, and excepting a few turf magnates who know each other well, everybody who in these days wishes to bet, looks out for a 'bookmaker.

The respectable bookmaker is generally—almost invariably—a self-made man. One of them, a man who could write a cheque (and, what is more, have it cashed) for fifty thousand pounds, was once a waiter in a well-known West end hotel famous some ten or a dozen years ago as the resort of military men given to betting, and for the sanded floor of the coffee room. Another, whose word is good any day among turf men for twenty-five or thirty thousand pounds, was, about half a dozen years back, butler and valet to a well-known sporting nobleman. A third once kept a small grocer's shop in a country town in the north of England. A fourth was a journeyman printer. A fifth used to drive a hansom cab. All these men began with small beginnings, and rose, upon their capacity for, and knowledge of, figures. The writer is no advocate of betting. If any one asked his advice how to lay out his money on a horse race, he would recommend to his client to leave the thing alone. In fact, the very winnings of the new calling are of themselves proofs enough that, as a rule, the public must lose its money, and the bookmakers must win.

There are two rules which no respectable bookmaker ever breaks. The first is, never to risk a single shilling over and above what he can pay down in hard cash 24 hours after the race. The second is, never to stand too much upon any one horse without hedging his money. It will hardly be believed what perfect confidence betting men among the general public—and in these days, particularly among what may be termed the lower middle classes, to bet is the rule, and not to bet the exception—will repose in bookmakers whom they know.

Among the outside public there is an idea that the whole betting world regulates its financial operations very much by relying on information obtained from the training stables, through persons who betray the trust reposed in them, and who divulge secrets respecting this horse beating his stable companion at a trial; that filly breaking down at exercise, or the other colt going wrong at his fetlock. This means of gaining information, however, is altogether a thing of the past. Ask any bookmaker what rule he observes in his betting throughout the years and he will reply that he 'follows the money'. He means that the market price of each horse guides him in all his speculations, and that of the quality or qualification of the horses he knows little or nothing. The said 'money' or 'market price'—the betting odds, in fact—are much more influenced by the owners of the horses wanting to pull up or push down the betting, than by any capabilities, or want of the same, in the horses themselves. Of course, when the owner of a really good horse thinks that the animal has a good chance to win a certain race, he backs him; but rarely without making his money safe by hedging upon some other horse in the same race.

There was a time when welshers and such like unmitigated rascals were to be found only in London, but now, thanks to cheap trains, they are to be found in every large town in England. Nay, in even small towns such as Cheltenham, Leamington and Bath. The nature of their frauds and the intense rascality of their calling, oblige them to be rolling stones. When the metropolis is too hot for them, they take themselves to Liverpool, or Leeds, and when those become too hot they emigrate to Manchester or Birmingham. After two or three years of provincial life he returns to London, and ends up in a police office and a jail.

Racing as now conducted is a pure matter of money making, and races might just as well be run by costermongers' donkeys as by the best blood in England, so far as it is conducive to any improvement in the breed of horses, apart from racing purposes.

All square said Stevens,
They back him at evens.
The race is all over,
Bar shouting they say.

I remember the wintry morn
And the mist on the Cotswold Hills
Where I once heard the blast of a huntsman's horn
Not far from the Severn rills
                    'How We Beat The Favourite' by ADAM LINDSAY GORDON

Cheltenham had its own poet. Adam Lindsay Gordon, a founder pupil at Cheltenham Boys College in the 1840s, had an aptitude for verse. He became a champion amateur rider, famously winning a steeplechase at Birdlip on a horse borrowed from Black Tom Oliver. That was his proudest moment.

His poem 'How We Beat The Favourite', describing a race over ditches and stone walls at Noverton, a short walk from the Cheltenham course of today, has been described as a classic of the genre. It describes either the Loamshire or Cheltenham Hunt Cup during the 1850s, poignant and eloquent verse constructed with melancholy, philosophical lyrics and jaunty sporting rhymes.

Expelled from Cheltenham College, Lindsay Gordon was banished to Australia by an embarrassed father, a professor of oriental languages, anxious that his son was frittering his life away on the turf. He became in turn a mounted policeman, an itinerant horse breaker, a gentleman steeplechaser, a provincial MP and land speculator until his infant son died and his stable burned down. Then, at the age of 37, he shot himself.

He was unstable and improvident, a classic Byronic *poète maudit*. Even his brief apotheosis as 'Australia's poet' on a memorial in Poets' Corner, Westminster Abbey, London, unveiled in 1934, was controversial, as he rarely wrote on Australian themes. He preferred to write about the Cheltenham steeplechases of his childhood.

He was the nearest thing England had to a racing poet.

Nor am I in the least disposed to sneer at gentlemen who like sporting and talk about it: for I do believe that the conversation of a dozen foxhunters is just as clever as that of a similar number of merchants, barristers, or literary men. But to this trade, as to all others, a man must be bred; if he has not learnt it thoroughly or in early life, he will not readily become a proficient afterwards, and when therefore the subject is broached, had best maintain a profound silence.
                                        WILLIAM THACKERAY

Steeplechasing was even more prominent in the Irish literature of the age, as even Henry Beresford was affectionately name checked in one of the more endearing passages about nineteenth-century Irish racing culture, William Thackeray's passage about being stuck in a horse racing conversation in his 1845 *Irish Sketch Book*:

> The town of Killarney was in a violent state of excitement with a series of horse-races, hurdle-races, boat-races, and stag-hunts by land and water, which were taking place, and attracted a vast crowd from all parts of the kingdom.
>
> All the inns were full, and lodgings cost five shillings a day—nay, more in some places; for though my landlady, Mrs. Macgillicuddy, charges but that sum, a leisurely old gentleman whom I never saw in my life before made my acquaintance by stopping me in the street yesterday, and said he paid a pound a day for his two bedrooms.
>
> The first sight I witnessed at Killarney was a race-ordinary, where, for a sum of twelve shillings, any man could take his share of turbot, salmon, venison, and beef, with port, and sherry, and whiskey-punch at discretion.
>
> Here were the squires of Cork and Kerry, one or two Englishmen, whose voices amidst the rich humming brogue round about sounded quite affected (not that they were so, but there seems a sort of impertinence in the shrill, high-pitched tone of the English voice here). At the head of the table, near the chairman, sat some brilliant young dragoons, neat, solemn, dull, with huge moustaches, and boots polished to a nicety.
>
> And here of course the conversation was of the horse, horsey: how Mr. This had refused fifteen hundred guineas for a horse which he bought for a hundred; how Bacchus was the best horse in Ireland; which horses were to run at Something races; and how the Marquis of Waterford gave a plate or a purse.
>
> We drank 'the Queen', with hip! hip! hurrah! the 'winner of the Kenmare stakes'—hurrah! Presently the gentleman next me rose and made a speech: he had brought a mare down and won the stakes—a hundred and seventy guineas—and I looked at him with a great deal of respect. Other toasts ensued, and more talk about horses.

The Beresford tradition continued for more than a century. Marcus Beresford, who ran Edward VII's stables in England, is a leading source on racing history. Patrick Beresford and his brother were leading polo players in the 1960s and 1970s and Patrick himself rode Blunt's Cross against Arkle in his surprise January 1962 victory in Navan.

Ireland produces nothing worthy of mention other than corn and excellent horses.

ELIZABETHAN SOLDIER

Thoroughbred sires were increasingly crossed on grade mares of various types. The notion of matching these faster hunters against each other, without the fox, was irresistible.

While steeplechase horses were bred from hunters, the English relied more on flat thoroughbred stallions to breed theirs, and soon thoroughbreds, or at the very least thoroughbred sires, were being used in breeding hunters and chasers.

Through judicious crossing of mares who were not completely thoroughbred or who at least could not be traced back to foundation mares listed in the *General Stud Book*, a number of half-bred mare families were established, especially in Ireland. They have provided steeplechasing with some of its greatest winners.

The arrival of thoroughbreds in Ireland came at a time of turmoil and had no lasting impact. Six stallions from the stud of Charles I, King of England, which had fallen into parliamentary hands, were sent to Colonel Michael Jones as a reward for defeating James Butler, Duke of Ormond, in the fascinating and complicated three-sided war of the 1640s. Five of these ended up in the hands of the O'Briens, Earls of Thomond, according to family tradition, or at least Edmund O'Brien's 1830s version of it.

The Byerley Turk, one of the four stallions from which all the world's great racehorses have descended, was used in the Battle of the Boyne in 1690. (On the opposite side, King James I is credited with the saying, 'All Irish horses are papists.') But the Turk too ended up back in Newmarket.

It was more than a century before Ireland acquired a reputation for breeding anything other than hunters. Athgarvan and Brownstown Studs were two of the earliest retirement homes for the champion stallion. It appears that only the fees have changed since the days when Sir Hercules covered mares in Harristown for five shillings and a glass of whiskey for the groom. Sir Hercules got most Irish thoroughbreds.

At Brownstown, Co. Kildare, he sired Birdcatcher who, in one legendary race at the Curragh in 1836, could not be stopped and ended up a mile further up the turnpike road to Newbridge. Birdcatcher's proud family included the first of the Irish-bred winners of the Epsom Derby, Daniel O'Rourke, two winners of the Doncaster St Leger and two winners of the Oaks. The studbooks start here.

> Being geldings, national hunt horses don't have much to look forward to in retirement. They aren't getting their oats in a figurative sense.
>
> ANDREW BAKER, *Independent*, 17 March 1996

Another reason to call upon thoroughbreds: there were no hunter sires. Steeplechasers were gelded, almost without exception. Removing the testicles was a standard practice for jump horses throughout the history of steeplechasing. The tradition goes back to Greek times, and with the growth of hunting and jump racing from the end of the seventeenth century, it became an accepted part of horselore.

So common is the practice that in 200 years of formal steeplechasing only a handful of horses which have not been castrated have won over jumps. Some colts have won over hurdles at the age of 3 and 4, and sometimes older. But they become reluctant at the age of 4, so most owners geld their colts as yearlings before they become reluctant to risk their colthood over thick fences. Those that have not been gelded can brush a fence with a delicate part of their anatomy and, understandably, become reluctant participants. The best time to geld is in the autumn after the flies have gone and before the wintry weather sets in. Proponents (which is everyone involved in steeplechasing) claim that the operation, done with a local anaesthetic, is quick and painless. The horse is back out in the field without realising what he is missing. A colt that is gelded too late is difficult to train.

Just one Cheltenham Gold Cup winner was an entire horse, the French 6-year old Fortina, who won in 1947 and retired to Grange Stud in Fermoy to replace Cottage as the leading sire of national hunt horses. His progeny included a son (Fort Leney 1968) and a daughter

(Glencaraig Lady 1972), who won the Gold Cup for Ireland, and dozens of other top-class chasers.

The Champion Hurdle, on the other hand, has been won seven times by entires. Monksfield, who won in 1978 and 1979, spent nine years at stud before his death in 1989. His best-known winners include Lakendara, Garrylough and It's a Snip.

Four mares have won the Gold Cup: Ballinode (1925), Kerstin (1958), Glencaraig Lady (1972) and Dawn Run (1986). And three mares have won the Champion Hurdle: African Sister (1939), Dawn Run (1986) and Flakey Dove (1994).

Arkle almost became the first horse in Cheltenham history to geld himself. On 20 April 1958 he was attracted by some fillies who had broken out of their paddock in the bottom field at Mary Baker's farm and decided to escape from his own home in the pond field by jumping the fence, topped with blackthorn and barbed wire. The barbed wire caught his small foreleg and tore open the skin, leaving a great gaping flap a foot long down his off-fore cannon-bone. It took 40 stitches to repair by his vet Maxie Cosgrove.

> He took over a portion of the same line as last day, by Mr Hope's of Castlewarden house to the tenth milestone on the Dublin road, over Mr Pidgeon's Hill, and down through the splendid grass field; across by the large demesne, where he went to ground in the wood. Boston Covert, the property of Lord Cloncurry, was then tried, with its usual successful result. Reynard went to the canal, then bent to the left, and over the scene of the last sportsman's race. Crossed the road up to the Hill of Oughterard to Mr David Ritchie's residence, through the garden at the rear of the house, on by the old churchyard, down through the large pasture field on the hill which faces Bishopscourt House; wheeled again to the right, and over to the quarries at Ardclough, and here the hounds were drawn off, owing to darkness setting in, and home was in order.
>
> *The Irish Times*, 7 January 1876

The hunt meetings of rural Ireland were more than social events. Some of the reportage in the newspapers tracked the movements of foxes, horses and hounds like a military report. The vigour with which those with time on their hands pursued the sport is impressive. *The Irish*

Times of 25 November 1867 reported: 'A lover of plenty of fox hunting should reside in County Kildare, as three days a week is generally considered good, but when it comes to four (out yesterday and today) I begin to think a man should be nurtured in pigskin to be able for it. Such is the love Baron de Roebeck (the master) has for the noble sport he is determined that each man that hunts should do so in the true acceptance of the term, namely, to be always ready and willing.'

'If he be a fox hunter,' the *Dublin Review* said of visitors to the country in May 1841, 'a few days with the Kildare, Kilkenny, Ormond, Limerick or some of the Connacht hunts, or with that prince of good, though also of queer fellows, the Marquis of Waterford, in Tipperary, will serve to show him the nerve and spirit of Irish men, horses, dogs and foxes.'

Celebrity tourists were invited to hunt as an important activity of their visit, such as Empress Elisabeth (Cissi) in 1879 and Prince Heinrich, the younger brother of Crown Prince Willem of Prussia, in 1902.

Point-to-point (or sportsman's races as they were known at an early stage) was a natural development from hunt meetings, by all accounts a derivative of the pounding matches with their own haphazard rules. Fairyhouse (Ward Union) and Punchestown (Kildare hunt) evolved from sportsman's courses.

Point-to-point race meetings began around 1860 just as steeplechases and hurdle races were being regulated. These races were run under the stewardship of the master of the foxhounds in the area over which they hunted. The cards began to take on a form, usually a farmers' race, a hunt race, a lightweight open and a heavyweight open race. They were officially recognised in 1889.

In point-to-points the object was to get to the finish over four miles of open country in the fastest time possible; the course route was left to each individual rider. In addition, the races were designed for horses that hunted, ridden by amateurs, although professionals began to take part in increasing numbers.

Some of the temporary courses became established venues in their own right, only to die out in the 1960s. The beautifully named Bracelet Stakes, confined to lady riders, was galloped over Windgates on the field where Istabraq spent his youth, one of the north Kildare point-to-point meetings held between 1912 and 1954.

Flickering newsreel coverage records Mrs Arthur Wall's victory in the event of 24 February 1924 in the midst of civil war. South County

Dublin hunt held their last point-to-point over nearby Boston Hill in 1962. Most point-to-points were eventually confined to enclosed grounds, although visitors will always claim that Punchestown and Fairyhouse have an aura of point-to-point about them. One of the events at Punchestown is still disparagingly referred to as the 'Farmers' Race'. Dan Moore, Tom Dreaper, Paul Carberry, Ruby Walsh and Adrian Maguire made their names on the point-to-point circuit.

The point-to-point has a romantic past, but the enthusiasm is not shared by all. Limestone Lad's owner and trainer Jim Bowe has an account of a long and injured walk back from a distant fall at a rural point-to-point.

In 1937 point-to-points were brought under the control of the National Hunt Committee, which does not allow professional riders in these races. They continue to serve as a source of income for local hunts and as a training ground for both horses and riders. Cheltenham Gold Cup and Grand National winners such as Teal, Merryman II, Four Ten, The Dikler, Cool Ground, Mr Mulligan, Cool Dawn and War Of Attrition all started as point-to-pointers. Florida Pearl and Best Mate competed at the same point-to-point meeting in Lismore.

> The farming classes, with very few exceptions, from Enfield to Celbridge, are strongly in favour of sustaining the hunt as absolutely necessary to the well being of the general community.
> Statement at public meeting during the War of Independence
> 'stop the hunt' campaign

National hunt racing skirted around the high politics of the Anglo-Irish War. The Easter Rebellion in 1916 coincided with the Irish Grand National and de Valera's General Strike of 1918 coincided with the first day of the Punchestown festival.

The English authorities told Irish race organisers that no race entries were to be accepted 'for horses the property of any persons being German, Austrian, Hungarian, Bulgarian or Turkish subjects or in which such persons have any interest whatsoever'.

When racing was banned in Ireland in May 1917, Edward Kennedy of the Irish Breeders, Owners and Trainers Association told a protest meeting that by banning racing the authorities were acting as recruiting sergeants for Sinn Féin in Ireland and for socialism in England. On

4 July the British government withdrew the April edict. Government sanction was required for all race meetings in 1918, and the number of race days was down to 112 (from 128 in 1915), and further down to 85 in 1918. Coal shortages and railway restrictions were the principal cause of the cuts, although provincial stewards chided the Turf Club and the National Hunt Committee for not giving them the option of running meetings independent of the rail services.

Hunting created an added difficulty during the national struggle. It was supported by the conservative colonial gentry and officers of the occupying British forces, but also by supporters of the independence movement.

Hunt gatherings targeted during the Land War of 1879–84 were often responding to local conditions, as in Kildare when the evicting land-lords Robert Bourke (Earl of Mayo) and Valentine Browne Lawless (Lord Cloncurry) took over as master from the less politically partisan (despite being a defeated electon candiate) Baron John de Roebeck.

In 1919 a new campaign went further with the deliberate disruption of national hunt racing as well as hunt meetings when Punchestown's entire festival and the 5 April point-to-point meeting at Windgates in Straffan were halted. By the end of February hunting outside of Ulster was brought to a halt by local activists who called on hunts to stop until there was a widescale release of prisoners.

Edwin Somerville was told by the Skibbereen Thomas McDonagh Sinn Féin Club that no member would be allowed to hunt or trespass on lands in the parish of Skibbereen until the prisoners were released. Joe Widger, an outstanding horse breeder in east Waterford, acceded to a request to stop hunting there. Hunting in Westmeath was sus-pended. Mr Watt took home the hounds when he met with a protest in Meath headed by Sean Boylan, the father of the later Meath football manager.

A confrontation in Batterstown, where a large number of police escorted the Ward Union, passed off without incident when the hunt was postponed.

The huntsmen who protested cited economic reasons and their aloofness from politics: the Irish Farmers Union branch at Maynooth, Kilcock and Donadea claimed that £80,000 was spent on hunting in Kildare alone. The Navan show set for 5 August was postponed, on the other hand, because of labour troubles in the town.

There was one major racing fatality during the War of Independence. The Turf Club's senior steward, Frank Brooke, an adviser to Lord Ffrench, was assassinated on 20 July 1920. The 1919 meeting of Miltown Malbay was postponed, and then on 14 April 1920, people gathered around a bonfire to celebrate the release of the Mountjoy prisoners were fired upon by police. Three men died instantly and many were injured in the stampede. Races scheduled for a fortnight later did not take place.

Upon the withdrawal of British troops it was feared the profile of events like Punchestown might suffer, where often more than half the Kildare hunt were British officers and the racecourse's officers' mess was a social fulcrum of the festival. The new government was anxious to confirm its alliance with racing and a Sinn Féin day was staged at Leopardstown soon after the ceasefire.

A less militaristic Anglo-Irish conflict would move to a different forum, and be cheered to the echo at Prestbury Park.

No county in Ireland, with the exception perhaps of Kildare, has been so hard hit by the removal of the British Garrison as this, and it has had a hard struggle for the past few years to keep going.

A. P. POLLOK, *Foxhunting in Ireland*

The degree of British army influence in hunting can be seen in a survey of the island's 23 clubs in the decades before the rise of the Cheltenham Festival and the personalities strongly associated with them: the Louth with Captain Filgate hunting the coverts at Mooretown, Cartown, Roger's Gorse and Silverstream; the Meath with Captain R. H. Fowler, Captain Hornsby, Captain Bob Dewhurst, John Watson (who hunted hounds five days a week for seventeen seasons) and Will Fitzsimons; Westmeath with Mrs Malone and Captain Winter; Kildare hounds with Baron de Roebeck, Francis Brooke and Major Mitchell; Kilkenny with Hercules Langrishe, Isaac Bell and Major Dermot McCalmont; Carlow with John Watson from 1808 to 1869, Robert Watson from 1869 to 1904 and Mrs Hall of Kellistown; Wexford hounds with Major Toby Lakin; the Island in north Wexford with Robert Watson and Colonel Hudson Kinahan; Coollattin with the Earl of Fitzwilliam and Dermot Doyne; Waterford with the Beresford family; West Waterford with Dorothy Musgrave; Tipperary with Thomas Ainsworth and Richard Burke; Limerick with Captain R. B. Brassey, Nigel Baring, Atty Persse and

A. Pollok; Scarteen (or the Black and Tans) with John Ryan, Dr McLoughlin and his nephew Major Walker; Duhallow with J. S. Shepherd; the Galway Blazers with Bowes Daly; East Galway with Mr Kenny; the Ormond hounds with Asheton Biddulph, G. S. Webb and L. H. Read; Laois (Queen's County) hounds with M. P. Minch and Major M. C. Hamilton; the United Hunt Club (Cork) with Major A. H. Watt; the Muskerry hunt with Captain A. H. Hornby; the Carberry with Patrick O'Driscoll; and the South Union (Cork) with C. A. Love. With partition, all the hunts ended up in the 26 counties; the six counties had staghounds and harriers.

After independence it is worth noting that three of the first twelve taoisigh were accomplished horsemen who rode to hounds (as was a Prime Minister of Northern Ireland). Charles Haughey (whose surname, *eachaidhe*, means 'horseman') had a third place in the Foxhunters Chase at Cheltenham with Flashing Steel in 1998, having won the Irish Grand National three years earlier. Finance Minister between 1997 and 2004 Charlie McCreevy is a Cheltenham veteran and a horse he part-owned, Chorelli, was considered a Gold Cup possibility until breaking a leg in the final race before the 1983 festival.

This compares with one taoiseach who played rugby to a high level and two who were knowledgeable followers of the game, with two taoisigh who played Gaelic games to inter-county level (one of whom, Jack Lynch, ranks among the greats of the games), and two more who were knowledgeable followers (one equally of soccer and Gaelic football), another taoiseach who was a knowledgeable follower, mainly of soccer, and a last taoiseach whose lack of knowledge on all things sporting was a national embarrassment. In addition, two tánaistí played soccer to League of Ireland level and another played international rugby. Two deputy first ministers in Northern Ireland also played Gaelic games to inter-county level.

The industry should have formed a mainstay for the new state's prestige. At the time of the treaty, Tetrarch, bred by Edward Kennedy in Ardclough, stood at Dermot McCalmont's stud in Mount Juliet and was for a time the world's leading sire. The number of meetings and prize money was increased. The Irish 2,000 Guineas was created in 1921 and the 1,000 Guineas in 1922.

The equine industry fared badly out of independence. Racing people were optimistic at first, but prize money began to decrease. The government's betting tax was only avoided after the cancellation of the Leopardstown meeting in 1925, and disillusionment with the quality and reputation of Irish race meetings reduced attendances. This was to be an important factor in shifting the focus of Irish racing away from Punchestown to Cheltenham.

The 1929 Totalisator Act which established the Tote under the control of the Turf Club and the Irish National Hunt Steeplechase Committee could have turned the situation around, especially as R. C. Dawson's Cloghran Stud in Co. Dublin produced four Derby winners sired by Blandford, but when, during the land annuities crisis, the British government put a 40 per cent tax on imported bloodstock, most Irish horses were shifted to England in advance of the measure.

In the following decade recession knocked the oats out of horse breeding in Ireland. After 1933 Irish horses, in common with all live-stock, largely went unsold. It took the boost of the wartime suspension of racing in England, the large-scale shift of horses in training to Ireland by Dorothy Paget and others, and the establishment of the Irish Racing Board in 1945 to counter the chronic decline of Irish breeding stock and a return to fortune for Irish-bred and trained horses.

Horses take flight and leave the earth, and hang for a half-second in a cloud of uncertainty before they know what the future will bring.
BILL BARICH, *A Fine Place to Daydream* (2005)

Under the new rules the jump game was divided into two types of races.

Hurdlers tackle three and a half foot high wooden frames tightly packed with gorse. Steeplechasers tackle four and a half foot high fences. A horse can often knock down a hurdle and keep going. A fence leaves much less room for error. Irish and British courses used to delight in adding further hazards for the steeplechaser. For every mile there must be at least one ditch, six foot wide and two foot deep on the take-off side, guarded by a band and a rail. A water jump at least twelve foot wide guarded by a fence is also compulsory. Jockeys and trainers argue that water jumps are unnecessary hazards. A fair proportion of falls occur when horses fail to clear the water and slip on landing.

Hurdle races are faster than steeplechases and usually shorter. Most of them are run over the minimum jumping distance of two miles. Irish and British rules state that there must be at least eight flights of hurdles over two miles, and an additional flight every quarter-mile after that. A two mile steeplechase contains at least twelve fences with at least six more obstacles for each additional mile.

Jumping races are held for ten months of the year, from August to June, on 40 tracks scattered across Ireland and Britain. An added attraction is the addition of hunter chases confined to horses that have been regularly hunted. In the early days of the sport hunter chases attracted horses which were not in the same class as racehorses, but after World War II they unearthed some top-class horses such as Freddie, Halloween, Teal, Oxo, Merryman II and Highland Wedding.

Flat races, being devoted to speed, are over quickly. But jump races were rich in subplots and dramatic reversals of fate. Plus they had a pastoral aspect that was transcendent, and entirely beautiful.
                        BILL BARICH, *A Fine Place to Daydream*

While flat racing is essentially an industry concerned with bloodstock breeding and high finance, steeplechasing remains a pure entertainment. The prospects of personal gain in this highly dangerous sport are so remote that the usual motivation for entering is a love of horses and the spirit of competition. Luck, good or bad, so governs the steeplechasing world that every contestant soon learns to lose graciously and be happy for another's success.

The spirit of camaraderie that exists on the jumping circuits is almost unknown in flat racing, where the greater sums of money at stake are liable to make every rival a deadly enemy and defeat something to be dreaded. Steeplechase trainers and jockeys do professional jobs while retaining the spirit of amateurism they have inherited from previous generations. Many of them carry on through sheer enthusiasm, with no hope of making more than a bare living.

Spectators too often show their preference for steeplechasing over the frenzied dash, often lasting little more than a minute, of flat racing. A race over fences or hurdles offers a prolonged promise of drama and heroics. For those who bet, jumps are no barrier to success. Form counts over jumps as much as it does on the flat. The additional factor of jumping ability counts too, but the uncertainty that the jumps add is a lure to the betting man.

With no international bloodstock industry behind it, because most horses are geldings and useless for breeding, jumping has spent its entire history extremely short of money.

> The sport of kings is our passion, the dogs too … nothing human is foreign to us, once we have digested the racing news.
>
> SAMUEL BECKETT

The decision to give the 1902 National Hunt Festival to Cheltenham would eventually lead to a seismic change in the nature of jump racing.

Cheltenham's initial tenure as host to the National Hunt Festival lasted only two years before the race moved to Warwick in 1904. But Cheltenham was determined to win the right to stage the race again, and after a seven year gap the National Hunt Chase, a four mile national hunt steeplechase, then open only to maidens ridden by amateurs, returned to Prestbury Park in 1911, and there it stayed.

Alongside the National Hunt Chase, innovative clerk of the course Frederick Cathcart introduced several new and extremely valuable races at Cheltenham. They included an important Grand National trial, the National Hunt Handicap Chase, the Gloucestershire Hurdle for novices, the County Handicap Hurdle and the revived Grand Annual Chase. In 1923 the festival was extended from two to three days.

In 1924 a new race was added to the programme, to offer a chance for long-distance chasers to compete against each other under level terms in a weight-for-age race. Despite its grandiose title, the Cheltenham Gold Cup was not regarded among the most important races of the meeting. Three years later Cheltenham introduced a weight-for-age hurdling championship, the Champion Hurdle.

The timing could not have been better. Within a few years the two races had captured the imagination of the racing public, thanks to some Irish-bred horses, Irish owners, Irish jockeys and Irish trainers who were at the heart of that achievement. Steeplechasing was enjoying a revival in the 1920s. Wealthy new owners entered the fray: Jock Whitney, Ambrose Clarke, Vivian Hugh Smith (the first Lord Bicester) and Whitney's cousin, the deliciously eccentric Dorothy Paget, who injected impossibly large amounts of money into the sport, money they could never hope to win back.

Ireland, birthplace of the steeplechase, was at the heart of the transformation of Cheltenham into the most entertaining event in horse racing.

Chapter 3 ⌒

| MECCA OF MARCH

This annual tribal gathering is invariably spoken of in an affectionate, sometimes reverent manner. Criticism of it is tantamount to blasphemy. Cheltenham is also used as a key reference point in the tribal calendar. Just as we might speak of something happening 'before Christmas' or 'after Easter', Racing Tribe enthusiasts will say, 'We must get together after Cheltenham.'

KATE FOX, *The Racing Tribe*

Cheltenham in mid-March, and there is not an empty hotel room or bar stool in sight. By 2009 there were 26 races overall and 450 horses competing over the four days in some of the most hotly contested races of the entire racing calendar. The races are each distinctive, and the characteristics are not immediately apparent from the title or even the list of those eligible. There is a hierarchy of achievement. Each race represents a carefully delineated stratum of society that is unique to itself.

Money counts. In a sport in which just one in ten horses yields their owners any sort of profit, they compete for £3.5 m of prize money in grade 1 events including the Champion Bumper, Triumph Hurdle, Ryanair Chase, Supreme Novices Hurdle, Ballymore Properties Novices Hurdle, Arkle Challenge Trophy, Royal & SunAlliance Chase, Champion Hurdle, World Hurdle, Queen Mother Champion Chase and the feature race, the Cheltenham Gold Cup.

The festival is a diverse and eclectic affair, with novices, veterans, amateurs, professionals, converted thoroughbred flat horses, classic steeplechasers, hunters and point-to-pointers all sharing the sward.

Each race is a biggie in its own context. One of the two biggest hunter chases of the season, the Foxhunters, is run on the Friday over the same course as the Gold Cup and is also known as the amateurs' Gold Cup.

The festival was traditionally run over three days. An experimental fourth day was added in 1995 because drainage works at the track would prevent further meetings being held that year. It attracted a disappointing crowd of 16,835 (compared with a Gold Cup day attendance of 57,804 and attendances of 42,875 and 38,450 the first two days).

After much procrastination, a fourth day proper was added in 2005 and the Gold Cup was transferred to the Friday. This time the idea worked, although it had many critics, and still has.

The organisers say there are options for new races, like a two and a half mile hurdle, a long-distance chase or another bumper, but Edward Gillespie, Cheltenham's managing director, says he doesn't want to be accused of 'diminishing quality or thinning things out'.

The Cheltenham formula is being replicated everywhere, not least Cheltenham itself for its winter festival. Festival racing is the norm, as days are added and pots increase. Amid all this, Cheltenham remains entrenched at the heart of Irish popular culture.

―――

Soft day, thank God. The first day of the festival is ideal when the going is softest. As the course has become firmer in recent years the organisers have turned on the taps to soften up the ground.

The ground can contribute to injuries, so the intention of the organisers is to have it always on the slow side of good. Throughout the history of the festival there have been concerns about the high number of injuries and fatalities to horses. This was brought to a head in 2006 when eleven horses died. Nine died during the four-day meeting and two more later succumbed to injuries sustained there.

An inquiry by the Horse Racing Regulatory Authority into last year's rash of fatalities concluded, in effect, that it was a statistical blip, although a fence on the far side of the course has been moved back a few yards and is no longer on an incline. It is speed that kills horses; soft ground slows them down.

―――

The Supreme Novices Hurdle (1.30 pm on Tuesday) is traditionally greeted by the 'Cheltenham Roar' which signifies the beginning of the festivities. The race was sponsored by Anglo Irish Bank from 2006 to 2008.

The race has a reputation for showcasing stars of the future. Hors La Loi III, winner in 1999, and Brave Inca, winner in 2004, went on to win the Champion Hurdle in 2002 and 2006. Three times Gold Cup winner Best Mate was second to Sausalito Bay here in 2000, Kicking King was second to Back In Front in 2003 and War Of Attrition was second to Brave Inca in 2004.

Every second year the race is won by horses with two or fewer runs over hurdles. It was the scene of one of the great Irish betting windfalls in 1991 when Destriero, owned by Dublin carpet millionaire and former world poker champion Noel Furlong, yielded £1 m for its connections at 6/1.

The race has been won by Irish-trained horses 38 times throughout its history, and by the French once. Remarkably, horses trained at nine different Irish stables have won eleven of the last eighteen (and six out of the last eight) races, including Noel Meade with Go Native (2009), Edward Harty with Captain Cee Bee (2008), Willie Mullins with 40/1 shot Ebaziyan (2007, a horse formerly trained for the flat by John Oxx) and Tourist Attraction (1995), Colm Murphy with Brave Inca (2004), Edward O'Grady with Back In Front (2003), Christy Roche with Like A Butterfly (2002), Noel Meade with Sausalito Bay (2001), Pat Flynn with French Ballerina (1998) and Montelado (1993, the only horse in festival history to have won two successive races, having won the finishing race in 1992), Andy Geraghty with Destriero (1991), Mouse Morris with Buck House (1983), Dessie Hughes with Miller Hill (1982), Mick O'Toole with Hartstown (1981) and Mac's Chariot (1977), Liam Browne with Slaney Idol (1980), Des McDonogh with Stranfield (1979), Edward O'Grady with Golden Cygnet (1978), Padge Berry with Bannow Rambler (1975), Christy Grassick with Noble Life (1972), Paddy Sleator with Ballywilliam Boy (1970) and Havago (1965), Dan Moore with L'Escargot (1968) and Tripacer (1962), Tom Dreaper with Flyingbolt (1964), Kilcullen-based Paddy Murphy with Clerical Grey (1962), and Vincent O'Brien with ten winners, Admiral Stuart and Prudent King (1958), Saffron Tartan (1957), Pelargos and Boys Hurrah (1956), Illyric and Vindore (1955), Stroller (1954) and Cockatoo (1952), and Danny Morgan with Assynt (1953).

Until 1974 the race was known as the Gloucestershire Hurdle after the county in which Cheltenham is situated. Prior to 1972 it was split into separate divisions, usually two, but in 1946 and 1963 there were three races. Of the sixteen divisions from 1952–59, Vincent O'Brien won ten. It was the race which rescued Irish hopes at the festival in 1957 when Saffron Tartan, in the words of *Irish Times* columnist John Healy, 'carried many a boat and air fare on his back after they had taken a fair gruelling beforehand.' Ireland kept a stranglehold on the race for seven years, 1977–83.

The 1964 winner Flyingbolt, a stable companion of Arkle, won the Cotswold Chase in 1965 and the Queen Mother Champion Chase and Irish Grand National in 1966. The 1968 winner L'Escargot later won the Cheltenham Gold Cup in 1970 and 1971 and the Grand National in 1975. The 1970 winner Bula went on to win the Champion Hurdle in 1971 and 1972.

It is run over the Champion Hurdle course with a distance of two miles and about half a furlong. The race is open to novices aged 4 years old and upwards, and the total prize fund is £120,000. There are eight hurdles to be jumped in the race.

———

The Arkle Challenge Trophy (2.05 pm on Tuesday) is the champion chase for novices. Inaugurated in 1946 as the Cotswold Chase, it was given its present name in 1969 to honour Tom Dreaper's great Cheltenham hero Arkle. Fittingly, Dreaper was the first to win the race for Ireland with Fortria in 1958 and went on to win it five times in all. Irish trainers have won it fifteen times, including Tom Cooper with the wittily named Forpadydeplasterer (2009, owned by Charlie Chawke and the Goat racing syndicate), Jessica Harrington with Moscow Flyer (2002), Arthur Moore with Klairon Davis (1995) and The Brickshee (1982), Edward O'Grady with Ventana Canyon (1996), Andrew McNamara with Boreen Prince (1985), Francis Flood with Bobsline (1984), Bill Durkan with Anaglog's Daughter (1980), Mick O'Toole with Chinrullah (1979, who passed the post first in the following year's Champion Chase, only to be disqualified some time after the event because of a positive drug test), Tom Dreaper with Alpheus (1971),

Flyingbolt (1965), Ben Stack (1963), Mountcashel King (1961) and Fortria (1958), and Pat Rooney with Arctic Stream (1967).

The race provided one of the great Anglo-Irish battles in Cheltenham history when Noddy's Ryde, ridden by Neale Doughty and trained by Gordon Richards, represented England against the Francis Flood-trained Bobsline, ridden by Frank Berry in 1984.

Noddy's Ryde took up the pace six out and only Bobsline could stay with him coming down the hill. The two jumped the last together and stayed together up the hill until Bobsline forged ahead near the line to win by a length and a half.

Bobsline went on to contest the 1985 Champion Chase, only to fall at the third last in and break a small bone in his hind leg, and though he subsequently won many more races, he was never as good again. Noddy's Ryde tragically broke a leg at Exeter in the Haldon Gold Cup at the start of the following season.

It has also had three Irish sponsors: Waterford Crystal from 1991 to 1993, Guinness from 1994 to 1999 and the *Irish Independent* since 2000. The novices have to travel and jump faster than they ever have before and there has been just one winning favourite since 1991. The fields for this event tend to be smaller than for most of the other races at the festival.

The 1979 Gold Cup winner Alverton won this race a year previously, while the 2005 (Kicking King) and 2006 (War of Attrition) Gold Cup winners had also run in this race the year previously. And Best Mate would have too, were the meeting not abandoned due to the outbreak of foot and mouth disease.

Since 1991 six winners of the race have gone on to win the Queen Mother Champion Chase, including Flagship Uberalles, Moscow Flyer, Azertyuiop and Voy Por Ustedes, while a further five winners have been placed. Arkle's stablemate Flyingbolt was the only winner to subsequently win the Champion Chase. The 1956 winner, Sir Ken, was a previous triple Champion Hurdle winner.

The race is run on the Old Course over two miles and is open to horses aged 5 years and upwards. The total prize fund is £170,000. There are twelve fences to be jumped in the race.

The William Hill Trophy (2.40 pm on Tuesday) is the first big handicap of the meeting and is therefore a very popular betting race. One of the first Irish successes at Cheltenham when Charlie Rogers won with Dorothy Paget's Dunshaughlin (1946), it has come to Ireland just seven times since, including Tony Martin with Dun Doire (2006), Christy Roche with Youllneverwalkalone (2003), with three Tom Dreaper and one Vincent O'Brien victory in the 1950s and 60s.

As with all the handicaps run at the festival, the race often features a large field and is fiercely competitive. Antonin in 1994 was the only favourite to win since 1977, and punters emphasise the importance of picking an improving horse which is well handicapped for the run.

The race has become a stepping stone to the Grand National rather than the Gold Cup (something that was originally intended for the Gold Cup itself), although only Rough Quest has done the double in recent years.

It is a class A grade 3 chase run over three miles and about half a furlong. It is open to horses aged 5 years and upwards. The total prize fund is £90,000. No horse aged more than 11 has been placed since 1997 from 27 runners, and the last ten winners have all carried less than eleven stone.

—

The Champion Hurdle (3.20 pm on Tuesday) is the highlight of the first day of the Cheltenham Festival and the most prestigious hurdle race on the calendar. A huge cheer rings out from the grandstands when the runners pass the enclosures for the first time. However, it is often the jumping out in the country that sorts the field out, and the pace quickens as the contenders turn off the final bend and face the killing quarter-mile climb to the finish.

It became an Irish sponsored race in 1990 when the Smurfit Group stepped in to replace a major banking group which withdrew its sponsorship. Kappa was added to the title in 2006 to reflect the company's new corporate identity.

First won for Ireland by Maxwell Arnott with Distel (1946), some of the greatest names in Irish sporting history have won the race, including Hatton's Grace, Monksfield, Dawn Run, Hardy Eustace and

Istabraq. Ireland has won seventeen out of the 79 renewals, including Maynooth-based John Carr with Sublimity (2007), Colm Murphy with Brave Inca (2006, when Ireland provided the first three past the post for the second successive year), Dessie Hughes with Hardy Eustace (2004 and 2005), Aidan O'Brien with Istabraq (1998, 1999 and 2000), Paddy Mullins with Dawn Run (1984), Michael Cunningham with For Auction (1992) and Des McDonogh with Monksfield (1978 and 1979), who fought a series of key Anglo-Irish battles with the Peter Easterby-trained Sea Pigeon (runner-up in 1978 and 1979 and winner in 1980 and 1981).

Before that you to go back to the 1963 champion, the one-eyed Winning Fair, trained in County Tipperary by George Spencer, father of champion flat jockey Jamie Spencer, to Paddy Sleator with Another Flash (1960) and further back to Vincent O'Brien's treble with Hatton's Grace (1949–51).

When Dawn Run won the race in 1984, she was the first mare to do so, two years before she became the only horse to date to win both the Champion Hurdle and Gold Cup at Cheltenham. The 1947 runner-up Le Paillon went on to win that year's Prix de l'Arc de Triomphe, the most prestigious flat race in Europe.

Horses with previous course form, and especially previous festival form, have fared particularly well in the event. Punters need to pick a horse that stays further than two miles, and recent SunAlliance (later Ballymore Properties) Novices Hurdle winners have a good record in the race.

The race is open to horses aged 4 years and upwards and carries a total prize fund of £370,000. It is run over a distance of two miles 110 yards (3,319 m) on the Old Course. Prior to 1980 the distance was about 110 yards further. There are eight hurdles to be jumped in the race.

————

The Cross-Country Chase (4.00 pm on Tuesday) has become an Irish speciality, or rather a speciality for the trainer who was once one of Ireland's greatest point-to-point jockeys, Enda Bolger, and the top female jockey Nina Carberry. Enda has trained the winner of this event four times in five years—Spot The Difference (2005), Heads On the Ground (2007) and Garde Champetre (2008 and 2009). All were owned by J. P. McManus. The last three were ridden by Nina Carberry. Bolger trained and McManus owned the first three home in 2009.

The cross-country course takes racing at Cheltenham back to its roots with a selection of natural and man-made obstacles incorporating banks, ditches, hedges, water and timber rails. While steeplechase fences are constructed from dead materials, the fences on the cross-country course are living, growing trees, shrubs and bushes, which are regularly trimmed.

Designed by Mike Etherington-Smith, who was responsible for the three-day event cross-country course at the Sydney Olympics in 2000, the configuration of the course deliberately weaves around the centre of Prestbury Park, with turns to the left and right leading competitors on a variety of routes and directions.

The inaugural Cross-Country Chase was won by one of the most popular equine stars of the sport, cross-country specialist Spot the Difference, who was retired at the age of 14 after a glittering career. The J. P. McManus-owned gelding won seven times at Cheltenham in cross-country races and also won Punchestown's La Touche Cup twice, the first of them in 2003.

It has been dominated by one of the most popular jockeys at the festival, Paul Carberry. When Paul talked about his father's career as a jump jockey and the family after Bobby Jo won the Grand National in 1999, he said his sister Nina was 'the best of all of us'. She was 14 at the time.

It was the first of the new races to be added to the programme in 2002 to create the new four-day festival. It is run over three miles seven furlongs of the cross-country course. It is open to horses aged 5 years and upwards and has a total prize fund of £50,000.

————

The David Nicholson Mares Hurdle (4.40 pm, last race on Tuesday) is a mares only event added in 2009 and named in honour of David Nicholson, described by Cheltenham racecourse MD Edward Gillespie as 'both Cheltenham's strongest supporter and fiercest critic'. The inaugural race was won by Willie Mullins with 2/1 favourite Quevega, ridden by Ruby Walsh. She won by fourteen lengths despite a poor start when she was off last as the tape went up. The race is a grade 2 hurdle run over two miles and about four and a half furlongs (4,124 m). It is open to mares aged 4 and above. The total prize fund is £100,000. The inaugural race attracted 21 runners, showing the level of interest.

——

Wednesday's programme begins with the National Hunt Chase Challenge Cup (1.30 pm), a class B chase run over four miles, the longest and oldest race at the festival and known as the 'amateurs' Grand National'.

It is the race around which the festival was originally built. Until the 1930s only the Grand National was more important than the National Hunt Chase in the jump calendar. It was run at a number of venues until it became part of the new two-day National Hunt Festival at Cheltenham in 1911.

After 139 runnings it is also considered the most difficult to predict. There has been only one winning favourite in recent times. Owners sometimes cite this race as the weakest in the festival in terms of class and therefore the easiest to win.

Famously, it was the first target of J. P. McManus at the festival when he sent out his first horses, Jack of Trumps (1978) and Deep Gale (1979) in the race, heavily backed but unsuccessfully, before Edward O'Grady won the race for him with Bit of a Skite (1983). McManus hadn't backed the successful horse.

The Cork-born though now locally based Jonjo O'Neill has trained four of the last seven winners. No 6-year old has won since 1989 and no successful 5-year old has won it for over 30 years.

Notable Irish winners include Ian Duncan with Another Run (2005), Michael Hourigan with Deejaydee (1999), Eddie O'Grady with Loving Around (1996), Bit of a Skite (1983) and Mr Midland (1974), Homer Scott with Omerta (1986), Paddy Mullins with Macks Friendly (1984) and Hazy Dawn (1982), Dan Moore with Arctic Ale (1979) and Mick O'Toole with Gay Tie (1977). The previous Irish winner was Pat Taaffe's father Tom with Dorimant in 1964.

Roly Daniels burst into a verse of Danny Boy as his horse Hazy Dawn entered the winner's enclosure after winning in 1982. He had bought the horse in 1980 on the recommendation of his brother-in-law Terry Casey, a former jump jockey who was head lad at the time with trainer Pat Hughes, because her initials HD coincided with the initials of his hit record 'Hello Darling'.

The race is open to novices aged 5 years and upwards. All horses have to be ridden by amateurs. The total prize fund is £75,000. There is now a safety limit of 24 in the field. Amateur jockeys have to be category B (Britain) or category C (Ireland) riders to take part in the race.

———

The Ballymore Properties Novices Hurdle (2.05 pm on Wednesday) was introduced in 1971 as the Aldsworth Hurdle and is registered as the Baring Bingham Novices Hurdle. The insurance company SunAlliance began sponsoring the race in 1974. It became the SunAlliance Novices Hurdle and, confusingly, the sponsors changed the name of the race three times in as many years eventually to Royal & SunAlliance Novices Hurdle after the merger of Royal Insurance and SunAlliance in 1996. Sponsorship was taken over by the Irish property developer Sean Mulryan in 2007.

The 1975 winner Davy Lad went on to win the 1977 Cheltenham Gold Cup. The 1997 winner Istabraq became the first winner of this race to go on to win the Champion Hurdle. Hardy Eustace was the second. In 1983 Sabin du Loir (one of Peter Scudamore's favourite rides) defeated future Champion Hurdle and Cheltenham Gold Cup winner Dawn Run into second place and future Grand National winner West Tip into third place. Sabin du Loir also won the John Bull Chase ten years later.

The victory of Edward O'Grady's Mister Donovan launched the career of one of the great Cheltenham personalities. John P. McManus backed Mister Donovan from 6/1 to 9/2 on the day to take £250,000 out of the ring. Tom Foley's 1994 winner, Danoli, was also the subject of a massive gamble by McManus and was sent off the 7/4 favourite to win. An even shorter priced winner was Liam Browne's Mr Kildare at 8/11 in 1978. But such big bets are fraught with danger. When Harcon was beaten in the SunAlliance Chase of 1995, bets included £70,000 to win £40,000 and another of £35,000 to win £20,000. Favourites have been successful in just twelve of the 36 runnings.

Just one winner from well over a hundred runners since 1974 was aged older than 6. Six-year olds have won seven of the last nine runnings. Unlike the Supreme Novices Hurdle, this race suits both top-class stayers from the flat and the more old-fashioned chasing type.

The fourteen Irish winners (including six consecutive victories from 1973–78) include Willie Mullins with Mikael D'Haguenet (2009) and Fiveforthree (2008), Noel Meade with Nicanor (2006), Dessie Hughes with Hardy Eustace (2003), Aidan O'Brien with Urubande (1996) and Istabraq (1997), Tom Foley with Danoli (1994), Edward O'Grady with Mister Donovan (1982) and Dromlargan (1980), Liam Browne with Mr Kildare (1978), Mick O'Toole with Davy Lad (1975) and Parkhill (1976), Paddy Osborne with Brown Lad (1974) and Adrian Maxwell with Willie Wumpkins (1973).

The race is a class A grade 1 hurdle run over two miles five furlongs (4,225 m) on the Old Course. It is open to novices aged 4 years and upwards. The total prize fund is £120,000. There are ten hurdles to be jumped in the race.

———

The RSA (formerly the Royal & SunAlliance) Chase (2.40 pm on Wednesday) takes its name from its sponsors, the insurance company Royal & SunAlliance. It is the race where Arkle first showed his prowess to the Cheltenham multitude. The sponsorship dates back to 1974— prior to the merger of Royal Insurance and SunAlliance in 1996, the race was known as the SunAlliance Chase. The only previous sponsor of the race was the Tote (the Totalisator Champion Novice Chase, 1964–73), before which the race was called the Broadway Novices Chase.

Joe Osborne first won the race for Ireland with Conneyburrow in 1953. Since then the fourteen Irish winners include Willie Mullins with Cooldine (2009), Rule Supreme (2004) and Florida Pearl (1998), Pat Hughes with Antarctic Bay (1985), Dan Moore with Tied Cottage (1976), Jim Dreaper with Ten Up (1974), Paddy Mullins with Herring Gull (1968), Tom Dreaper with Proud Tarquin (1970), Arkloin (1965) and, most notably, Arkle (1963).

Arkle, Ten Up, Master Smudge, Garrison Savannah, Looks Like Trouble and Denman all subsequently won the Cheltenham Gold Cup.

Master Smudge was awarded victory in the Gold Cup after Tied Cottage was disqualified for failing a drug test.

Twelve of the last fourteen winners were aged 7 or 8. Just two 6-year olds have won since 1978. Until recently shocks were often a feature of this event.

Cheltenham is always a tough place for novice chasers, and the quicker pace of festival races and the stamina-sapping trips have all probably contributed to this statistic. Some trainers prefer to avoid the race altogether and target their best staying novices at other festivals later in the year.

A grade 1 national hunt chase for 5-year-old and above novices, it is run over a distance of three miles 110 yards (4,929 m) on the Old Course. The total prize fund is £170,000. There are nineteen fences to be jumped in the race.

The feature race on the second day of the festival is the Queen Mother Champion Chase (3.20 pm on Wednesday), a great demolition Derby of a race which started as a novelty 50 years ago and has emerged as the highlight of the festival, just as the Gold Cup and Champion Hurdle did in their turn.

It is also the race associated with Flyingbolt, arguably the greatest Irish chaser never to have won the Gold Cup, and Crisp, the greatest English chaser never to have won it either. TV personality Ted Walsh won the race as a jockey on Hilly Way in 1979, leading to one of the great apocrypha of Irish broadcasting when he declared: 'I rode the Queen Mother.'

Ireland's twenty winners include John Murphy with Newmill (2006), Jessica Harrington with Moscow Flyer (2003 and 2005), Arthur Moore with Klairon Davis (1996) and Drumgora (1981), Mouse Morris with Buck House (1986), Peter McCreery with Hilly Way (1978 and 1979), Brian Lusk with Skymass (1976 and 1977), Dan Moore with Inkslinger (1973) and Quita Que (1959), Jim Dreaper with Lough Inagh (1975) and his father Tom with Straight Fort (1970), Muir (1969), Ben Stack (1964), Flyingbolt (1966) and Fortria (1960 and 1961).

The race was first run in 1959 as the Champion Chase. The title was changed in 1980, the year of her 80th birthday, as a mark of appreciation to George v's wife and queen consort Elizabeth Bowes-Lyon-Windsor, the mother of England's Queen Elizabeth Windsor, a woman credited with setting the tone for the modern less-formal monarchy, in recognition of the profile she brought to the Cheltenham Festival. Before 2007 the race was not sponsored, but since then it has been run with the sponsored title of the Seasons Holidays Queen Mother Champion Chase.

Given the pace as the best two mile chasers in the business attack the twelve Cheltenham fences at speed, surefooted jumping is more important in this race than any other at the festival. The pace is un-relenting from start to finish, and even the slightest mistake can cost a horse more than a length. Ditches out in the country and the second and third last fences coming down the hill provide key moments in the race, the scene of epic battles between Edredon Blue and Direct Route in 2000, or Viking Flagship, Travado and Deep Sensation in 1994, and the emotional triumph for One Man in 1998 when Brian Harding's winning ride subsequently won the Lester Award for 'Jump Ride of the Year'.

Favourites have a great record in the race. Nine of the last eleven Arkle Trophy winners were first or second in the Queen Mother the following year. Kauto Star fell in the 2006 Queen Mother Champion Chase. Many winners of the race have been rated higher by the handicapper than the winner of the King George or the Gold Cup.

The race, a class A grade 1 chase open to horses aged 5 and upwards, has fewer entrants than the other grade 1 events. The total prize fund is £320,000. It is run over a distance of two miles (3,219 m).

——

The Coral Cup Handicap Hurdle (4.00 pm on Wednesday) is the first of the big handicap hurdles run at the meeting and is therefore a big betting race. Some huge gambles have been foiled by relatively uncon-sidered outsiders and only two favourites have won the race, Olympian in 1993 and Xenophon, which was backed down from long odds to 4/1 favourite in 2003.

Punters watch out for a well-handicapped horse. Veteran gamblers wait until the day of the race to see where the money is going before choosing.

The six Irish winners include Tom Taaffe with Ninetieth Minute (2009, a popular win under jockey Paddy Flood), Edward O'Grady with Sky's The Limit (2006) and Time For A Run (1994, when he famously instructed Charlie Swan to 'ride with balls of steel'), Tony Martin with Xenophon (2003), Christy Roche with Khayrawani (1999, when Irish horses filled the first three places) and Pat O'Donnell with Chance Coffey (1996, when Ireland also filled the first three places).

Open to horses aged 5 and upwards, the race is a class A grade 3 handicap hurdle run over two miles four and a half furlongs (4,124 m). The total prize fund is £80,000.

The Fred Winter Juvenile Novices Handicap Hurdle (4.40 pm on Wednesday) is named after arguably the greatest jump jockey of his era and later a great trainer, champion jump jockey four times and champion trainer of steeplechasers and hurdlers eight times between 1971 and 1985.

The two Irish winners were Mick Quinlan with Silk Affair (2009, a first success for both trainer and jockey Tom O'Brien) and Paul Nolan with Dabiroun (2005, ridden by Nina Carberry).

Nina Carberry became the first female jockey to win a race at the festival since Gee Armitage on Gee-A in 1987, just hours after her brother Paul had been jeered by punters after his exaggerated waiting tactics had cost Harchibald the Champion Hurdle.

It is a long-odds race. Just three horses priced at under 10/1 have finished in the first seven in five runnings of this race. A listed race run over two miles and about half a furlong, the race is open to 4-year-old novices only and carries a total prize fund of £80,000.

The Weatherby's Champion Bumper Open NH Flat Race (5.15 pm on Wednesday) was added to the programme in 1992, almost certainly to create more interest among Irish trainers after the catastrophic festival for Ireland in 1989 that did not produce a single Irish winner.

Flat races over national hunt courses, or bumpers, were an Irish trait. Few English racecourses staged them until the late 1970s, and Cheltenham's was instantly the most prestigious in national hunt racing.

Like all bumpers, this event has often featured horses which subsequently became leading hurdlers or chasers. This makes it worthwhile keeping an eye not just on the placed horses but also on some of those further back in the field. Best known was Florida Pearl, Willie Mullins's 1997 winner, who went on to win a host of grade 1 steeplechases in Britain and Ireland.

Irish-trained horses have won thirteen of the sixteen runnings since, and all of the first eight horses home in 2009 were trained in Ireland, led by Philip Fenton who had a first festival success with Dunguib. Mullins, who had eight horses in the 2009 race, has trained six winners. He rode his first winner of the race, the 1996 scorer Wither Or Which, while his son Patrick was in the saddle when Cousin Vinny won for the stable in 2008.

The winners include Cousin Vinny (2008), Missed That (2005), Joe Cullen (2000), Alexander Banquet (1998), Florida Pearl (1997) and Wither Or Which (1996). Ireland's other winners include Jessica Harrington with Cork All Star (2007, after which owner Cathal Ryan, son of the Ryanair founder, tragically died of cancer within months of his father), Joe Crowley with Hairy Molly (2006), Tom Cooper with Total Enjoyment (2004), Edward O'Grady with Pizarro (2002) and Mucklemeg (1994), Homer Scott with Rhythm Section (1993) and Pat Flynn with Montelado (1992).

Trabolgan, French Holly, Iris's Gift, Thisthatandtother, Rhinestone Cowboy, Wichita Lineman, Albertas Run and Fiveforthree, to name but a few, were all beaten here but subsequently went on to make big names for themselves over hurdles or fences.

The race is a class A grade 1 flat race open to horses which are aged 4 to 6 years old. It is run over a distance of two miles 110 yards (3,319 m) on the Old Course and has a total prize fund of £60,000.

Unlike most bumpers, professional jockeys are allowed to ride. Jockeys from flat racing sometimes take part. Jamie Spencer rode the winner in 2002.

———

The Jewson Novices Handicap Chase (1.30 pm on Thursday) was one of the new races introduced to the four-day festival in 2005. It was won for the first time for Ireland in 2008 by Tom Taaffe with Conor Clarkson's Finger Onthe Pulse. 'Cheltenham is the know all and be all to me,' said Taaffe. 'It's the mecca and has been since I was a kid. To win by a neck here is as good as a mile elsewhere.' It has been won previously by two Irish-owned horses, J. P. McManus's Reveille (2007) and Mary Durkan's L'Antartique (2008).

———

The Pertemps Final Handicap Hurdle (2.05 pm on Thursday) is a big betting race and there have been rumoured coup attempts down the years with the suspicion that certain horses have been laid out specifically for the race.

This is a race known for attracting a monster gamble on the morning of the race, often on an Irish runner. J. P. McManus's two 50/1 victories in the race with Creon in 2004 and Kadoun in 2006 were the famous gambler's longest priced victors. After Kadoun's victory McManus said: 'I had a little bit on him. You never have enough on them when they win. I'd forgotten he was in this race!'

Despite this, there have been only five Irish winners, including Michael O'Brien with Kadoun (2006), Dessie Hughes with Oulart (2005), John Hassett with Generosa (1999), Harry de Bromhead with Fissure Sea (1993) and Michael Purcell with My View (1992).

In order to participate in the race, all runners have to have competed in one of the qualifying races that are run throughout the year. The final is a class A listed hurdle run over three miles open to horses aged 5 and upwards who have qualified for the final. The total prize fund is £80,000. Despite the mythology of giant gambles and raids on the bookmaking fraternity, two of the last six winners were priced at 50/1.

———

The Ryanair Chase (2.40 pm on Thursday) was first run in 2005 as a new race when the festival was increased from a three-day to a four-day meeting. It was initially sponsored by the *Daily Telegraph* and has been run as the Ryanair Chase since 2006.

The Cathcart Chase, last brought to Ireland by Arthur Moore with Second Schedual (1993) and Edward O'Grady with Rusty Tears (1977), was run over the same distance and was restricted to novices and second-season steeplechasers. It was discontinued and effectively replaced by two separate races, the Festival Trophy, open to all chasers, and the Jewson Novices Handicap Chase, also run over two miles five furlongs.

It was first run with grade 1 status in 2008, before which it was contested at grade 2 level. The 2008 race was run on Cheltenham's Old Course over a distance of two miles four furlongs (4,124 m) with fifteen fences, about a hundred metres and two fences shorter than the original length of the race on the New Course. The race is open to horses aged 5 and upwards and the total prize fund is £220,000.

There were those who feared the race might detract from the Queen Mother Chase or the Gold Cup. However, the five runnings of the event have shown there is room for a separate championship race over this distance and has attracted plenty of top-class two and a half mile chasers who specialise in the distance and the course. Despite two second places, Ireland has never won the race. Mossbank in 2008, trained by Michael Hourigan, was owned by the chief executive of the sponsor airline, Michael O'Leary, who came within five lengths of winning his company's money. Races such as the Paddy Power Gold Cup, Boylesports Gold Cup, the Turf TV New Year Chase and the Chronicle Bookmakers Trophy Chase are the acknowledged form guides for this race.

———

The Ladbrokes World Hurdle (3.20 pm on Thursday) was first run with its current conditions in 1972, when it was known as the Stayers' Hurdle. Before that it was known as the Spa Hurdle. Waterford Crystal sponsored the race from 1978 to 1990.

It is open to horses aged 4 and upwards and has grown in prestige in recent years. It has benefited from the trend towards better ground at the festival, which means the race has become less of a slog and a forum for classier horses to dominate. A total of eleven favourites have been successful.

It has been boosted by the exploits of the great French champion Baracouda, who won the race twice and then finished second twice, and the subsequent three-time winner Inglis Drever. Ireland has not won it since 1995.

Six of the twelve winners up to 2009 were bred in Ireland, and nine of the winners were trained in Ireland, notably Michael Hourigan with Dorans Pride (1995), Paddy Kiely with Shuil Ar Aghaidh (1993), Mouse Morris with Trapper John (1990), John Mulhern with Galmoy (1987 and 1988), Edward O'Grady with Mountrivers (1980) and Flame Gun (1978), Mick O'Toole with Bit Of A Jig (1976) and Jim Dreaper with Brown Lad (1975).

Until 1992 it was run over a distance of three miles one furlong (5,029 m) on Cheltenham's Old Course and it was scheduled for the opening day of the festival. In 1993 it was moved to the third day and run on the New Course over three miles (4,828 m).

There are twelve hurdles to be jumped in the race which carries a total prize fund of £260,000. The 1992 winner Nomadic Way, owned by Robert Sangster, had previously finished runner-up in the 1990 and 1991 Champion Hurdle. The 1996 winner Cyborgo hadn't run since finishing second in the same race a year earlier.

——

The Freddie Williams Plate (4.00 pm on Thursday) has Ireland's poorest record of the entire festival with only one winner in 56 runnings, Andy Geraghty with Doubleuagain (1982).

It was formerly known as the Mildmay of Flete, then the Festival Plate, and was subsequently renamed to honour the legendary festival bookmaker Freddie Williams in 2009. Novice chasers have a good record in the race as they often turn out to be well handicapped compared to their more experienced rivals. Some say the introduction of the Jewson Handicap specifically for novices will reverse that trend in the coming years. French-bred horses have won five of the last nine runnings and have been runners-up in the other four.

The race is a class A grade 3 handicap chase run over two miles five furlongs and is open to horses aged 5 and upwards with a total prize fund of £90,000.

There has been only one winning favourite since 1981. Of the last fourteen winners, twelve carried no more than eleven stone.

―――

All horses are ridden by amateur jockeys in the Kim Muir Challenge Cup (4.40 pm on Thursday), regarded as one of the hardest races of the festival to predict, with nine double figure price winners in the last thirteen years and five in the last six years.

Charlie Rogers first won the race for Ireland with Astrometer in 1946. Ireland's five winners include Michael Cunningham with Greasepaint (1983), Edward O'Grady with Prolan (1976, ridden by Ted Walsh), Peter McCreery with Castleruddery (1974) and Charlie McCartan with Irish Coffee (1959).

The race, a class B handicap chase run over three miles and about half a furlong, is open to horses aged 5 and upwards with a total prize fund of £60,000. It is not a good race for the Irish. The 2008 winner High Chimes was the first Irish-trained winner for 25 years.

―――

The final day of the festival gets under way with a race that is virtually a cavalry charge, the JCB Triumph Hurdle (1.30 pm on Friday). One of the most competitive races of the festival, it once had a field of 31 (1970) and has never had fewer than fourteen in recent years.

The race, only open to 4-year-old novices, was first run in 1939 at Hurst Park Racecourse and was transferred to Cheltenham in 1965 following the closure of its original venue. It has been staged as part of the Cheltenham Festival since 1968, having previously been run in April.

The six Irish winners include Willie Mullins with Scolardy (2002), Ted Walsh with Commanche Court (1997), Michael O'Brien with Shawiya (1993), Dermot Weld with Rare Holiday (1990), Edward O'Grady with Northern Game (1984) and Adrian Maxwell with Meladon (1977).

The most successful of these was the 1997 winner Commanche Court which went on to win the 2000 Irish Grand National as a maiden chaser and came second in the 2002 Cheltenham Gold Cup.

The 2007 winner, Katchit, was the first winner of this race since Kribensis in 1988 to go on to win the Champion Hurdle. Paddy's Return became a top-class staying hurdler. Katarino won the Fox Hunters' Chase at Aintree over 2m 5½f two years in a row. The 1974 winner, Attivo, owned by the BBC commentator on the race, Peter O'Sullevan, was the only odds-on winner in the history of the race at Cheltenham.

Inexperience was once a major determinant in this race, but that is changing as more horses come to the juvenile ranks straight from lengthy careers on the flat. The race always attracts a large field, which means luck plays a big part in the result.

Of the most recent winners Detroit City was rated 100 on the flat, Penzance was rated 86, Made In Japan 87 and Spectroscope 73. Scolardy was rated 83 in Ireland.

Snow Drop was trained in France and Katarino had run three times over obstacles there (including once over fences) before he even began his juvenile career in England. Racehorses in France begin schooling and racing over obstacles much earlier than their Irish or English counterparts.

The race is a class A grade 1 hurdle run over two miles and a furlong (3,420 m) on the New Course with a total prize fund of £40,000. There are eight hurdles to be jumped in the race. There have been three sponsors of the race since the move to Cheltenham—the *Daily Express* (1965–1996), Elite Racing Club (1997–2000) and JCB (2002–present).

————

The Vincent O'Brien County Handicap Hurdle (2.05 pm on Friday), once the traditional festival 'getting out stakes', has now been moved forward to be one of three hurdle races run before the Gold Cup on Friday to ensure fresh ground on the chase course.

The ten Irish winners include Tony Mullins with Pedrobob (2007), Jessica Harrington with Spirit Leader (2003), Edward O'Grady with Staplestown (1981), Rosses Point-based Billy Boyers with Kilcoleman (1977), Delma Harty with Khan (1970, the first success at the festival by a woman trainer), Dan Moore with Bahrain (1963), Clem Magnier with Albergo (1960) and Teapot II (1953), Joe Osborne with Friendly Boy (1958) and Michael Dawson with Bold Baby (1954).

Its former billing associated this race with the battle for leading jockey and trainer at the festival, and this race frequently used to determine who won those prizes. In 2003, for example, the event proved to be a showdown between Barry Geraghty and Richard Johnson for champion jockey, with the Meath man coming out on top. In 2006 Ruby Walsh pipped Tony McCoy to the title by winning the race on Desert Quest.

A class A grade 3 hurdle run over two miles and a furlong, open to horses aged 5 and upwards and with a total prize fund of £50,000, this race is often the most competitive of all the events run over the four days. Of the last 34 runnings, 32 were won by a horse starting at no more than 16/1.

——

The Albert Bartlett Novices Hurdle (2.40 pm on Friday) is a class A grade 2 hurdle run over three miles. Sponsored by 'England's largest grower of root potatoes', it is open to novices aged 4 and upwards and has had two Irish-trained second-placed horses so far. The total prize fund is £100,000.

Another race created by the changes in racing trends, in this case the tendency of the Ballymore Properties Hurdle to attract more flat-bred horses, the expectation is that the Albert Bartlett Hurdle will develop into the main target for long-term chase prospects during their novice year over hurdles and could also prove a pointer to future World Hurdle winners.

——

The Totesport Cheltenham Gold Cup (3.20 pm on Friday) is the event that everyone wants to win. The race remains the focus of the festival and the entire jumping season, and continues to serve up great drama.

Although run over three and a quarter miles (5,331 m) over 22 fences, the pace of the race is more like a two and a half mile contest, placing even greater emphasis on stamina. Horses have to have not only the speed to stay in contention, but they also have to jump well.

From a jockey's point of view the two key fences are the ditch at the top of the hill, four out, and the third last, which is taken on the down-hill and where many Gold Cups have been decided. The second last and last have also seen their share of drama as horses tire. There is a longer run-in on the New Course. The fourth last has now been moved back fifteen metres, meaning it is jumped on a slightly flatter part of the track. But the distinguishing feature of the race is the last uphill half-furlong that has so often changed a possible victory into defeat.

The trend has been for second-season chasers to win the race, and for horses placed in the previous year's Gold Cup not to win, Bregawn in 1983 and Kauto Star in 2009 being the exceptions.

Until the 1940s the race used to be considered little more than a trial for the Grand National. As the importance of the festival has grown, so has the significance of this race. In equine circles it is now the biggest event on the chasing calendar.

To add to the appeal of the race, every second year an outsider makes the frame in the Gold Cup, like Norton's Coin, a 100/1 winner in 1990. Welsh farmer turned trainer, Sirrell Griffiths, started the day by milking his herd of cows in Carmarthen.

Down the years it has provided some of the most unforgettable dramas and achievements in sporting as well as racing history.

Desert Orchid's success in the mud and rain of 1989 was voted by readers of the *Racing Post* as the greatest ever race, and Michael Dickinson's first five home in 1983 as the greatest training feat of all time. But there have been other incidents which have won their place in four-legged folklore: the sequential victories of Golden Miller, Cottage Rake, Arkle and Best Mate, the dramatic finishes such as Golden Miller v Thomond II in 1935 and Arkle v Mill House in 1964, Dawn Run's recovery from a fading third to exuberant victory in 1986, and the might have beens, such as Tied Cottage's unexpected fall in 1979.

Arkle was the shortest-priced winner of all. He won once at 10/1 on (you won £1 for every £10 you bet).

The race which started life at three miles two furlongs from 1924–28 was lengthened to three miles three furlongs from 1928–36, came back to three miles two furlongs from 1936–39, was shortened further to three miles in 1940–45, then extended again to three miles two furlongs from 1946–58, to three and three-quarter miles and 130 yards from 1959–64, and finally three miles two furlongs and 75 yards since 1965. It is open to horses aged 5 and upwards. The total prize fund is £475,000.

The 1978 Gold Cup, abandoned because of snow, was eventually run in April instead. Cancellations have been due to frost (1931), flooding (1937), World War II (1943, 1944) and most famously the foot and mouth crisis of 2001. Day two of the festival was cancelled in 2008 due to high winds with all Wednesday's races moved to Thursday and Friday.

——

The Christies Foxhunter Chase (4.00 pm on Friday) is the amateur riders' Gold Cup and the highlight of the hunter chase season. This being Cheltenham, major stables come to contest the race with the traditional point-to-point trainers.

The race is run over the course and distance of the Gold Cup and has been won by some top-class steeplechasers such as Double Silk, Kingscliff and Sleeping Night. Ireland's winners include Ray Hurley with Whyso Mayo (2006), Enda Bolger with Elegant Lord (1996), Eugene M. O'Sullivan with Lovely Citizen (1991), Mouse Morris with Attitude Adjuster (1986, ridden by Ted Walsh) and Barry Kelly with Eliogarty (1983). Eliogarty was ridden by owner Caroline Beasley, who became the first woman to ride a winner at Cheltenham.

At one stage the race was known as the Buttevant Hunters Chase, after the town where steeplechasing originated, and an invitation was sent to the Mayor of Buttevant to present the trophy.

The field tends to be a combination of older experienced chasers nearing retirement and young pretenders from the point-to-point circuit looking to make the leap to racing under rules. Earthmover burst on to the scene when winning in 1998, went on to compete for many of the biggest prizes in the sport, then returned to hunter chasing in the twilight of his career and sprang something of an upset when winning this race for the second time aged 13 in 2004.

The race is a class B chase run over three miles and about two and a half furlongs. It is open to horses aged 5 and upwards who have met various qualifying criteria. The total prize fund is £40,000.

——

The Conditionals Hurdle Handicap (4.40 pm on Friday) became the latest addition to the Cheltenham Festival and is run over two miles and about four and a half furlongs (4,124 m). The total prize fund is £50,000.

It was designated as a race for potential champion jockeys of the future and an opportunity for some of the large number of horses which are eliminated from the Coral Cup each year to have a run at the festival.

It was announced in January 2009 that this race would be named in honour of Martin Pipe, the most successful national hunt trainer of all. The first winner, Andytown, was a 25/1 shot.

——

The Johnny Henderson Grand Annual Chase (5.15 pm on Friday) is the new getting out stakes, the last race of the festival, in place of the County Hurdle that was switched to earlier in the day.

It is an ancient race, first run in April 1834 at Andoversford, near Cheltenham, over three miles of open country that has a reputation for being kind to fancied horses. Nine of the last thirteen runnings have been won by horses who started at 8/1 or shorter and 29 of the last 34 runnings were won by horses that started at no bigger than 10/1.

The race died out in the 1860s, like much of the English steeple-chasing calendar, but was revived at the turn of the century. For some time it was the single most important national hunt race, surpassing even the Grand National. During the early 1900s it was held at Melton Mowbray, Leicester and Warwick before finally returning to Cheltenham in 1913.

Ireland's nine winners include Arthur Moore with Tiger Cry (2008) and Fadoudal (2002), Mouse Morris with Fota Island (2005), Jessica Harrington with Space Trucker (1999), Michael Cunningham with

Churchfield Boy (1983), Mick Burke with Khan (1971), Jimmy Brogan with Monsieur Trois Etoiles (1960), Clem Magnier with Top Twenty (1958 and 1959) and Charlie Rogers with Loyal King (1946).

The race is a class A grade 3 chase run over two miles and about half a furlong. It is open to horses aged 5 and upwards with a total prize fund of £90,000. The name of the race was extended in 2006 to commemorate the life of Johnny Henderson, father of Nicky and the man who saved Cheltenham Racecourse from developers in 1963 by forming Racecourse Holdings Trust, a non profit-making organisation, and raising £240,000 to purchase the racecourse and safeguard its future.

As they return home the followers can ponder that, without him, there might not have been a Cheltenham today. The Gold Cup would have gone the way of the Lancashire, and Prestbury would have followed Manchester, St Albans, Croydon, Gatwick and the others which have been lost to the sport.

But there is a group of people who were even more crucial to the survival and prosperity of Cheltenham—the Irish.

Chapter 4 ~

| THE MILLER'S MILE

It is very seldom that Irish racing and hunting people
make a determined attack on an English meeting without
paying, at least their expenses. One gathers that they did
more than that yesterday.
        London Times, Cheltenham Report, 10 March 1922

The prospect of money, prizes on a scale not available at home in an industry that was contracting rather than expanding, brought that small group of Irish to Cheltenham in the 1920s. They were also enamoured by the prospects of two shots at a similar pot at a time when festivals were few and far between. Many an Irish horse would be entered in two races on separate days.

'Today a beginning will be made with the National Hunt festival in Cheltenham,' the *Irish Independent* of 8 March 1922 reported, 'which as a sporting event pure and simple stands out alone in our list of fixtures—something like our own Punchestown and Fairyhouse fixtures. Record entries were obtained for the present meeting, and the executive are enabled to offer stakes and cups valued at nearly 7,000 sovereigns, which is unique for a two day fixture under these rules. Horses of all classes are catered for, and it will not be surprising if a field of record extent for a steeplechase goes to the starting post today for the National Hunt Chase, which will be of record value in this particular event.'

The Irish racing fraternity would be happy to enter their horses on both days. Then in 1922 there was success, inaccurately recorded as the first success for an Irish horse in Cheltenham, and it was achieved by Ireland's only Cheltenham-born trainer.

Algernon 'Algy' Anthony was a three-time champion Irish jockey who had famously ridden the 1900 Grand National winner. It was said of his Grand National win on Ambush II (certain records show him as the trainer) that he did everything but sleep in the horse's box. He had started his apprenticeship with Samuel Darling at Beckhampton and had come to Ireland to ride for Gratton Lushington at Conyngham Lodge in the Curragh.

Having established himself at Westenra Lodge on the Curragh, he trained another Grand National winner Troytown in 1920. In 1922 he returned to his native Cheltenham with Mr Hutton's Connemara Black. Despite its expectation of a good showing, Connemara Black came a cropper in the chase.

But the cost of the passage could still be saved. Connemara Black returned the following day to win the Foxhunters Challenge Cup Steeplechase from the back, a 'steeplechase run over four miles and a real fox catchers race'. The winner was 'a beautiful stamp of hunter and probably capable of better things', *The Irish Times* reported. It also boasted one of the most massive trophies ever given for a sporting event. All three placed horses were Irish owned. Be Careful was trained in Ireland and Mouse ii was Irish owned.

'Connemara Black had been expected by the numerous Irish visitors to win the big race of the previous day,' the *London Times* reported. 'In that event he had fallen in the water.'

The same report noted that 'the meeting is not officially settled permanently at Cheltenham, but it will occasion amazement if, so long as it is so well conducted as it is at present, it should ever be moved to another course.'

The *London Times* correspondent paused to fire a broadside at the arrival of Totalisators Limited, of which at least three of the directors are owners, S. W. Beer, Major Alexander and Captain Davy.

Cheltenham's first Irish winner returned unsuccessfully in 1923. A few months later his trainer was dead. He had fallen ill while attending a meeting in Limerick, underwent two operations but never fully recovered and died at his home on 30 November 1923.

Algy's fame included the fact that he was first to identify the talent of Castlefin-bred Master Robert, the plough horse Algy had used to help prepare Troytown for his 1920 Grand National success and who went on to win the 1924 Grand National at 25/1. Ten girls in Dublin restaurants won £235, and four Liverpool girl clerks £1,000 when he romped home for one of the most romantic Grand National victories of all time. A big number of clerks in Dublin government offices benefited from a Friday morning tip-off.

Mares seldom, if ever win the Grand National. Ballinode must have an excellent chance of following Shandon Lass.

London Times, 12 March 1925

The *London Times* told a shocked public in March 1925 of a small but shapely Irish mare and a very clever jumper, Ballinode's five-length victory over the fancied Alcazar to win the Gold Cup at Cheltenham.

Owned by Christopher Bentley and trained by Frank Morgan, she had arrived as the 3/1 second favourite and 'showed not only stamina but also fine speed that she was always able to keep within a few lengths of the fast Alcazar'. Conjuror II and Patsey V were both ignored by the market, and the *London Times* correspondent felt he 'need not comment on their running except to say that in my opinion they will have to experience Glenside's luck if they are to win at Aintree. Each of the two horses gave an admirable display of jumping. Alcazar was in front until the fence at the bottom of the hill, when Ballinode joined him. For a short time they galloped side by side, until just before the straight was reached, Alcazar's stamina gave out, and Ballinode went on to win easily.' Because Frank Morgan had not got his riding licence in time, the mare was ridden by Ted Leader.

The speculation immediately was whether Ballinode would follow another mare, 1889 Aintree Grand National winner Frigate and 1902 winner Shannon Lass, into the record books. She was backed to 10/1 but fell.

It was a personal triumph for Frank Morgan of Waterford and Epsom. 'Her trainer Frank Morgan, to whom great credit is due for her excellent condition, was delightfully enthusiastic about her success and rushed out on to the course to lead the mare in.' Ballinode's stablemate Louvima had won the opening race of the afternoon.

Morgan was born in Waterford in July 1887, and was apprenticed at the age of 12 to the Tramore-born J. J. Parkinson, the Maddenstown-based trainer who headed the list of owners in 1914 and 1917 and was champion trainer in 1914, 1917, 1919, 1923 and 1926. Morgan won the Leopardstown Grand Prize on St Brendan and the Irish Derby on Royal Arch in 1924.

His brother John was awarded £1,740 compensation for the burning of his home, Mount Neil, in Waterford on 1 January 1924.

Frank Morgan died on 29 September 1970, aged 83, in his home in Reigate Road, Epsom. Four of his sons were steeplechase jockeys, Dick,

Frank, Tom and Joe. His nephew Danny Morgan rode the Cheltenham Cup winner of 1938, Morse Code, and in 1959 trained the Gold Cup winner Roddy Owen.

Irish horses seem to do well over this course.

London Times, 11 March 1926

In 1926 Frank Barbour, a wealthy owner/trainer from Trimblestown, Co. Meath, won the Gold Cup with 100/8 outsider Koko. Koko made the running from the start and was challenged by the 6/5 favourite Ruddyglow after a mile, then by Viuve. Old Tay Bridge was backed to 8/1 second favourite. Alongside Ruddyglow, Old Tay Bridge was challenging Koko between the last two fences. Koko held off the challenge fairly easily and won by four lengths. 'It is not easy to give any definite reason why Koko should not again beat Old Tay Bridge in the Grand National,' the *London Times* reported. 'He jumped admirably yesterday and stayed well.'

Koko didn't make it to the Grand National, for which Cheltenham was regarded as a warm-up at the time. The Irish challenger there, Sprig, was fourth.

Barbour sold Koko to Captain Guest for 10,000 guineas and sold another horse, Easter Hero, to Captain Alfred Lowenstein for £7,000, 'absurd sums of money', according to the *London Times*. Easter Hero 'caused all the trouble' after leading at Becher's in the chaotic 1928 Grand National, a race in which all the horses fell except 100/8 outsider Tipperary Tim and the second placed Billy Barton, whose rider re-mounted after falling at the last. Easter Hero managed to bring down an estimated twenty of the 42 starters at the open ditch at the Canal Turn. A few months later Easter Hero's owner was killed in a fall from an aeroplane and the jinxed horse was sold on to Jock Whitney, later American Ambassador in London, and placed with trainer Jack Anthony in Wales and jockey Dick Rees.

So when the 1929 Cheltenham meeting was postponed from 5 March to 12 March because of frost and snow, it was Easter Hero, moving from hurdles to fences for the first time, who was backed to 7/4 favourite.

The bright sunshine made the distinguishing of colours on the course rather difficult. The going was good. Rees took his horse to the front and established a 30-length lead, allowed two horses to catch him and took off again to win by twenty lengths. In 1930 he took off once more and won at 11/8 by twenty lengths from Grakle, ridden by Lester Piggot's father Keith, having shaken off the challenge of Gib, a faller at the last fence.

The days of big cross-channel sales were brought to a halt on 11 July 1932 when the Whitehall government slapped a 20 per cent tax on live animals exported from the Irish Free State, one of a series of measures in an attempt to cripple the Irish economy that was to become known as the 'economic war'.

Stables were reduced and attendances at race meetings fell. Navan Racecourse was closed for two years and the Irish invasion of Cheltenham was halted. By then the most successful Irish horse of all time had already landed in Cambridgeshire. Golden Miller, the horse described by racing journalist Sidney Galtrey as 'a God on four legs', was trained out of England and was not by now an Irish horse at all. But his exploits in winning five Cheltenham Gold Cups and becoming the only horse to capture the Gold Cup and the Grand National in the same year merit him more than a passing mention.

The ups and downs of his career captured the imagination of the two islands and elevated steeplechasing to a new peak in popularity.

> Miss Paget undoubtedly has a very useful young steeplechaser in Golden Miller—he is only four years old—and one which should make a big name for himself.
>
> *London Times,* 5 December 1931

Julius Solomons, a respected Dublin businessman and leader of the city's vibrant Jewish community, became the breeder of Cheltenham's most successful horse somewhat by accident.

He took the mare Miller's Pride, probably as a debt settlement from her owner James Nugent, and left the mare at Pelletstown, Drumree, Co. Meath, the farm of Laurence Geraghty, to be covered by a virtually unknown sire, Goldcourt.

The bay foal that was born in 1929 was of unpromising lineage. Goldcourt stood at a fee of five guineas and had never run. He was by Goldminer who had also never seen a racecourse. Goldminer was, however, by Gallinule and there was Melbourne blood in his line. Golden Miller's dam, Miller's Pride, had never won. Her best effort was to be placed second in a £22 steeplechase at Pilltown. But she had Barcaldine blood and had bred at least one winner, May Crescent, owned by Basil Briscoe at Longstowe Hall in Cambridgeshire. Their offspring was born on 30 April 1927.

Geraghty was effectively the breeder, but after about a dozen years when no keep or stud fees of any kind had been paid, Geraghty began to record himself as the breeder of her foals. However, when Golden Miller's older brother May Crescent began winning, Solomons instructed Weatherby's to record him as the breeder in the next stud book and thereafter was able to claim his place in racing history. The Geraghtys of Drumree deserve to get their place in history back. A great Irish racing family, they have since provided one of the outstanding jump jockeys of the modern era, Barry.

Golden Miller was sold for £100 as a yearling to Mr Quinn of Fethard, who sold him on for £300 to Galwey Greer, and two years later, still unbroken, he was purchased by Dick Farmer for £500 and came into the hands of Basil Briscoe, who was interested in tracking down May Crescent's brother.

In his first race, a Southwell hurdle in September 1930, Golden Miller ran with little distinction, but by the end of the season he had won twice over hurdles and performed well in his first attempt over fences. He was then sold to Phillip Carr, father of a future England cricket captain, for £1,000.

After he was beaten a head by a 10-year-old Rolie, when Golden Miller was only 4, the eccentric Dorothy Paget bought him for £6,000 as part of perhaps the most valuable two-horse lot in history. It included Insurance, who was to win the Champion Hurdle in 1932 and 1933.

After four more races over hurdles the gelding reverted to fences, including a controversial disqualification at Newbury in December 1931 for carrying the wrong weight. He opened 1932 with a second and a win, and arrived at Cheltenham as the only young horse in the race, with Ted Leader as the chosen jockey and the pundits thinking he would not have enough to beat horses such as the Grand National winner of 1931 (and favourite for the 1932 event), the Tom Couthwaite-trained Grakle, and Gib, who had fallen so tragically at the last fence in 1930. The punters were cannier, backing Golden Miller to 8/1, against 11/10 on Grakle and 3/1 against Kingsford, who was ridden by Billy Stott and testing the distance. As it happened, Gib fell at the second fence and

Kingsford fell at the first fence of the second circuit, bringing down Grakle with him.

The going was excellent. Inverse made the running to the bottom of the hill. Ted Leader made a fine recovery at a fence on the far side of the course and then joined Inverse before taking the lead with two fences to go and winning by four lengths. After winning he rode on, caught the riderless Grakle and brought him back to the paddock.

Miss Paget is to be congratulated on her great double. She is a young owner of the very best type who is to be encouraged in every way, as is her young trainer.

London Times

The chain smoking chain store magnate Dorothy Wyndham Paget didn't need much encouragement.

Her eccentric high-spending habits added glamour to depression-era racing. She spent £3 m on her horses and sustained vast gambling losses. She bet huge sums daily. Her largest recorded bet was £160,000 to win £20,000. According to folklore her reputation as a woman of honour meant bookies would accept night-time bets after races had been run. Between 1934 and the outbreak of World War II the two biggest racecourse gamblers were women. Dorothy Paget and Mrs J. V. Rank would bet £10,000 on their horses whenever they ran.

Dorothy's mother Pauline Payne Whitney was a daughter of William C. Whitney in New York, one of the most prominent thoroughbred racing and breeding families in American racing history. Her father was Almeric Hugh Paget, first Baron Queenborough (1861–1949), politician and yachtsman. She was a cousin of Jock Whitney, owner of the dual Cheltenham Gold Cup winner Easter Hero and later American Ambassador in London.

In her teenage years she had gloried in being expelled from six schools, beginning with Heathfield School at Ascot, before finishing her formal education in Paris at an establishment run by Princess Meshchersky, a Russian émigré.

Her wealth, inherited from her maternal grandfather, allowed her to indulge in expensive leisure pursuits, starting in 1931 by backing the motor racing team of the 1929 Le Mans winner Tim Birken to the tune of £32,000.

She became the godmother to Cheltenham, as enthusiastic about chasing and hurdling as she was about the flat. She was the leading national hunt owner in England in 1933–34, 1940–41 and 1951–52 and English flat racing champion owner in 1943, the year one of her horses won the Epsom Derby. Golden Miller was responsible for five of her seven Cheltenham Gold Cup successes, with one each by Roman Hackle in 1940 and Mont Tremblant in 1952. Her four Champion Hurdle winners were Insurance in 1932 and 1933, Solford in 1940 and Distel in 1946. Her horses won a total of 1,532 races in both flat and hurdling.

Paget is notably responsible for the establishment of the Sainte Geneviève-des-Bois Russian Cemetery in France. Beautiful in her youth, she has not been served well by the newsreel footage of her 20 stone figure, dowdy and overweight, leading in her later Derby, Grand National and Cheltenham winners. According to folklore she wore the same shapeless blue tweed coat and French beret year after year for superstitious reasons. She smoked 100 cigarettes a day and cared nothing for public recognition, declaring, 'The public doesn't pay my training bills.'

On her way to and from race meetings she would hire a railway compartment to ensure her privacy and always took two seats at the theatre or Wimbledon, one for her handbag. She referred to her staff by a colour code rather than by name and often communicated with them by memo.

Quintin Gilbey claims in his 1973 biography, *Queen of the Turf: the Dorothy Paget Story*, that Paget found male company distasteful and claimed she was sometimes physically sick in the presence of men. When she congratulated Golden Miller, it was remarked that this was the first male she had ever kissed—though it was noted that he was a gelding.

When she died of a heart attack on 9 February 1960, an acerbic obituary in the *Sporting Life* created a new controversy in death to match those in life. 'Too much money too soon,' it went. 'An appropriate epitaph for the Hon. Dorothy Wyndham Paget, dead at the age of 54, 43 of her years had been spent in pleasing herself. She became a millionairess at the age of 11. That was her tragedy. Poor little rich girl, that phrase might have been written for her. Her glory? Mostly reflected. She chose the turf as her playground, and, by chance became associated with Golden Miller, one of the greatest horses of all time. We shall remember her as the bulky, Glastonbury-booted figure which appeared on the racecourse surrounded by a retinue of servants. We shall reminisce about her bad manners, enormous appetite and extraordinary clothes. And we shall miss her.'

The obituary led to a spirited defence from her closest companion, Olga (Olili) de Mumm, niece of Princess Meshchersky, taking issue with the way her many kindnesses were disregarded and her abruptness emphasised.

He is not, in my opinion, so good a steeplechaser as seems the general view.

London Times, 7 March 1933

Dorothy Paget allayed the nervousness about the status of Cheltenham among racing people as prize money, attendances and interest plummeted in the early 1930s.

Paget's famous double double (Insurance won the Champion Hurdle on the same day as Golden Miller's Gold Cup in 1932 and 1933), achieved by the two horses she had purchased as a double lot for 12,000 guineas, were won from fields of three and six respectively in 1932, and five and seven respectively in 1933. Could it be that the Golden Miller legend was built on the fact that he had to contend with mediocre opposition?

Golden Miller's unbroken success in 1932–33 helped rebuild confidence in the meeting and, now favourite at 7/4, he won by ten lengths in 'the style of a great horse, at last he must be admitted to be that,' according to the *London Times*. 'He took a few fences slightly sideways and appeared to get rather close to a few fences, but he never made a serious mistake, and he is such a clever and intelligent horse that such slight delinquencies mean nothing to him, for he can recover from them so easily that it seems he almost makes them on purpose. The cheering and clapping of hands were renewed when he came back into the paddock.'

Cheltenham was still seen as a build-up to the Aintree Grand National, and the Aintree course was unsuited to Golden Miller's habit of jumping to the right. He tired on the second circuit and fell at the Canal Turn.

Now 7 years old, in 1934 he moved to Briscoe's new stable at Newmarket (something that was to prove significant in the aftermath of the Aintree Grand National a year later), remained unbeaten for twelve months and then achieved the unprecedented double of the Cheltenham Gold Cup and the Aintree Grand National, a feat rarely attempted nowadays, never mind matched.

Golden Miller started the 1934 Gold Cup at 6/5 against and won from the front by six lengths, jumping the last 'with his ears pricked and raced away up the hill to win with ease from Avenger. Over this course Golden Miller is not only as good as ever he was but an exceptionally good horse.'

He was 8/1 against for the Grand National and was one of a group of three which had drawn away from the field by the second Canal Turn, and later joined by a fourth horse. Golden Miller hit the top of the second last fence hard. 'It is very rare for a horse to hit a fence in this race at so late a stage and still stand, let alone have anything left, but Golden Miller did not fall, and ran on as if nothing had happened. By the time he reached the last fence he had regained ground on Delanaige, landed in front and drew away to win by five lengths.'

I have never seen a better national and I know of no owner who more deserves to win such a race, for Miss Paget has entered wholeheartedly into racing under National Hunt and Jockey Club rules. Wilson rode a great race, as one would expect of a man who has spent a long time hunting with the Whaddon Chase, thus showing once more that the ideal rider over this course is a hunting man.

London Times, 1935

The impact of Golden Miller's celebrity status was being felt in Cheltenham. In 1935 the Gold Cup was moved from Tuesday to Thursday. It was a new birth for the competition. Golden Miller started at 2/1 and won by three-quarters of a length from Thomond II (bred by George de Stacpoole in Tobertynan, Co. Meath, and owned by Dorothy Paget's cousin Jock Whitney) in a race occasionally described as the 'steeplechase of the century' and feted 35 years later as the greatest steeplechase ever run.

'Two fences from the finish the pair were side by side,' the *London Times* reported. 'Then, approaching the last fence, Speck, on Thomond II, felt for his whip and took it up. Though Wilson never felt for his whip, Golden Miller was all out to win. What a great horse he is in every way.'

Golden Miller started the 1935 Aintree Grand National at the absurdly short price of 2/1, not entirely because of his unbeaten record (as has been claimed), but because a number of punters doubled him with Flamenco, the winner of the Lincolnshire Handicap.

He set off with rumours of a temperature and an unbelievable handicap of 12 st 7 lb—the handicap is capped at twelve stone nowadays. At the tenth fence he unseated his jockey Gerry Wilson. Next day he confirmed his dislike of Aintree by throwing Wilson at the first fence of the Champion Chase.

Wilson said that the horse felt sore and was not going his usual self, but felt the Saturday morning workout had gone well. Miss Paget then blamed her trainer for the double catastrophe, claiming he had been over-galloped on the hard ground at Newmarket.

As the row almost developed into a national scandal, Dorothy Paget claimed that the trainer had criticised the rider after the Grand National and she had responded with some questions for the trainer after the Champion Steeplechase. She was famously acerbic, and according to biographer Quintin Gilbey, she described herself as 'desperately fussy'. Briscoe responded by asking her to remove Golden Miller from his yard, and the horse was trained by Owen Anthony at his yard in Letcombe Bassett for the rest of his career.

Former Aintree winning jockey and trainer Jack Anthony had agreed with Paget that the Grand National had been left at Cheltenham as far as both Golden Miller and Thomond II were concerned. The priorities of the mid-1930s were still that the Gold Cup was a warm-up for Aintree.

In 1936 Golden Miller won his fifth consecutive Cheltenham Gold Cup by twelve lengths (having started at an unbackable 21/20), but failed at Aintree. Pundits were now claiming he should not be started at Aintree, although 'over his own country Golden Miller is the best steeplechaser in the land'.

Meanwhile, the Balbriggan-bred Reynoldstown, a brother of Easter Hero by My Prince, went on to retain the Grand National the following year. The horse had been bred by Richard Ball and was now owned by a Leicester-based Cork man Noel Furlong, trained by the owner and ridden in 1935 by Furlong's son Frank. Another of My Prince's offspring, Royal Mail, won the Grand National in 1937.

Golden Miller continued to win in moderate company in the 1936–37 season, but bad weather caused the cancellation of the Gold Cup, and in the Grand National he refused at the fence where he had ditched his jockey two years before. There were three more victories in the 1937–38 campaign, but in his sixth Gold Cup attempt Golden Miller was beaten two lengths by the younger Morse Code, his first and only defeat at Cheltenham. He started once again as favourite at 7/4 and had acquired legendary status among the public. The first-class special train from London had an extra coach and more than 500 passengers were carried. 'I have never seen a larger attendance,' the *London Times* wrote, 'and there was not a visitor present who did not wish he had won this Gold Cup for the sixth time. There was no race last year and that was the pity of it, for he was then a year younger. Yet in his defeat he showed what a grand horse he is, and his reception as he came back to the enclosure was greater than that of the winner.'

After eleven months he returned to run a listless race at Newbury and at last Dorothy Paget retired him to her farm in Essex with a record of 29 wins from his 52 national hunt races and £14,922 in prize money. He remained there for eighteen years until he was put down on 11 January 1937 at the age of 30.

Miss Paget has been described as the fairy godmother of racing. Her enthusiasm for racing in this country is best shown by the fact that her percentage of entries in chases invariably totals a third of the total entry at any meeting. In Charlie Rogers, she has a trainer who is possibly one of the best judges in this or any other country of a horse, whether in training or as a potential winner.

The Irish Times, 21 November 1944

With the advent of war, Dorothy Paget transferred many of her thoroughbreds to Ireland. They arrived in three shipments in early 1940, one to Frank Rogers at Glascairn Stud, Ratoath, one to his brother Charlie of Balfestown, Kilbride, Co. Meath, and 25 two-year olds to the renowned jockey Tommy Cusack at Brownstown, Co. Kildare.

Charlie later leased Ms Paget's stables at Crotanstown in January 1941, and Nugent trained there. Former Minister for Agriculture Joe McGrath purchased the Brownstown stud.

In 1946 Rogers won Ireland's first Cheltenham Champion Hurdle in her colours.

That same year she purchased Ballymacoll, a stud four miles from Maynooth but in Co. Meath. It was at Ballymacoll that Arkle was sired.

Chapter 5

HOW THE IRISH SAVED CHELTENHAM

*Prince Regent's fame effectively began the mass exodus
from the Emerald Isle to Cheltenham that we now take
very much for granted. While post-war rationing
continued through to England to 1950, the invading army
of punters brought over their own strings of sausages.*
BOB HARMAN, *The Ultimate Dream, the History of
the Cheltenham Gold Cup,* 2001

Cheltenham was outgrowing its landscape. Until the 1950s the entire steeplechasing industry was probably the original one-trick pony. Or rather, it was a one-race steed with every trainer, owner and jockey's eye on the Aintree Grand National.

By 1959 the Grand National was no longer the target; Cheltenham was. How did the bridesmaid become the bride?

The finance of the sport had changed. For all its growing reputation, the Gold Cup was a poorly endowed championship. Prince Regent won £1,130 in 1946, Fortina in 1947 and Cottage Rake £1,911 in 1948. The 1949 Gold Cup prize fund was increased to £3,258. 'The new figure is more in keeping with the importance of the race, the huge cost of present-day chasers, and the great crowds attending the national hunt meeting', the *London Times* wrote.

The profile was growing. The 1953 Cheltenham Gold Cup was broadcast on BBC radio. The 1955 Cheltenham Gold Cup was broadcast on BBC television, bringing the festival to a new audience.

But first to Tom Dreaper's yard in Greenogue, Killsallaghan, on the Dublin-Meath border, from where Prince Regent began his journey to capture the 1946 Gold Cup. Prince Regent's success at Cheltenham and failure at Aintree was to bring about a change in how everyone regarded the Cheltenham Festival.

Irish visitors to Cheltenham find it difficult to believe that Poor Flame has a chance of beating Prince Regent in today's race for the Gold Cup.

London Times, 15 March 1946

Seven Irish horses left on the mailboat from Dublin on the evening of Friday 5 March 1946. They had a happier journey than the three that had represented Ireland a year earlier, who had a delayed and stormy passage and came home empty handed.

The undoubted star of the 1946 lot was Prince Regent, already backed at 17/2 to win £155,000 in the Grand National. A big 16.3 hand horse, he was bought as a yearling at the Ballsbridge Sales of 1935, then resold as a 2-year old for 320 guineas by Harry Bonner on behalf of James Voase Rank, the milling millionaire and older brother of film magnate J. Arthur Rank.

He was boarded out until he was 3 to Bobby Power, who sent him on to Tom Dreaper's yard. Dreaper kept him until he was 5 before racing him, riding him to his first win himself in a bumper in Naas in 1940.

The horse was due to return to Bobby Power, but Power was killed in a road accident on his way to the Dublin Horse Show. Gwyn Evans, who was due to train him at Rank's Druids Lodge in England, also died in tragic circumstances. Dreaper declined Rank's invitation to go to England as a private trainer. Rank decided to send the horse to Meath instead.

He won three races in 1941, one of them a hurdle. In 1942 at the age of 7 he was saddled by former showjumper Timmy Hyde for the first time after his jockey Jimmy Brogan was injured. He won four races including the Irish Grand National carrying an enormous weight of 12 st 7 lb. A 1939 Grand National-winning jockey on Workman, Hyde rode Prince Regent 28 times in five seasons before a fall at the 1951 Clonakilty Show that left him in a wheelchair. It was unfortunate that he peaked in the middle of a war which denied him the chance of showing off his greatness at Cheltenham.

The advantage was the number of high quality horses in training in Ireland sent over from England by owners such as Dorothy Paget because of restrictions in the movement of bloodstock. According to Hyde, 'It was the heyday of Irish steeplechasing. Good horses were a penny a dozen.'

Dorothy Paget's Golden Jack set up a terrific rivalry with Prince Regent by beating him at Leopardstown, then lost to him in the 1942 Irish Grand National. So too did Prince Blackthorn, beaten by Prince Regent in Baldoyle in January 1943 in a race reckoned to be one of the best steeplechases ever seen in Ireland.

Carrying 12 st or over throughout his career, Prince Regent was beaten into second place by Golden Jack in the 1943 Irish Grand National. He was sent to race in England after the war had ended but was, according to Hyde, well past his best. He missed the 1945 Gold Cup because of a warble behind his ears that made it impossible to place a saddle on him. After a win in Wetherby he was installed as Gold Cup favourite. So it came to pass that a past-it Prince Regent won the 1946 Gold Cup.

A record 35,000 crowd turned out to see the new Irish hero. In the paddock Prince Regent looked fit and well muscled. He had been backed down to 11/10 from 7/4 before racing on Tuesday, with Lord Stalbridge's unbeaten novice Red April at 9/2 and Poor Flame, trained by Tom Rimell, at 5/1. 'He is a big horse, nearly 17 hands, with great depth through his shoulder and powerful quarters,' the *London Times* wrote. 'Alongside him the French grey Lalgreya looked small and poor, though quite a good type. Prince Regent has a lazy, kind head, and he races with a lazy, long stride. So easy was his action that he gave a false impression of moving much more slowly than he really was.'

Elsich, the 200/1 outsider described as 'a fruitcake of a horse' by Cheltenham historian Bob Harman, set off in front of Poor Flame. They had not gone a mile when Prince Regent jumped to the front. For a time Red April stayed with Poor Flame and Prince Regent, but at the end of two miles he was beaten. From then to the finish Prince Regent lobbed over the fences as if they were hurdles. Fred Rimell on Poor Flame, who had been told that the Prince might not stay and tried to run him off his feet, continued to do so until the third fence from home, when Poor Flame made one of his characteristic errors. He had given a good performance but looked tired. Prince Regent jumped this fence as effortlessly as ever and came round the turn into the straight with his rider Tim Hyde looking behind him. 'It took me a minute or two to beat that fellow today,' Hyde told his trainer.

As he cleared the last fence he was greeted with a great cheer and went steadily up the final rise to win by five lengths. The race was relayed to radio listeners in both countries, Micheál O'Hehir and Raymond Glendenning pairing up for the BBC commentary. 'He was his usual exuberant and efficient self in putting over his part of the story of how Prince Regent snuffed out Poor Flame', Hugh Brett wrote in the *Sunday Independent*.

'Hundreds had rushed down from the stands to see him led in,' *The Irish Times* reported, 'and, as he came along with Hyde all smiles, the cheering broke out and lasted for a considerable time.'

'He is a worthy champion, and the large number of Irish visitors who came to see him may well be proud of him', the *London Times* reported. The sporting artist Snaffles described Prince Regent as the ultimate horse after the victory. But he was not to ride the Gold Cup again. Instead his owner's attention strayed north to Aintree. Prince Regent was installed as 9/4 favourite for the Grand National despite the 12 st 5 lb the handicapper allotted him. His owner, James Voase Rank, who had once vowed he would win the Derby, the Grand National and the Waterloo Cup (the Cheltenham Gold Cup did not figure in his ambition), now believed he was never going to get a better horse to deliver the Grand National.

Tim Hyde disagreed. While he was publicly quoted as saying 'he jumped like a fellow who will take Aintree in his stride', privately he wrote: 'I felt at last the edge was beginning to go off the great horse's speed and I realised that now, at eleven, he was past his best.'

The betrayal of Prince Regent to the hardship of Aintree helped bring an end to the Gold Cup's reputation as a stepping-stone to Aintree and its emergence as the pinnacle of steeplechasing in its own right.

A largish Irish following came to Aintree and sent Prince Regent away as favourite. Hyde could not believe he was still on his feet doing the second circuit, he had made so many mistakes. He was hampered by loose horses, and Hyde said he had to ride three finishes to stay in the race at all. Though he jumped the last in front, he was caught by Fermoy-bred Lovely Cottage, receiving 25 lb, and Jack Finlay also passed him.

Prince Regent never won the National. In 1947, again as favourite and again in front of even stronger Irish support, he went up 2 lb to 12 st 7 lb and finished fourth to the surprise winner Caughoo, bred in Wexford by Patrick Power and trained by Herbert McDowell on the sands at Sutton.

In 1948, carrying 12 st 2 lb, he was out of the race when he was carried off by a loose horse at Becher's. Rank moved him to England and teamed up with veteran jockey Jack Molony. Under Dreaper he had won 21 races out of 49 in five seasons. He would have won more Gold Cups than Golden Miller but for the war and the Aintree obsession of his owner. Instead he won just one.

He won once more at Cheltenham before retiring at the age of 15.

Whatever one may think about Prince Regent's Grand National chances it is as difficult to get away from his credentials in the race today as it was with Distel on Tuesday. All through his racing career he has been asked to give away great weights and he has attempted to do so with success. His maturity coinciding with the war years limited the scope of his endeavour, and it is only for the first time today that he has the opportunity to vindicate the opinion which has long been held of him by those who know him best.

London Times, 14 March 1946

It was not the only cause for celebration, for in 1946 Distel became the first Irish-trained winner of the Champion Hurdle at odds of 4/5.

A small 5-year-old bay with three white socks, he won the 1944 Cesarewitch for Colonel A. J. Blake of Heath House stable in Laois before being purchased at the top price of 1,800 guineas on behalf of Dorothy Paget by her Irish racing manager Charlie Rogers.

He was trained by Maxwell Arnott (as was another of Ms Paget's runners, Lady Juliet) at Greenmount in Clonsilla and ridden by Bobby O'Ryan.

O'Ryan can take much credit for the victory. The pacemaker Odette had been swallowed up by the field after a mile. Turning for home with three-quarters of a mile to go, O'Ryan sent Distel into the lead, went on to jump the last hurdle clear from Robin o' Chantry and won by five lengths.

Distel returned as 5/1 second favourite for the Champion Hurdle in 1947 but flopped and never realised the potential he had shown in victory as a 5-year old. He was found to have suffered chronic heart disease caused by overstrained heart muscles and was put down in 1948. This, Ms Paget declared, 'should exonerate the horse from his peculiar lapses towards the end of his career.'

It was a good meeting for Rogers and Dorothy Paget. Bobby O'Ryan also rode Dunshaughlin to a five-length victory in the Cotswold Chase.

Captain Denis Baggalley from Kiltale rode the Kim Muir Memorial Chase winner for Rogers. Astrometer had won the 1941 Cesarewitch for a young Vincent O'Brien, only to be purchased for Ms Paget for 750 guineas after the death of O'Brien's father.

Ratoath jockey Dan Moore, apparently back in favour with Dorothy Paget after one of her characteristic fallings-out, rode Loyal King to win the Cheltenham Grand Annual Steeplechase, carrying a 10 lb penalty and beating another Irish challenger Keep Faith by two lengths.

This gave Ireland an impressive five wins out of 30 runners in eighteen races, one by Tom Dreaper, one by Maxwell Arnott and three by Rogers (and his assistant Tommy Nugent). Confusingly, official records list Distel as trained by Rogers and Loyal King as trained by Fulke Walwyn, to whose stable the notoriously cranky Ms Paget moved the horse immediately after Cheltenham.

> As a whole the runners looked hard trained, as if prepared solely for the task on hand, with no regard for the future.
>
> *The Guardian*, review of Cheltenham Festival, 7 March 1948

About 25 years after the event, someone decided that the triple victory of Cottage Rake between 1948 and 1951 began the Hibernification of Cheltenham.

Not exactly. The numbers travelling over to attend the Rake's Gold Cup successes were unlikely to be greater than the small but enthusiastic group who supported Prince Regent's assault on the Cheltenham Gold Cup in 1946, and certainly smaller than his ill-fated obsessive attempts to win Aintree.

While Cheltenham historian Bob Harman traces the demise of Aintree 'as a prestige event' to Prince Regent's failure to win there, it seems to have had a more telling impact on the Irish fan base of national hunt racing, who turned their attention back to the Cotswolds.

Harman wrote that Prince Regent was the greatest horse of his generation and his failure to win the Grand National carrying heavy weights exposed the event as a lottery.

The big Irish following that went to Aintree to back him were also becoming conscious that their time and money might be better spent at Cheltenham.

Aubrey Brabazon came into the paddock wearing Miss Shortiss's colours of white with a blue V. He was lucky to be wearing anything at all. Miss Shortiss left her colours behind in Dublin and had spent the last four days mostly standing at the door of the Railway Hotel waiting for the registered parcel to arrive.

The Irish Times, report of Galway races, 3 August 1944

The large Irish following that came to see Prince Regent was the subject of much comment in 1946.

Cheltenham buffs prefer to nominate 1948 as the date Cheltenham turned green. It fits a time when Ireland's sporting profile was growing, if only within the peculiarly acerbic Anglo-Irish arena.

While Vincent O'Brien was sending his star horses by converted bomber from Shannon, a small charter plane carried Irish followers for the first time in 1948, including jockeys Jimmy Brogan and Dan Moore, and one of the great characters among Irish racehorse owners, the red haired chain smoking racehorse owner Betty Shortiss from Tramore, owner of Gold Cup contestant African Collection, and her sister Pauline.

It was expected to land near the course, but fog forced it down near Liverpool. The *Irish Independent* reported that the racing 'was enjoyed by a huge crowd, only a small proportion of which was Irish', and when Cottage Rake won the Gold Cup the same writer reported: 'The cheer that greeted the winner was reminiscent of that accorded Prince Regent two years ago.'

Fred Daly's 1947 British Open victory, Ireland's 1948 Rugby Union Grand Slam and Ireland's achievement at Goodison Park in Liverpool in 1949 in becoming the first team from outside Whitehall's territorial claims to beat England on home ground, all coincided with the emergence into the public spotlight of Cottage Rake, his trainer and, more importantly, the hilly racecourse on which Cottage Rake's successes were being played out.

Anglo-Irish rivalry was going through a peculiar phase of its own. The relationship had attained a certain edge because of Ireland's neutrality in World War II and the attitude of Winston Churchill.

Churchill, whose unhappy childhood in Dublin fuelled an increasingly intemperate Hibernophobia, had devoted two pages of his World War II victory address to an attack on the Irish people and Taoiseach

Éamon de Valera. Although Churchill had been voted out of office the previous July 1947 and de Valera voted out in February 1948, anti-Irish feeling was still high in England. What better place to explore new opportunities for friendship than on the racecourse at Cheltenham?

Major Geoffrey Harbord wrote after Prince Regent's victory in 1946 that 'the meeting clearly proved, if proof were needed, that Irish form is 10 lb better than ours, not 21 lb worse, as the handicappers have assessed it throughout the season'.

> It is not easy in these days to buy horses likely to make good steeple-chasers. Many trainers of jumpers have been in Ireland during the summer and autumn trying to buy possible Grand National and Gold Cup winners and they have found prices high and the selection small. More and more breeders have devoted their land to mares whose produce can be sold as yearlings at Doncaster, Newmarket and Ballsbridge. Since the reward is generally greater for 18 months keep for these prospective winners on the Flat than for about four years keep for the chasers, their decision is hardly to be wondered at.
>
> *London Times*, 2 December 1948

English buyers had several strong sires in mind when they crossed the channel. Steel Point, standing in Waterford, and Mr Toots, who sired in Tipperary, had a handful of winners each. But Cottage, who had died in 1942, was the best known.

The sire of Cottage, Tracery, was a champion on the flat. He had been bred in Kentucky by Mr Belmont but was sent to race in England where he won the St Leger in 1912 and might well have won the Ascot Gold Cup (he was two or three lengths clear of the field), had not a man named Harold Hewitt of Hope End, Herefordshire, run across the field with a revolver and a suffragette flag.

Cottage himself was bred in France by Baron Edouard de Rothschild in 1918. Sent to race in England, he won only once, a small race in Doncaster worth £168. He had, according to contemporaries, a savage temperament, and when put up for sale at the Newmarket Bloodstock Sales of 1924, he was knocked down to the only bidder, Michael Magnier of Grange Stud, Fermoy, Co. Cork. According to folklore someone commented, 'there goes twenty five thousand pounds worth of trouble' as he left the ring.

Michael Magnier tamed him, and he sired three Grand National winners: Workman (1939), Lovely Cottage (1946) and Sheila's Cottage (1948); and Brendan's Cottage, winner of the Cheltenham Gold Cup in 1939. Unusually, when he won in 1939, Workman was Irish owned, bred, ridden (by Tim Hyde) and trained by Jack Ruttle out of Hazlehatch Stud.

By the time Cottage died in 1942 the £25,000 worth of trouble had supplanted My Prince as the leading sire of steeplechasers in Ireland.

During the 1948 jump season the progeny of Cottage won three times as much money as that of his nearest rival. The latest of his progeny was about to make Cheltenham history.

> The Southern trainer, Vincent O'Brien, saddled the winner of the Corinthian race, Cottage Rake. He is a fine type of horse who will be heard of again.
>
> *The Irish Times* report from Leopardstown, 16 February 1946

Dan O'Brien, the enthusiastic horse breeder and farmer from Churchtown near Mallow in Co. Cork, passed away in 1943.

He had been a breeder and trainer of high-performance horses like Astrometer, the winner of the 1941 Irish Cesarewitch (and a Cheltenham winner for Charlie Rogers), and Astrologer, a winner of the 1943 Irish Cambridgeshire. And he had a worthy successor.

His son Vincent was born in 1917, learned to ride as a boy and hunted with the Dashing Duhallows, which claims to be Ireland's oldest hunt club. He had no interest in formal education and dropped out at 15 to join Fred Clarke's stables at Leopardstown. He began looking after the point-to-pointers and eventually became assistant to his dad, a very successful one, leading the Cesarewitch winner Astrometer into the enclosure in 1941. He had plans to emigrate, but his father persuaded him to stay at home and help him with the horses. When his dad died in 1943, the farm was left to another son by his first marriage. His best horses were sold off.

Many great Irish national hunt trainers remember the trauma of having to part with a great horse when the owner dies—Paddy Mullins never forgot how Nicolaus Silver was sold out of his yard a few months before winning the 1961 Aintree Grand National.

Astrometer and all the other great horses from Dan O'Brien's stables in Churchtown were snapped up by leading owners, including Dorothy Paget.

The young O'Brien learned that a good stable needed loyal owners with a proper financial foundation. It was to become a driving force in his life from which the whole racing industry in Ireland would benefit.

Vincent persuaded his half-brother to lease him back the stables and gallops. He was given a horse to train by a family friend, wool merchant Frank Vickerman of Glenageary. With horses such as Cotty he built up Vickerman's trophy cabinet and attracted more owners, most notably Joseph McGrath of the sweepstake family, owners of the *Irish Independent* newspaper. More importantly, he spotted Good Days and Drybob at the Newmarket Sales.

He knew that the income from training horses would not be enough to sustain him. In complete contrast to Tom Dreaper, who remained a farmer who did a bit of training throughout his life, O'Brien was essentially a punter who did a bit of training all his life. The two men who turned Cheltenham into an Irish festival came from opposite sides of the same game.

First the 27-year-old O'Brien and his owners took on the Irish bookmakers. His first coup was a double at long odds in the 1944 Irish Cambridgshire (where Drybob dead-heated at 50/1 in October) and the Cesarewitch (when Good Days won at 20/1). It left Vincent O'Brien with 45 winners in his first season, seventeen ahead of his nearest rival, and a sound financial base from which to work. And thus began the career of Ireland's greatest trainer of racing horses.

To achieve that sort of success again, he would need to look beyond Ireland, where the prize money was greater. He knew that the betting rings of Cheltenham, and of England in general, were awash with black market currency after the war, and where a bookmaker's cheque was an ideal way of laundering anything earned on the fringes of the regulated and rationed society.

O'Brien could take advantage of his youth, his distance and his seclusion. He set in motion several plans to sting the bookies with ante-post wagers on his little known horses.

The name of Cottage Rake has been added to the list of winners of the Mickey Macardle Cup, a name that bids fair to be written with honour in the annals of Chasing.

Irish Independent, report from Dundalk, 19 April 1947

Vincent O'Brien knew Dr Otto Vaughan from Mallow, who had brought his big horse Cottage Rake to Limerick show to win second prize. The doctor had hunted Cottage Rake, whose line was traced to Stella, with the Mallow hounds, and he was keen to sell him as a racehorse but unable to find a buyer in the restricted wartime conditions. O'Brien agreed to train the horse for the County Plate Hurdle in Limerick in December 1945. He won by six lengths and followed up with another win in Leopardstown in February. O'Brien took him for training. A few flat races later he was more saleable.

The final part of the Cottage Rake story was added when Aubrey Brabazon rode Cottage Rake in his first steeplechase at Leopardstown on St Stephen's Day in 1946. They won by twenty lengths.

Aubrey Brabazon was the son of the trainer Cecil, who originally trained in Kilcumney before moving to Rangers Lodge on the Curragh. He had already won the Galway Plate three times and his ride on Cottage Rake was instrumental on his catching Martin Molony to finish level in the jockeys' championship of 1946.

O'Brien persuaded Frank Vickerman to pay £3,500 for the horse. But Cottage Rake was failed by the vet. A second vet failed the horse and Vickerman changed his mind. O'Brien persuaded Vickerman to hire a third vet, but the deal went through anyway. A cheque for part payment of the horse had already been cashed. And so, against his better judgment, Frank Vickerman was stuck with the horse that ultimately changed the lives of his owner, jockey, trainer and indeed the entire history of Cheltenham.

A feature of the race was the skilled and intrepid riding of the two Irish jockeys, particularly the loser. Both horses and jockeys were greeted with a storm of cheering as they were led in.

London Times, 5 March 1948

By March 1948 Cottage Rake was 9, woefully (or for O'Brien and his fellow bookie-bashers, fortunately) inexperienced, and had never run further than two and a half miles. He had won four of his eight steeplechases, including the Irish Cesarewitch, but had fallen in his last outing at Leopardstown. 'Though he may forget that mishap and jump the Cheltenham course he must be written down as unlikely to do so', the *London Times* predicted. A week later the same newspaper reported the race to be 'the most open for many years. Unless there is heavy rain the going will be dry and fast. This will suit horses like Cool Customer and Cottage Rake, who have brilliant speed.'

The portents were not good with a week to go before the 1948 festival. Snow and frost brought all racing to a halt. Trainers who were getting ready for the festival were in trouble with their winding up gallops.

However, it was a glorious sunny day in Cheltenham, with perfect visibility. The course rode with slightly more yield than in previous races, but it was still firm. The 7/2 favourite, Cool Customer, looked game but impetuous in the paddock. Red April, as usual, was rather light. Revelry had lost a lot of weight since Lingfield and wore a breastplate. Happy Home, another Irish bred, looked 'finer drawn than usual' according to Meyrick Good, *Sporting Life* correspondent, the doyen of racing correspondents and the BBC's first racing commentator, but 'was everything that a good chaser should be'. According to another writer, Freddy Fox, 'though a charming little horse, he looked too small when compared with some of his opponents'. He and Cottage Rake, said the *Guardian*, 'appeared the most unconcerned of the party, most of whom were sweating slightly.' Cottage Rake, at 10/1 the fourth favourite, was last to enter the ring, a fine deep horse of class who 'compared favourably in looks with any of the champions of the past twenty years'.

The story of the race is easily told. Cool Customer got too close to the first fence and fell. On the last turn Cottage Rake locked with Happy Home down the hill. Realising he had not the speed to cope with Cottage Rake on the flat, Martin Molony flung Happy Home at the last fence and gained a couple of lengths on the inside. Aubrey Brabazon allowed his horse a moment to balance and then made use of the speed Cottage Rake had shown previously to pass Happy Home.

Martin Molony was to finish behind Cottage Rake twice more before saddling Silver Fame to victory in 1951.

It would have taken a super horse to catch Cottage Rake. Neither made any blunder either at this speed or the early part of the race. At one moment we had all expected to see a great match, and in the next it was over.

London Times, report of Cheltenham Gold Cup, 10 March 1950

Frank Vickerman, Cottage Rake's owner, was undecided on whether he would enter the Aintree Grand National in 1949. He said he was pulling his horse out of the entry list on 18 January 1949. The effect was to diminish the chances of horses who would have had to carry 10 st down by six or seven pounds, to push the remaining horses nearer to those at the bottom of the handicap. No one grumbled, the *London Times* said, 'except the owners of those less good entries, for the most popular result is always a win for one of the top weights.' But Vickerman changed his mind.

Jack Frost made the decision for him. The Cheltenham Gold Cup and the last day of racing on 10 March 1949 was abandoned after O'Brien's horses had been flown to Cheltenham at great expense, chartering a converted bomber to bring Hatton's Grace and Cottage Rake on the three hour journey from Shannon to Bristol. The horse tried to lie down while the plane was taking off, according to Vickerman, and 'will not travel by air again'.

With a decision to hold the Gold Cup at the next Cheltenham meeting, Vickerman pulled Cottage Rake out of the Grand National. The fact that the Gold Cup prize money had more than doubled to over £3,258 made the decision easier. It was the first signal from the racing world that the Grand National was not the only show in town.

When the Gold Cup was held on 11 April, it was in front of a smaller crowd and on firmer ground. Cottage Rake was 6/5 on for his long-awaited duel with the young pretender Finnure (starting at 11/2, his first ride back in Ireland had been by a very young Pat Taaffe) and old master Cool Customer (13/2), another Irish bred.

Aubrey Brabazon, knowing his mount's turn of speed, allowed Cool Customer a slight lead coming to the last fence, just as he had done with Happy Home in 1948. As soon as they landed on the flat, he challenged. Cottage Rake drew up alongside the leader amid a storm of cheers and sprinted past him.

In January 1950 the pundits were claiming that Cottage Rake was too old, but the punters were having none of it. The rival of previous years, Cool Customer, was laid up. In the history of the Gold Cup no horse older than 11 had won, although three of the winners were actually 11 and the average age until then was 8.4. A new rival had emerged, Irish-bred Finnure, who was unbeaten in five outings and who had an 11 lb advantage when he beat Cottage Rake over three miles at Kempton

Park. It was going to be another battle between Aubrey Brabazon and Martin Molony. Cottage Rake was 6/5 on, Finnure 5/4 against.

The early pace was slow. Cottage Rake was forced into the lead on the second circuit by Molony's determination to sit behind him. He continued slowly over the water, over the open ditch and up the hill with Finnure about three lengths behind him. Then when they turned the top corner to take the second open ditch, Brabazon let the champion go. He jumped the fence like a hurdle and flew down the hill, eating up the ground with his long stride. Before Molony could move there was a distance of about eight lengths between the horses. Both jockeys charged the next two fences at full tilt unerringly. Instead of a close race, spectators were treated to the spectacle of a great horse winning more easily than he had ever done in his previous Gold Cups. He turned into the straight with a ten-length lead and swept up the hill to the winning post with every part of the gigantic crowd cheering him to the echo.

'He and his jockey received the reception they deserved in the winner's enclosure. Brabazon's face was a picture of relief and happiness as he repeatedly acknowledged the holloas of the crowd.'

'No community loves a good horse more than those who come to this meeting,' the *London Times* wrote. 'It was apparent that they have taken this lean, leggy champion to their hearts. He is a quick, easy jumper with speed and stamina, and is possessed of a most likeable kindly disposition.'

The prospect of a fourth successive Gold Cup lay open until January 1951, when the news that Cottage Rake would not run led to all betting being cancelled. Even in late 1951 there was a rumour of his return. Cottage Rake moved over to Gerald Balding's stable in England, but the change of scenery could not reverse the decline.

The 1951 Gold Cup was an all English affair held in late April, Silver Fame beating Greenogue in the last stride.

I think he would have beaten National Spirit. But we were robbed of a fine race between the veterans. Hatton's Grace is 11 years old and National Spirit 10.

London Times, 7 March 1951

O'Brien had his eye on another Cheltenham prize, the Champion Hurdle. And here is where the story of Mrs Harry Keogh begins.

Bred by Mrs J. W. Harris, Hatton's Grace was bought by J. Kirwan for 50 guineas at the Dublin Sales. Trained by B. Nugent, the horse started winning amateurs' races on the flat at Bellewstown and the Phoenix Park. Kirwan sold a half-share to Dan Corry, the international show-jumper. Eventually Mrs Keogh bought both shares in Hatton's Grace as a 6-year old. It was a further two years before she sent him down to Mallow to be trained by Vincent O'Brien.

Hatton's Grace won one of his two races in 1946–47 and two of his eight in 1947–48. O'Brien sent him by air for his first attempt at the Champion Hurdle in 1948 and finished fifth. After being very far behind in the opening stages, he made up so much ground that he finished only four or five lengths behind the winner, National Spirit.

He then won a solitary hurdle race at Naas before being dispatched to Cheltenham for the 1949 Champion Hurdle and won the race at 100/7. O'Brien and his colleagues had backed him at ante-post odds of 33/1, 25/1 and 20/1.

He was among the oldest winners of the Champion Hurdle; only two others had won it at 9 years of age on 8 March 1949. Remarkably, Hatton's Grace went on to win three in a row.

A strong cold wind dried the course in patches, but some of it rode heavy. Looking up at the stands as the race was about to begin, it seemed a much smaller attendance than usual. The uncertain weather was no doubt to blame. At the turn into the straight it was clear that either Hatton's Grace or Captain Fox would win. Aubrey Brabazon secured the inside position on Hatton's Grace and, with his mount showing a great finishing burst, came right away to win by six lengths. The defending double champion National Spirit was fifth.

The following year, 1950, Hatton's Grace started as the 5/2 favourite. A cold ground fog covered the country around Cheltenham, but just before racing it lifted, and for the rest of the afternoon the sun shone hot in a cloudless sky.

Twice champion, the Vic Smyth-trained National Spirit made the running to the last hurdle. Over the second last flight he was still a length clear, but by the time he reached the last, three horses including Hatton's Grace were closing down on him. Up the hill it was Martin Molony on Harlech against Aubrey Brabazon on Hatton's Grace. Hatton's Grace stayed up the hill with superb grit.

Hatton's Grace was ridden by Aubrey Brabazon for the first two of his three Champion Hurdle victories. In 1951, Tim Molony rode him to complete the treble, substituting for his injured brother Martin.

After two days of rain, a watery sun shone while racing was in progress, but the course rode very heavy indeed. An hour before the first race, some of the car parks were full up and queues of traffic stretched for four miles on the London road and nearly as far on some of the others.

Hatton's Grace was 4/1 second favourite behind 11/4 Average, with the other veteran National Spirit back at 11/1.

It was the veterans who thrived in the mire. National Spirit charged past the two French entrants and gave them and the rest of the field a brilliant and exhilarating lesson in jumping. He gained at every flight, taking off yards back and putting all the power of his big frame into the race. The French horses succumbed on exceptionally boggy ground at the foot of the hill about three furlongs from home. National Spirit lost his feet on landing at the last fence and fell on his side. Hatton's Grace, who had been closing with a superlative run, dashed up the hill with unabated energy, 'leaving us all with the impression that age is no bar to him, and so long as the rain keeps falling he will keep winning'.

In February 1952 he was beaten out of a place in a handicap hurdle at Naas. It was clear the party was over. The winner, Killala, was a 9-year old who had not won previously.

Hatton's Grace went to the Champion Hurdle, the race he used to own, for the last time. He was rated second favourite by the faithful punters who backed him to 13/2 and he finished fifth behind 3/1 favourite Sir Ken, a horse sired by a French government stallion and bought in post-war France, where the breeding industry was in more distress than in Ireland,

It was with astonishment and admiration that we watched the young Irish trainer, M. V. O'Brien, saddle the champions over both types of jumps for the second year in succession, a remarkable feat indeed. He has bought a new establishment in Tipperary to which he will move the horses later in the year.

London Times, 10 March 1950

Vincent O'Brien was different from the sort of Irish trainer that the English media commentariat were used to deprecating. He had learned to effect an accent which sounded more like an Ascot owner than a

Cheltenham trainer. He was also managing his media deftly, building up a relationship with the right people.

All the time he was taking every opportunity to use his horses to ambush the bookies. He pulled off a joke at the Curragh bookmakers' expense on 1 April 1950 when Knock Hard, after a bumper and two chases, and two weeks after winning over fences, returned to the flat to win the Irish Lincoln. Jumpers had won the Cesarewitch before because of its length. The one mile Lincoln was another story.

Thanks to Knock Hard's strange credentials and the hefty 8 st 12 lb on his back, O'Brien had got some of his money on at 6/1 with an army of followers queuing up behind. An avalanche of money forced Knock Hard back to 2/1 with scarcely a shilling on his twelve opponents.

T. P. Burns brought the favourite home by five lengths. According to Burns, Knock Hard 'was really a flat horse that turned to chasing'. O'Brien afterwards said that Knock Hard 'had no natural aptitude for jumping'. Despite this, Knock Hard managed to win eight steeplechases throughout his career including the 1953 Cheltenham Gold Cup.

What do you think drove Vincent in those days? Burns asked rhetorically in his biography, *A Life in Racing*. 'Money. You have to realise that Vincent started out with nothing, nothing at all. The family farm had gone to his older half-brother. He had nothing but ability and ambition. To get to the top was going to take money. He didn't have any, so it had to be got somehow. Anyhow.'

Knock Hard, it was estimated, would not have been far behind the winner and well ahead of the rest of the field, had he not fallen at the second last fence in 1952 when chasing eventual winner Mont Tremblant. Mont Tremblant, a novice, won a first Gold Cup for the gloriously named Fulke Walwyn, whose 40 winners at the Cheltenham Festival between 1946 and 1986 set a standard for every trainer.

On 9 February 1953 the *London Times* racing correspondent wrote that O'Brien, for a young man, had truly remarkable success with steeplechasers and hurdlers in big races. 'With Hatton's Grace and Cottage Rake now passed into history, he was still able to win the big races at Haydock Park and Doncaster with Galatian and Knock Hard last week, and to send Lucky Dome to Dublin to win the valuable Leopardstown Steeplechase.'

A few weeks later Knock Hard was to win the Cheltenham Gold Cup, and Vincent O'Brien was to send out the first of three successive

English Grand National winners, Early Mist, Royal Tan and Quare Times.

Mont Tremblant was not the horse he had been in 1952. He tired at the last fence allowing Galloway Brae to pass him, while the redoubtable Tim Molony drove Knock Hard past both of them on the outside. A mighty leap at the last sealed it for Vincent O'Brien, Tim Molony and Harry Keogh, the owner, who also liked a bet.

'Knock Hard is game and he certainly put an end to the doubts of his stamina,' the *London Times* wrote. 'Knock Hard must be the most versatile horse ever to win the Gold Cup. He has won good races on the flat and over hurdles, and seems able to return occasionally from steeplechasing to win again on the flat. He and Tim Molony were greeted with round after round of cheers when they came back to the winner's enclosure.'

What the public did not know was that O'Brien had discovered that Knock Hard had a heart condition that could have caused him to drop dead at any time. Tim Molony fearlessly agreed to carry on in the saddle.

'Vincent O'Brien from his far-away stables in the green fields of Tipperary is becoming almost a legendary trainer. It is the fourth time he has won the blue riband of steeplechasing in six years. Not even the fog lying in its accustomed strength could reduce the stature of this race.'

Tim Molony, who was in the saddle, had a quiet season until just before the Cheltenham Festival, and then he seemed to carry all before him, riding Sir Ken to a second Champion Hurdle and then Knock Hard to victory at 11/2 in the Gold Cup.

The now defunct Gloucestershire Hurdle, which was run in two divisions, was won ten times by Vincent O'Brien. Between 1950 and 1959, O'Brien sent out ten horses to contest one or other of the divisions. Of the two who failed to win, one was beaten a short head and the other a head. In 1958 he had eight winners at the festival and Saffron Tartan was favourite for the 1959 Gold Cup until he had to pull out on race morning.

And that was where Vincent O'Brien and Cheltenham effectively parted company. Soon after he moved to Ballydoyle, near Cashel, Co. Tipperary, O'Brien took charge of a colt, Ballymoss, owned by Philadelphia building contractor John McShain. Ballymoss cut a swathe through the flat racing circuit, winning the Irish Derby,

England's St Leger and France's Prix de l'Arc de Triomphe in 1958, becoming European Horse of the Year.

In 1962 he won his first Epsom Derby with Larkspur and followed up with Sir Ivor (1968), Nijinsky (1970), Roberto (1972), The Minstrel (1977) and Golden Fleece (1982).

During the 1970s he and owner Robert Sangster, along with O'Brien's son-in-law John Magnier, established what became known as the Coolmore syndicate, centred on Coolmore Stud in Co. Tipperary and stud farms in Kentucky and Australia. By purchasing some of Northern Dancer's progeny, they created a supply line of champion flat horses that reinvented Irish horse racing.

In 2001 Dr Michael Vincent O'Brien was voted the greatest influence in horse racing history, according to a worldwide vote hosted by the *Racing Post* newspaper.

> R. Mansbridge was killed at Cheltenham yesterday by a kick on the back of his head when his mount, Siren Light, was brought down in the long distance hurdle race.
>
> *London Times*, 12 April 1956

During the 1950s Aintree's fortunes began to suffer. It was a bleak time for the course and for steeplechasing in general. Of the 57 fatalities in Aintree history, the 1950s accounted for nearly a quarter of them.

The 1954 Aintree Grand National, won by a neck by Vincent O'Brien's Royal Tan, was the most disastrous of all, with four equine fatalities, two of them Irish trained, Pat Taaffe's mount Conneyburrow and Tim Molony's mount Dominick's Bar, as well as Legal Joy and Paris New York. One jockey also lost his life as a result of injuries sustained in the race.

Shabby and run down after years of military use, a few coats of paint could not disguise the fact that the stands and enclosures were slowly falling apart. The owners of the course, the Topham family, invested money in a new steeplechase course with scaled down versions of the National fences, named after the popular amateur jockey Lord Mildmay, who had helped in the design process.

The replica National fences were not a success and were eventually replaced by conventional park fences. The Tophams also funded the building of a motor racing circuit on the inside of the National course which hosted the British Grand Prix.

Even the honeypot Grand National was in trouble. Year by year the standard of the race dropped. Rank's obsession with the race and the experience of Prince Regent helped end the days when the Gold Cup winner would automatically take his place in the line-up.

Mirabel Topham tried to sell the course, sparking a long-running drama over the future of the National. For many years it appeared as though the race was doomed. A transfer to another course such as Doncaster or Cheltenham was considered.

By the 1960s Cheltenham had become acknowledged as the most important jumps race meeting in the calendar. The Gold Cup and the Champion Hurdle were the undisputed championship races for chasers and hurdlers.

In 1960 the Queen Mother Champion Chase became, for many purists, the new highlight of the festival, an exhibition of jumping at speed by the top horses in the industry. New championship races were introduced for novice chasers and hurdlers, a champion flat race and a new generation of competitive handicaps. The TV cameras came to Cheltenham in 1955 bringing a new audience to the sport.

Thanks to TV and sponsorship, for the first time horses could earn significant sums of money for their owners without having to risk the perils of the Grand National.

> His stamina and liking for the course proved more decisive than the mathematics of the form book.
>
> *London Times,* 15 March 1957

Tractor magnate David Brown flew in from New York to see his tiny Irish-bred colt Linwell win the 1957 Gold Cup.

The 16 hand high horse was bought for £750 by Mr I. Herbert on behalf of Brown. He passed through the hands of P. Quinn in Tipperary, who once had Golden Miller on his farm. Brown hunted him in Oxfordshire and Mr Herbert rode him in point-to-points. Linwell won from the bottom of the handicap and continued winning to the top.

The first disaster occurred when Sir Ken fell two fences after the water and about a mile from home. Bryan Marshall said afterwards that he was going strongly at the time and that he had just pulled to the outside to pass tiring horses. Pointsman also made an error and lost a little ground. ESB, who had been Ireland's last winner of the Aintree Grand National for three decades when he won in 1956, and Gay Donald were both beaten shortly afterwards. Three fences out Kerstin and Linwell moved up to the heels of the leader. Pointswell cannoned off Kerstin's quarters, breaking his stride. Linwell and Kerstin passed Rose Park and Linwell jumped the last fence into the lead, holding his advantage to the post.

> Six Irish horses have won the Cheltenham Gold Cup since it was first run in 1924, but seldom if ever has there been a luckier winner of the race than Roddy Owen, given the cup on a platter by Pas Seul's sensational last fence fall. Not only was this brilliant novice going on the bit and in the lead when disaster overtook him, but he badly hampered Linwell and Lochroe, who were then in second and third places.
>
> Philip Clifford, *Daily Mail*, 1959

Without reaching the record heights of 1958, the 1959 festival was good for Ireland. They won the inaugural Champion Chase with Quita Que and achieved six wins from sixteen starts. Unlike 1958 though, they were expected to win the Gold Cup as well.

As it happened, Dan Morgan's victory with Roddy Owen was almost wholly unexpected, because 1959 looked set to be the year of Saffron Tartan and Vincent O'Brien. 'If the luck deserted one Irish stable with the news yesterday that Vincent O'Brien's favourite, Saffron Tartan, had been coughing and could not run in the Gold Cup,' the *London Times* reported, 'it returned in a dramatic last half-minute of the race to another Irish stable with the victory of Roddy Owen over Linwell and Lochroe.'

Roddy Owen was bred by the Nolan family at the Curragh and purchased as an unbroken 5-year old in 1953 by Oliver Plunkett, the twelfth and last Lord Fingall. He was named after the 1892 Aintree Grand National-winning jockey Captain Roderick Owen, who won 250 races as an amateur.

When Roddy Owen was beaten a short head in the 1958 King George, Bunny Cox, first choice jockey for Wicklow trainer Paddy Sleator, was on board. Plunkett recruited Cox in Britain when Sleator had no runners in a race. 'Bunny Cox did a tremendously generous thing in 1959 before that Gold Cup,' Michael Power told John Donohue of the *Meath Chronicle* in 2009. 'He was to ride Roddy Owen. He rang the owner the night before and said Bobby Beasley had no ride, and should ride Roddy Owen. The owner wasn't going to change, but Cox said the horse goes better for Beasley.'

Donohue, who knew the family, recalls that during his riding years Plunkett was easy to distinguish as he always wore glasses. It was said he 'was as blind as a bat and brave as a lion' and won the 1930 National Hunt Chase on Sir Lindsay. He served a record five periods as national hunt steward and was also joint master of the Ward Union and was on the original board of the National Stud.

Plunkett's sister, Lady Mary Kirk, was godmother to Mouse Morris, trainer of Michael O'Leary's War of Attrition, winner of the 2006 Cheltenham Gold Cup.

There had been considerable rain during the night after the first day, but it came down in full fury on Wednesday night and Thursday morning and left the new course so waterlogged that the steeplechases, except for the Foxhunters Challenge Cup, were run on the old course.

The sight of a tractor two hours before the first race pulling a car out of the mud in a car park gave an ominous indication of the conditions. The fence before the water, which is jumped twice for the Gold Cup, was cut out, and the horses returned looking as though they had been dragged through a mud bath, while the faces of the riders and their colours were scarcely recognisable.

The wild and stormy morning gave way to sunshine through most of the afternoon. Roddy Owen started at 5/1 with Linwell at 11/2 and Lochroe at 100-9.

It was a case of being in the right place at the right time for Roddy Owen. Taxidermist came down five fences from home, losing his feet on landing in the mud. Roddy Owen was fourth at the last fence when Pas Seul, a half-brother to the 1955 winner Gay Donald, with an advantage of two lengths and going well, came down in front of Linwell, bringing him almost to a halt, and interfering with Lochroe. Bobby Beasley was on his own on Roddy Owen and already well on his way up the hill to the winning post before Winter got Linwell going again. By the time they reached the post Roddy Owen was three lengths in front of Linwell with Lochroe ten lengths away third and Hart Royal fourth.

His time of 7 minutes 28 seconds was more than a minute slower than Silver Fame's 1951 record of 6 minutes 23 seconds.

Beasley said later he felt confident that he would have won in any case. Beasley was later to win an even more important battle against alcoholism and returned to pilot Captain Christy to another Gold Cup in 1974.

The Irish camp, a hilariously impious blend of God, in the shape of the entire priesthood, and Mammon, in the various disguises he takes upon himself among the laity over the water.

DEREK MALCOM, *The Guardian*, 6 May 1964

The cheers for the eight winners in 1958 and Roddy Owen in 1959 showed that the number of Irish followers had grown. Many were now English based after a decade of high emigration. But more had travelled especially for the event. The mailboats which conveyed Irish fans were uncomfortable by today's standards, but large enough to cope with the numbers of the time. The *Hibernia* and the *Cambria* could carry 1,000 passengers each from Dun Laoghaire to Holyhead. Both had come into service in 1949, replacing the smaller 1920–21 vessels of the same name, in time for the increased Irish interest in Cheltenham inspired by Vincent O'Brien's Cottage Rake.

'Invasion' was not yet the term. In a 1983 interview commentator Micheál O'Hehir said there were only a few dozen Irish supporters who had travelled to follow Tom Dreaper's Prince Regent in 1946, although a slightly larger number came to see him at Aintree.

Finbarr Slattery recalls travelling on the *Innisfallen* from Cork in 1958 to watch the Vincent O'Brien festival. The *Princess Maud*, the flat-bottomed ship that was infamously nicknamed 'Rock and Roll' because of the propensity of passengers to get seasick, was also used in 1958 to convey passengers to what was Ireland's most successful Cheltenham Festival, Vincent O'Brien delivering eight winners: Top Twenty, Springsilver, Admiral Stuart, Fortria, Sentina, Prudent King, Quita Que and Friendly Boy.

Seven Irish horses were entered for the Gold Cup in 1961, indicating the level of Irish interest even before Arkle came on the scene. The controversy over the eligibility of Paddy Sleator's Zonda, having failed a drug test in Ireland, ran for weeks before the race.

Irish bookmakers who were regulars at the festival now included Bill Quinlan, Malachy Skelly, Eddie and Jim Mulligan and Jim Murray.

The first air charter services for punters were also used that year, using an Aer Lingus BAC 111 to Birmingham, but fares were high and numbers small. Horses continued to travel on the Rosslare to Fishguard southern sea corridor.

Aer Lingus started a scheduled service, AT270 (Aer Lingus did not start using EI until the summer of 1950), to Birmingham Elmdon Airport on 2 May 1949, a Douglas DC-3 aircraft originally built for the US Army Air Force in 1943 fitted with 26 seats and bearing the name St Declan. Fares were expensive, £6-0-0 single, £10-16-0 return and £9-0-0 excursion return.

In the winter of 1959, the DC-3s were replaced by new Fokker F27 Friendship twin turbo-props. Vickers Viscount 800s replaced these in 1966, and Boeing 737 jets were used from 1970 until the fleet became an all-Airbus one in 2001.

Bristol was not, as yet, a major gateway. Until the 1990s most racegoers who travelled by air flew to London because there was a better service from there and they took special trains up to Cheltenham from Paddington.

Joe Tully, whose father Frank conveyed many of these Irish fans, explains that the timing of Cheltenham was particularly suited to the travelling punter. At a time when annual holidays were calculated by the tax year, unused days would have to be used up before the deadline of 5 April. It was a short break, less than a week long, and some would visit the festival according to whether they had one, two or three days to use.

The car ferries of the 1960s were to change the dynamic of the Irish support at Cheltenham, facilitating coach services from Irish towns. Paddy Dignam, who started the Stena coach service in 1976, recalls that Cheltenham was an ordinary race meeting when he first took bookings for the festival in 1952. In 1966 the overnight cabins on the Rosslare to Fishguard service, the *St David*, were gutted to fit a car deck and the sailings changed to daytime. It could hold only 150 cars, but the idea proved popular. In 1973 the *Avalon* was added on the Dun Laoghaire route.

When the giant 7,836 tonne *St Columba* commenced service in 1977 with capacity for 2,500 passengers and 400 cars and coaches, Ireland's

Cheltenham numbers shot up to above 3,000 for the first time. Famously, at the launch service in Aalborg, the mechanically launched champagne bottle looped around the site and missed the brow of the ship. The gents toilet at Aalborg dock was named the St Columba instead!

It might be regarded as an appropriate metaphor for the way the Irish economy was about to go, and the impact it would have on Ireland's record at Cheltenham.

Chapter 6 ～

ARKLE AND BEYOND

Who was born in a stable and has millions of followers?
Arkle.
> 1964 joke popular in the aftermath of the 'Bigger than
> God' Beatles controversy

When Ireland's television service opened in January 1962, it was natural that national hunt racing would feature prominently in the schedule. The first head of sport was Micheál O'Hehir, the most famous racing media personality who had commentated for the BBC Light programme at Cheltenham since 1946, teaming up with Raymond Glendenning and then Richard North, and he made sure Cheltenham was on the schedule.

The first two races for the Cheltenham Gold Cup relayed to the Irish audience were won by English horses with Ireland's (and Tom Dreaper's) best-known challenger in second place on both occasions. Both winners were trained by Fulke Walwyn. The popular 11-year-old Mandarin won in 1962, overtaking Pat Taaffe on Fortria, and returning to the winner's enclosure to the best reception for years, and Mill House won in 1963, thundering up the hill eleven lengths again ahead of Pat Taaffe on Tom Dreaper's Fortria. The ground was much softer than Fortria would have liked. His wealthy owner picked up £25,000 in bets.

At 17 hands high Mill House was known simply as 'the big horse' and by consensus was regarded as the outstanding prospect not just for 1964 but for the next decade.

Irish viewers wanted Taaffe to reverse the order of things in the coming years. The name of the horse that might do it, that could challenge Mill House, was already on everyone's lips. He had won the unusually competitive Broadway Chase at the 1963 Cheltenham Festival. The name had a ring to it. Arkle.

The feel he gives you is something different from any other horse. Even before he runs. Even when he's walking with his head up there.

PAT TAAFFE

Was Arkle the greatest steeplechaser there has ever been? No one can say for certain. It is always a fruitless and contentious task to compare racehorses of different eras. What can be said is that no other steeplechaser in the history of the sport established a wider margin of superiority over his contemporaries—or a firmer grip on the imagination of the sporting public.

He was the first four-legged celebrity, his picture regularly on the front of the tabloid newspapers, and a star of the new television age. His name was to become familiar to people who had never set foot on a racetrack.

Arkle ran in 35 races, three of them on the flat and six over hurdles. The rest were steeplechases and, in this, his true metier, he was beaten only four times—once by a luckless slip, twice by weight and once by the injury that ended his career.

Arkle did enough to convince most experts that he was the greatest steeplechaser who ever lived. No other champion has ever dominated his contemporaries so overwhelmingly that he made top class rivals look pedestrians.

JOHN RANDALL, Racing Post

Part of the mythology of Arkle is the claim that he was an unlikely champion, a gangly gelding, an unlikely winner by a sire who was a failed flat racer. 'He was well bred for his task,' his equographer Ivor Herbert wrote in 1966, 'but not superbly so. His maternal side were prolific winner-producers in a limited class. His sire, through bred in purple, was a racing flop. Arkle in his youth was far from being the paragon of equine beauty,' he added. 'He was sold in the open market inexpensively. He was not, at first, highly considered by his wise old trainer.'

Bright Cherry was covered by Archive at the Loughtown Stud near Clane, Co. Kildare, on 2 May 1956. Archive was a cheap stallion, standing at £50, and had failed to win once in two seasons on the racecourse.

But this was only partly true. Arkle's grandsire was the unbeaten

Italian thoroughbred champion Nearco (1935–1957), an outstandingly prepotent sire, eclipsed only by his grandson Northern Dancer. His granddam, Archive's mother, was also an outstanding mare, Book Law, winner of the St Leger and runner-up in the Oaks and 1,000 Guineas. At stud she had produced six winners. *Thoroughbred Heritage* says that Nearco was 'one of the greatest racehorses of the twentieth century' as well as patriarch of the most dominant sire line in thoroughbred history.

Nearco retired undefeated after fourteen races and was sold in 1938 by breeder Federico Tesio to Martin Benson of Beech House Stud in Newmarket, England, for £60,000, a world record price for a sire in those days.

Nearco's legacy comes primarily from three of his sons: Nasrullah, Nearctic and Royal Charger. His other sons included Dante, winner of the 1945 Epsom Derby, and Nimbus who won the Epsom Derby and 2,000 Guineas in 1949. From his daughters, Nearco was the damsire of the French multiple group 1 winner Charlottesville, and damsire of the 1948 Epsom Derby winner Arctic Prince.

Among Arkle's many important relatives are Ballymoss, Better Loosen Up, Fort Marcy, Invasor, Mr Prospector, Nasrullah, Never Say Die, Nijinsky II, Northern Dancer, Royal Palace, Secretariat, Shergar and Sir Ivor.

According to *France Galop*, the male bloodline of every Prix de l'Arc de Triomphe winner from 1994 through 2007 goes back to Nearco, his son Nasrullah and his grandson Northern Dancer. Bred in the purple indeed. It was just that the talent had skipped a generation.

> Arkle was a Rolls Royce of a horse. He was as clever as any hunter and he could always find a fifth or even a sixth leg.
>
> TOM DREAPER, interview with SEAMUS COUNIHAN,
> *Sunday Independent*, 19 December 1971

Mrs Mary Baker's mare Bright Cherry, herself a fast two mile chaser trained in her racing days by Tom Dreaper, gave birth to a foal at 3.30 am on 19 April 1957 in Dorothy Paget's Ballymacoll Stud, just across the Meath border from Maynooth. Mrs Baker raised him on a farm on the Dublin-Meath border, within an A330 roar of Dublin Airport. He was fed with oats rolled with a mineral supplement called Rosette. Two nights a week he was given bran mashes rolled with cod liver oil.

Dreaper had won point-to-points on the new foal's grandmother, Greenogue Princess. So it was not entirely guesswork when, at the 1960 August Goff Sales, he bought the big gawky bay 3-year-old Lot 148 for 1,150 guineas.

It was the best price of the sale, a surprise to the Bakers who had put a reserve of 500 guineas on him, enough to merit Arkle's photograph being taken for the *Irish Press*.

He was bidding on behalf of Anne Grosvenor, Duchess of Westminster. He had told her he had trained the dam who had a lot of speed, that the family had produced more than its share of winners, but he suspected the colt would not stay further than two miles. The under-bidder was Charles Radclyffe who liked the look of the horse despite his angular appearance.

Anne Grosvenor also bought Bray Flame for even more (2,000 guineas) at the same sales, before changing his name to Brae to add a Scottish flavour. She offered the choice of the horses between two trainers, Dreaper and Willie O'Grady from Killeens, Ballynonty, in Tipperary, father of Edward O'Grady. Dreaper chose bay gelding Lot 148, soon to be renamed Arkle after a mountain in the Grosvenor estate in Lochmore, Sutherland, in north-west Scotland.

> Arkle was a divine freak. Arkle possessed an athlete's physical attri-butes: power, speed, judgment, balance, a quick eye, stamina and the ability to learn, absorb and then react instinctively. Other good horses have had these talents, or most of them, in good measure. Arkle simply possessed them all in abundance.
>
> IVOR HERBERT, *Arkle: The Classic Story of a Champion*

Arkle's new owner was the Cork-born daughter of a British army officer, Edward Langford Sullivan.

Known as Nancy Sullivan in her childhood in Glanmire, she now had a title under England's hereditary peerage, Anne Winifred Sullivan Grosvenor, Duchess of Westminster. She was the childless widow of the richest man in England, a man 36 years older than she was. Hugh Richard Arthur Grosvenor was a guest of her father when they met. A horse race enthusiast, he was known as Bend'Or after his grandfather's chestnut stallion, an ancestor of Arkle on both sides of his pedigree, who won the Epsom Derby in the year he was born.

The second Duke of Westminster was a controversial character, a supporter of the Ulster Unionist Party (for whom his nephew held a parliamentary seat), the Mosley movement in England and other anti-Semitic and Fascist movements on the European mainland. He had helped complete the demise of the English Liberal Party in 1931 by leaking details of his brother-in-law's homosexuality. His own love life was flamboyant. Until 1930 he had been a lover of Gabrielle ('Coco') Chanel, showering her with expensive gifts to win her heart. Nancy was 31 and he was 67 when she became his fourth wife in 1947.

He died six years later and she inherited a life interest in his estates, including a 700 acre estate near Maynooth, the Grosvenor's Eaton Stud near Chester, from where famous horses such as Bend'Or, Ormonde and Flying Fox were bred, and Lochmore in Sutherland. She outlived her husband by 50 years, dying on 31 August 2003.

After her husband's death Anne began to indulge her interest in horse racing. Probably the best horse bred at her studs was Brioche, third in the 1957 St Leger. Apart from Arkle, her horses included Ten Up which won another Gold Cup for her and Tom Dreaper in 1970, Kinloch Brae trained by Willie O'Grady who won at Cheltenham and beat L'Escargot in the Power Gold Cup. She also owned Last Suspect, winner of the 1985 Grand National at odds of 50/1 when trained by Captain Tim Forster. Last Suspect only ran after some last-minute persuasion from jockey Hywel Davies, who was told by Grosvenor, 'It's your neck if you break it.'

Another famous horse, Foinavon, won the Foxrock Cup at Leopardstown for her in 1965, but she sold him long before his astonishing 1967 Grand National triumph, where a mass pile-up at a fence now named in his honour resulted in his victory at 100/1.

Nancy's love for Arkle was clear to everyone around her. She rode him at Bryanstown and the character of the two went hand in hand. Stablehand Paddy Murray used to tell the story of finding the two of them eating sugar lumps together, the horse lying down and not bothering to rise when she came round to see him.

I don't really know where I learned about training horses. I think you could say I accumulated it along the way. I made some awful mistakes at first. But I learned from them.

TOM DREAPER, interview with SEAMUS COUNIHAN, *Sunday Independent*, 19 December 1971

Arkle's trainer was already accepted as the best national hunt trainer in Ireland since Vincent O'Brien had gone to the flat. Born in September 1898, Tom Dreaper rode as an amateur between 1922 and 1940 and first began to train with two horses. He was a farmer as much as a trainer. His dad was a keen punter, but he believed that nobody made money from racing. The countryside around Kilsallaghan where they lived was dotted with fleeced punters.

'I think my father was correct,' Tom Dreaper said in 1971. 'All the people around the countryside at that time were stony broke because of the horses. They were either keeping horses they couldn't afford in the first place, or else betting on them. All the time they were getting deeper into debt.'

Dreaper became the country's leading trainer almost by accident. Mrs N. J. Kelly's My Branch gave him a valuable victory in the Clonard Steeplechase in March 1938, setting him up for the Irish Grand National. My Branch was beaten by Clare County at Fairyhouse, but a subsequent win at Punchestown was enough to inspire James Voase Rank to send him four horses in August 1938, horses which had unexpectedly become available due to the tragic death of his trainer Bobby Power.

They were a promising bunch including Royal Approach, whose career was tragically cut short, Shagreen and a young unmade horse that won a bumper which the young trainer rode himself. Prince Regent was to win the 1946 Cheltenham Gold Cup and made Dreaper the most famous national hunt trainer on the island. He recruited Tim Hyde as his stable jockey and built up a strong reputation on the Irish and English circuits, led by Prince Regent.

Dreaper was badly hit by the death of Rank in 1952 followed in 1956 by the death of his other wealthy owner, merchant banker Vivian Hugh Smith (the first Lord Bicester). But by January 1963 he had a promising stable of 30 horses in training, his preferred number throughout his career, led by Fortria, Olympia and two novices, Ben Stack and Arkle. That quartet of horses helped turn him into one of Cheltenham's leading trainers, the fifth most successful of all time and the leading Irish trainer with 26 winners, three ahead of Vincent O'Brien.

The trainer's most important part of the mythology of Arkle was his acceptance of horses that were slow to mature. By comparison, Arkle's sister Cherry Tang was sold as a 5-year old, was raced within ten weeks

The emergence of a new celebrity culture which coincided with his series of Cheltenham Gold Cup successes helped make Arkle the most famous racehorse in Irish, and indeed English, racing history. Here he is looking over the shoulder of the head lad at Rathsallagh, Paddy Murray. (*Racing Post*)

Cottage Rake with Aubrey Brabazon in 1949 winning the second leg of a Gold Cup treble for his young trainer Vincent O'Brien. 'Aubrey's up, the money's down,/The frightened bookies quake,/Come on my lads and give a cheer,/Begod 'tis Cottage Rake.' (*Topfoto*)

Hatton's Grace (No. 3) and National Spirit fight it out over the last hurdle in the 1951 Champion Hurdle. Hatton's Grace went on to win by five lengths, completing a Champion Hurdle treble for Vincent O'Brien to match Cottage Rake's in the Gold Cup. O'Brien, the horse's third trainer, completed a three in a row in the Aintree Grand National with three different horses before exiting National Hunt altogether in 1958, to become the most successful Irish trainer on the flat. The Tipperary-bred Hatton's Grace, which cost just 18 guineas in 1941 and became known as the 'ugly duckling' of the parade ring, was one of the most versatile racehorses in history, winning over distances varying from 1 mile on the flat to a 2 mile 3 furlong steeplechase. (*Topfoto*)

The greatest duel of all: Pat Taaffe on Arkle (*right*) and Willie Robinson on Mill House. Their rivalry transcended sport and brought two countries to a halt to watch their races on flickering black and white tv screens. (*Mirrorpix*)

History would have been very different for Arkle and the Gold Cup if he had come down after unexpectedly hitting the eleventh fence in 1966. Despite doubts that had arisen a few weeks earlier, when he won narrowly at Leopardstown, admittedly in hock deep mud giving away three stone all round, Arkle went on to win his third successive Gold Cup by 30 lengths, beating the 20-lengths record of Easter Hero in 1946 that Arkle had previously equalled. According to Taaffe in a post-race interview, 'If he had been extended he could have won by a furlong.' The race was run on St Patrick's Day, and Taaffe claimed the shamrock sprig on the horse never budged when he crashed through the fence. (*Mirrorpix*)

Pat Taaffe, now a trainer, brought more romance to the Cheltenham Gold Cup story in 1974 when his novice chaser Captain Christy and recovered alcoholic jockey Bobby Beasley won the Gold Cup. Beasley, whose life had fallen apart since riding Gold Cup winner Roddy Owen fifteen years earlier, made one of the most intuitive calls in the history of the race when he avoided the disaster that befell front runners High Ken and Pendil, three fences from home. (*Topfoto*)

Arkle's owner was born Nancy Sullivan in Cork and became entitled as a result of her marriage into the Grosvenor family, to be known as Anne, Duchess of Westminster. 'Judging horses is like judging cattle,' she said. 'You pick it up as you go along.' Arkle was buried beside the garden of his owner's home, before the skeleton was exhumed and put on display at the National Stud. (*Racing Post*)

Tom Dreaper, Charles Haughey and Pat Taaffe, at the Horse of the Year dinner in 1966. Dreaper, the master of Kilsallaghan, who won five Gold Cups with Prince Regent, Arkle and Fort Leney, said: 'Some men have great horses thrust upon them.' National Hunt enthusiast Haughey went on to own a third-place horse in the Foxhunters Chase at Cheltenham in 1998. Flashing Steel had won the Irish Grand National three years earlier. Taaffe's distinctive upright riding style helped create the celebrity cult of Arkle that gave National Hunt racing a higher profile than flat racing for the first time, and thrust both the Cheltenham Festival and Ireland's extended racing tradition into the heart of English popular culture. (*Topfoto*)

When Captain Christy won the Gold Cup in 1974, horse and rider both carried reputations as flawed geniuses. (*Topfoto*)

L'Escargot leading the field at Aintree. He became the first horse since Golden Miller to win the Gold Cup and the Aintree Grand National, although not in the same year as the Miller had done. (*Mirrorpix*)

Mick O'Toole's 14-1 victory with Davy Lad in 1977 was Ireland's sixth Cheltenham Gold Cup in eight years and a rare Irish one-two in the festival's top attraction, having beaten the 20-1 challenger Tied Cottage into second place. It was also one of the great betting coups in the history of the race. Mick O'Toole, who had moved his stable from Castleknock to the Curragh some years earlier, had backed his Gold Cup winner ante-post at 50-1. One of seven Irish winners at the 1977 festival, the Lad was bought as a three-year old in the Curragh by the McGowan family. (*Topfoto*)

Immortalised by his ride on Dawn Run in 1986, Jonjo O'Neill became one of Ireland's most famous ex-pat trainers when he set up a training stable beside his beloved Cheltenham.

Monksfield (*left*) and Sea Pigeon fought some of the greatest Anglo-Irish duels in Cheltenham history. Monksfield cost Des McDonogh just 740 guineas as a yearling, and won five times on the flat before initiating what has come to be regarded as a golden age for the Champion Hurdle. He finished second to Night Nurse in 1977 and then embarked on one of the great Cheltenham rivalries with Sea Pigeon, winning the 1978 and 1979 Champion Hurdle, but losing in 1980. (*Racing Fotos*)

Imperial Call was ridden by Conor O'Dwyer to an unexpected victory for Cork and Fergie Sutherland in the Gold Cup of 1996, sparking 'extraordinary scenes of celebration in the parade ring' and causing Cheltenham racecourse officials to revamp their security for future Irish wins. (*Topfoto*)

Trainer Paddy Mullins at Cheltenham in 1996. His victory with Dawn Run in 1986 was a bittersweet one, as his son was jocked off the horse by owner Charmian Hill. (*Sportsfile*)

Charlie Swan salutes the crowd after winning the first of three successive Champion Hurdles in 1998. Swan's alliance with the failed flat racer Istabraq, the rare and unexpected incursion into National Hunt racing by the emerging Irish champion trainer Aidan O'Brien, and the owner-gambler that bookies learned to fear, JP McManus, provided the festival romance of the 1990s. (*Racing Post*)

Istabraq in 1999. Bred for the flat, he was to become perhaps the greatest hurdler of all time and Ireland's most famous racehorse of his era. (*Racing Post*)

The Istabraq fan club at Cheltenham in 2000. Foot and mouth disease deprived him of the chance of a fourth successive Champion Hurdle in 2001. Istabraq was pulled up in the Champion Hurdle at Cheltenham in 2002. (*Racing Post*)

Jim Dreaper, son of Tom, took over the famous stable at Kilsallaghan and maintained the family tradition with a famous victory by Ten Up in 1975, at the age of 26, for owner Anne, Duchess of Westminster, with Tommy Carberry on board. Ten Up led from the first fence after the water on the first circuit in a victory that showed it was 'snatched from the jaws of the weather'. There were high hopes that Carvill's Hill would repeat the success in the late 1980s, but it was not to be.

Kicking King and Barry Geraghty after winning the Cheltenham Gold Cup for Ardclough and Tom Taaffe in 2005, renewing a Cheltenham connection with the Taaffe family that dates back to the 1940s. (*Racing Post*)

Barry Geraghty on Sky's The Limit, after winning the Coral Cup for Edward O'Grady in 2006.

Rupert 'Ruby' Walsh had one of the most spectacular starts possible to his career, winning the Aintree Grand National in 2000 at his first attempt, aged 20, on Papillon, trained by his father Ted. He twice won the Cheltenham Gold Cup on the English-trained Kauto Star and his seven wins at Cheltenham in 2009 included three championship events. He was paid tribute by fellow Kildare man Christy Moore in a ballad: 'Look at her up the jumps, be God, she's like a ballet dancer,/Over the last she hits the front, the other one's going to pass her,/Winner all right, it's up Kildare, follow me up to Carlow./Ruby hold her back, give her the crack, and up she'll go.' (*Racing Post*)

One of many Irish-born jockeys for English trainers who came to dominate the festival coming up to the turn of the twenty-first century: Cork-born Mick Fitzgerald's long association with Nicky Henderson and Cheltenham culminated in victory in the 1999 Gold Cup with See More Business. He was leading rider at the Cheltenham Festival in 1999 and 2000 before retiring through injury in 2008. By that stage Irish trainers were winning more than two-thirds of the prizes on offer at Cheltenham, as compared with a maximum of one-third won previously by Irish trainers. (*Racing Post*)

and raced three times unsuccessfully in 27 days before being retired. We never learned whether she had any of the same potential as her brother.

Michael Phillips wrote in December 1971: 'He might buy a horse as a three year old and not even run it for two years, simply because he needed time. As any trainer will know a patient policy needs the whole-hearted backing of the owner. Many will also be only too aware of the fact that the owner is not necessarily a particularly patient individual, especially when settling time draws near, but over the years Dreaper's judgment has been such that owners have never lacked faith in him.'

Dreaper planned the day for his horses differently from most other trainers.

'He is an exception to the rule,' Mill House's jockey Willie Robinson said of Dreaper in December 1971, 'if there is such a thing as a rule in the training of jumpers—because his procedure is entirely different from any other.' Patience was the over-riding factor in the Dreaper approach to training.

The programme of feeding began at 7.20 with 4 lb of dry oats, a midday feed of 4 lb at 11.40 am, earlier than the norm in other stables, an after lunch feed of a couple of carrots and a pull of grass at 2.30 pm, and then a main feed at 4.30 pm, early by training standards at the time. The contents of the main feed became a legend in its own lunchtime: mash, six freshly broken eggs, two bottles of instantly decanted Guinness and a few pounds of oats, all stirred together into a great con-gealed mess that the horse devoured. Arkle needed expensive time to find his true worth. Tom Dreaper and Anne Grosvenor gave it to him.

It will be a surprise if Arkle is beaten in the Broadway Novices Steeplechase. No young horse has made such an impression as he in winning his four races this season. He is a brilliant jumper and a determined galloper.

London Times, 12 March 1963

Arkle was broken in at Grosvenor's Cheshire home, Eaton Lodge, before going into training with Tom Dreaper. He was given plenty of time to mature and did not see a racecourse until he was nearly 5.

Arkle took some time to show even a glimmer of the brilliance to come. Mark Hely Hutchinson and Liam McLoughlin rode him in his early outings. His first two races, on the flat, were unremarkable. On

20 January 1962 he started an unconsidered 20/1 outsider in a hurdle race at Navan, for which the favourite was Kerforo, another of Dreaper's horses ridden by stable jockey Pat Taaffe.

The ground was very soft that day and as Taaffe struggled to keep Kerforo going after the last flight, he was astounded to see Arkle cruise past him. '*We* were at the finish,' he said. 'It was as if *he* had just begun.' It was the last time Arkle left Taaffe behind.

Ten months later they won their first steeplechase together—the Honeybourne Chase at Cheltenham—and from then on the names of Taaffe and Arkle were inseparable. No other jockey ever rode him over fences.

The first Gold cup was the best. The tension was terrific. That was *the* terrific thrill.

PAT TAAFFE

Pat Taaffe had been associated with Dreaper for fourteen years before Arkle came along. The son of a reasonably successful trainer, Thomas Taaffe from Rathcoole, Pat and his brother Toss were both teenage champions, descended from a family with a long association with national hunt racing.

Taaffe's public career began at the age of 10 when he rode his father's pony Magnolia in the children's jumping competition at the 1940 Dublin Horse Show. He was presented with second rosette by the American ambassador. He was 16 when he had his first ride under rules in 1946, riding Vivian Smith's (Lord Bicester) Finnure in his first race in Ireland. He rode a string of winners as an amateur, all trained by his father.

When Tom Dreaper's stable jockey, Eddie Newman, broke his knee in a fall in England in 1949, Dreaper asked Pat Taaffe to ride two of his horses at Leopardstown. Both were winners, and a 21 year association with Dreaper began. Taaffe suffered a broken leg in his first year as a professional that cost him his rides on Shagreen and Stormhead in the Irish and English nationals. Over the next few years Taaffe took over the better horses from Martin Molony: Roimond, Greenogue, Shagreen, Early Mist, Royal Approach, Storm Approach and Arkle's mother Bright Cherry, on whom he took third place at Naas on 12 May 1951.

Taaffe was tall, round shouldered and renowned for his sound tactics out in the country. He had a reputation for winning races by getting his horses to jump quickly, cleanly and safely, not by a flamboyant stretch at the finish.

Regarded by at least one critic as 'more a horseman than a jockey', his oddly upright style and characteristic waving arms was deprecated as amateurish at first. Taaffe answered his critics with his success. He won the 1955 Grand National on Quare Times and just about every other worthwhile prize in the jumping calendar. Despite a fall at Kilbeggan in 1956, in which he cracked his skull so badly he feared his career was over, he was back in the saddle within months and resumed an alliance with Dreaper that won four Gold Cups in five years in the 1960s. He rode another Aintree Grand National winner, Gay Trip, in 1971.

The relationship with Arkle started badly when he took one crashing fall while schooling over hurdles, but the great jumping expert took the young horse in hand. Thereafter jumping became one of the strongest weapons in his armoury. He never once fell in a race and in his entire career made less than a dozen serious mistakes.

One of those was crucial at the time, however, for it came at Newbury in the 1963 Hennessy Gold Cup, Arkle's long-awaited first meeting with Mill House, the young English-trained giant horse which had won the Cheltenham Gold Cup the previous season.

> You will soon be on the best horse in Britain, and quite possibly the world.
>
> PAT TAAFFE to WILLIE ROBINSON, stable jockey at Fulke Walwyn's stables in Lambourn after Mill House had joined the stable.

Fulke Thomas Tyndall Walwyn had good reason to be grateful to Ireland. His most notable victory as a jockey came as an amateur rider in the 1936 Grand National.

Because the 1935 winning jockey (and son of the trainer and owner) Frank Furlong was unfit, the Cork-born owner and trainer of Reynoldstown, Major Noel Furlong, asked Walwyn, an old army colleague in the 9th Lancers, to ride Reynoldstown. He won the race in style despite losing a whip and an iron.

Walwyn resigned from the army in 1937, due to adverse publicity from a court case involving a Soho night club fracas in which he appeared as a prosecution witness. He became a professional jockey until a near fatal fall at Ludlow in 1939 fractured his skull and rendered him unconscious for a month. He then turned to training, operating a small establishment at Delamere House in Lambourn and winning eighteen races before the outbreak of the war.

His successes were down to the support of Dorothy Paget, the grand dame of national hunt racing, owner of some of the best jumpers in England, but also famous for dismissing her trainers on a whim.

Walwyn trained for her for nearly ten years and it is thought he largely curbed her habit of late-night phone calls and nocturnal visits to the stables. He broke with Miss Paget in 1954 after having 'had enough' of her difficult behaviour.

Walwyn became one of the most successful national hunt trainers of all time. On one memorable occasion on 29 September 1948 Walwyn and jockey Bryan Marshall almost took her horses through the card at Folkestone, winning five and coming second in the last race.

He went on to train the winners of four Cheltenham Gold Cups, two Champion Hurdles, five King George VI Chases, seven Whitbread Gold Cups, seven Hennessy Cognac Gold Cups, two Scottish Grand Nationals and an Aintree Grand National, and was British jump racing champion trainer five times. He trained 40 winners at the Cheltenham Festival between 1946 and 1986, a record which still stands as of 2009. After his death in 1991 he was honoured by the posthumous renaming of the Kim Muir Memorial Chase—the three mile race for amateur riders on the opening day of the Cheltenham National Hunt Festival—as the Fulke Walwyn Challenge Cup Chase.

Walwyn had a reputation for treating each one of his horses as an individual animal. He was renowned for his treatment of doubtful legs, patient and determined never to hurry an injured horse back into serious training. When asked the secret of his success, he always acknowledged the contribution of his staff. The lads, he explained, were closest to the horses, and a good one could tell a trainer much about the animals for which he was responsible.

On the other hand he disliked delegation. As his obituaries pointed out, he had more patience with horses than with people. He gave a hard time to jockeys who failed to ride to orders or who were too hard on his horses.

He rode out every day until he was 66, only then choosing to accompany his horses to morning exercise in a Land Rover.

His favourite horse of all was the diminutive Mandarin who arrived in 1954 with a reputation as a poor jumper, but under Walwyn's tuition won the Hennessy and King George in 1957, the King George again in 1959, the Hennessy again in 1961, and the Cheltenham Gold Cup the following year.

Then in 1963 he retained the Gold Cup with a horse that was to become even more famous, winning the Cheltenham Gold Cup, the Hennessy and the King George. His name was Mill House. To many he was simply known as 'the big horse'.

The Arkle incident caused a number of his supporters to leave the course still convinced that he will beat Mill House in the championship.

London Times, 2 December 1963

Mill House was bred by the Lawlor family, hoteliers in Osberstown and Naas. Like his great rival, he was by a filed flat racer out of an excellent jumping mare. He was based for a while at Tom Taaffe's stables in Rathcoole and had been schooled over hurdles by Taaffe's second son, Pat, the man who ended up riding Mill House's greatest rival. He was bought by L. S. Dale for a rich advertising man new to racing, Bill Gollings, and transferred to Walwyn's stable in Lambourn.

Hence a horse bred just ten miles away from Arkle and ridden by Irish champion jockey Willie Robinson became the unlikely English hero in a great Anglo-Irish sporting contest.

Everyone was talking about it in the build-up, and history suggests that racegoers were right to be excited. They were, and remain, the two highest rated staying chasers of the post-war era.

At 212 Arkle's Timeform rating is the highest ever awarded to a steeplechaser. Only Flyingbolt, who was also trained by Tom Dreaper, had a rating anywhere near his at 210. The third highest is Mill House on 191.

Anticipation of the clash was already rife before the close of the 1963 Cheltenham Festival. 'Ever since the National Hunt festival at Cheltenham last March,' Tom MacGinty wrote in the *Sunday Independent* of 24 November 1963, 'when Arkle's astonishing twenty lengths win in the Broadway Chase was matched by Mill House's fluent Gold Cup victory, jumping enthusiasts have waited eagerly for the clash of these giants. Few dared to hope that they would meet before the Cheltenham Gold Cup but the sporting connections of both horses have adopted a fighting policy. The Hennessy is the first engagement of what promises to be a running battle through the winter and spring.'

'Those two race wreckers Mill House and Arkle are at work again over Christmas,' Jack Windsor wrote in the *Sunday Independent* of 22 December 1963. 'The handicapper has some chance to stop Arkle at Leopardstown on Thursday, but visitors to Kempton the same afternoon are promised only a public execution.'

To a growing tumult of excitement the horses eventually met in the 1963 Hennessy Gold Cup at Newbury. Mill House's followers considered him unbeatable, and when he came home alone with Arkle trailing eight lengths behind, they were understandably elated.

But it was not as simple as that. Three fences from home, moving up easily behind Mill House, Arkle had slipped on landing, sprawled and lost all his momentum. From the stands it did not look much, and neither Pat Taaffe nor Tom Dreaper was much given to hard luck stories. After Mill House's victory, Arkle's jockey Pat Taaffe insisted prophetically that Mill House would never beat him again. When he sat down with Dreaper, the two agreed that he would never attempt to kick Arkle into a fence again. Arkle was fast, an economical jumper. He didn't need any direction from the saddle. From then on Taaffe would rely on his devastating finishing kick.

> Not since Golden Miller met Thomond II in 1935 has the Gold Cup raised such an exhilarating prospect as the contest expected between Mill House and Arkle on Saturday. Golden Miller and Thomond II were in the air together over the last two fences with every watcher in the stands yelling, and it always has been thought the finest Gold Cup since the race was begun. The Cheltenham management could not have chosen a more propitious year to run the race on a Saturday.
>
> *London Times*, 3 March 1964

Both horses stepped up their preparations in anticipation of the big one. In the Thyestes Handicap at Gowran Park in January 1964, one newspaper re-echoed the most famous result in racing history by declaring: 'Arkle first, the rest nowhere.'

Then came a crucial change of timing that catapulted the duel into the living rooms of hundreds of thousands of households more than would have happened otherwise. The race was switched to Saturday for the first time in history. Even without Arkle and Mill House, this race was going to have a higher profile.

'A colder day for the Gold Cup has rarely been known', the *London Times* reported. The north wind carried snow showers all day and the ground had been white in the morning. The stewards were called and after an inspection they issued a statement that if more snow did not fall, racing would take place. That was the end of hopes for attracting the enormous crowd that might have made its way to the course. The cold and the doubt made many settle for the warmth of television.

There was little difficulty in approaching the course by car and the parks were not full. For all that there were many more than on the previous two days, and they were nearly a third up on the previous year.

Only two runners dared to take on the big two, with Mill House at 8/11, Arkle at 7/4, King's Nephew at 20/1 and eventual third place Pas Seul quoted at 50/1.

'When the great day dawned,' Derek Malcolm wrote in *The Guardian*, 'hellishly cold even for a Cotswold March, with great dabs of snow floating sideways in the air like unconvincing Christmas decorations it was possible to feel that something exceptional was going to happen.

'The crowd watched impatiently as a horse called Nesey won the Spa Hurdle to a positive crescendo of silence, through which a large Birmingham bookie was heard to complain that he might as well go home and get warm as watch the punters sticking glue on their wallets.

'Everybody had come to see the unbeatable Mill House versus the brilliant Arkle of Ireland, just for the thrill of it. The odds on either were scarcely worth the taking, and seemed for once beside the point.'

There were only four runners in the Gold Cup and Mill House made the running. However, he was joined by Arkle two out and Robinson was the first to go for his whip. Arkle was on top going to the last, drew away to win by five lengths, and thus the legend was born.

Malcolm wrote: 'By the time the moment came for the two stars to saunter disinterestedly around the paddock—there were two others in the race, but nobody bothered with them—one's reasoning had become a little clouded, and not only by the Guinness.

'The first half of the race lifted the fog. How ridiculous to think that Arkle could beat the horse that had brought more to racing than anyone ever thought possible. There was Mill House built like a barrel and with legs like Dorothy Ward, only four of them, striding lazily, but with a crippling pace out front.'

At the second last fence Mill House was still in front, but suddenly he was labouring and Pat Taaffe, poised two lengths behind him, had not moved. A moment later Taaffe gave Arkle his head

'And there was Arkle,' Derek Malcolm wrote, 'seeming to take two strides in Mill House's one, pounding several lengths behind, not jumping half as prettily. Even as the English champion pecked like a novice at the water he shrugged it off with a burst down the dip which increased his lead by another arrogant length. Then, with the two still away in the country, and the English entourage patting each other on the back in the enclosures, the crunch came. Mill House perceptibly quickened his consuming stride. Marvellous, ruddy marvellous, said a well-known trainer.

'But his face fell half a foot when the gap between the two remained precisely the same. Thereafter, and it all happened at the speed of lightning, all hell broke loose. Turning into the straight Mill House was still in front, with the challenger at his quarters. Before the last fence Willie Robinson, now whipless, was working like a dervish with Arkle and Pat Taaffe only inches behind.'

The time, 6 minutes 45.6 seconds, proved that Mill House did not have an off-day. It was four seconds faster than Saffron Tartan's 1961 record time on the same course on similar going.

'Such scenes have not been seen on an English racecourse before. The race was as near perfect as one could imagine', Richard Baerlein wrote in *The Guardian*.

'When it happened the wild demonstrations in the stands seemed to move bodily around to the unsaddling enclosure,' Hugh McIlvanney wrote in *The Observer*. 'The Irish had done down the English, and no one was being allowed to overlook the fact.'

The winning margin was five lengths, and no horse that met Arkle at level weights or anything like them was ever to get as close again.

After the fence Arkle was away. By the time the Irishman had crushed him on the cruel run-in up the hill, hardened veterans in the press box were seen to tremble so much that they could hardly hold their glasses on the race and even the imperturbable, impervious bookies clambered like monkeys to watch a legend being destroyed. It must have been like this when Moses parted the waters, said an Irishman within earshot.

DEREK MALCOLM, *The Guardian*

Arkle had hardly passed the post ahead of Mill House when there was a stampede from both the members' enclosure and Tattersalls to the winner's enclosure.

Exhilaration at the end of races is part of the national hunt meeting, but never has anything been seen like the elation on this occasion. And it was not only the Irish supporters of Arkle but the ordinary onlookers who were uplifted by this great match. Cheer after cheer broke out as the horses came in, one for Arkle, one for Pat Taaffe, one for Tom Dreaper, one for Mill House and Willie Robinson, and every one of them a heartfelt roar of appreciation.

The manner in which Arkle had made up the gap, opened by the stride and mighty jumping of Mill House as soon as asked, sticks in the memory of everyone who was there. Folklore has turned it into a greater rout than it seemed at the time. Would Mill House have done better had he not been alone in front until the second fence from the end? Would Arkle have found him more difficult to beat had the going been soft? As it was, the ground was perfect and Arkle proved that he had as much stamina as his big rival and greater acceleration.

'Arkle is not such an attractive horse as Mill House,' the *London Times* reported. 'He sticks his head forward and races mostly with his ears back rather than pricked. Built on a smaller scale than Mill House, he is more handsome, fully big enough and with a splendid deep girth.

'Crossing the water on the last circuit Mill House had established such a lead that everywhere in the crowd people were feeling and saying this was not going to be a race. Taaffe, something of a worrier when on the ground, is a cool and endlessly patient man in the saddle. He made no attempt to make Arkle go with Mill House, but he made a significant move to halve the distance between the two horses as they turned to go uphill at the beginning of the last mile.

'After that Taaffe approached no closer until they were coming to the third fence from home. Mill House made a fine leap there to make perhaps half a length. He set off for the corner about three lengths to the good. Then came the moment of truth.

'Taaffe, before our amazed gaze, gave away a second or two to turn Arkle slightly to the right, clear of Mill House's path, balanced him again, and went after the leader. Mill House is not slow, but his lead disappeared in a flash. The two horses jumped level at the next fence, and Arkle led by a length over the last. From there to the post he increased his lead to five lengths.'

Taaffe and Willie Fobinson had an agreement that, whenever they met, the winner would buy the loser a consolation prize. Taaffe was generous in victory and bought the air tickets for Robinson's honeymoon.

> He jumped on his back and he raised up his paw
> Three cheers for old Ireland said Master McGrath.
> 'Ballad of Master McGrath' (*c.* 1873)

Cottage Rake had a commemorative ballad written in his honour fifteen years before Arkle. Imperial Call was to have his own ballad 30 years later. It was appropriate that the ballad written for Arkle is one of the best in the Irish sporting folk canon.

It was written within days of the race by Dominic Behan, brother of playwright Brendan and nephew of Peadar Kearney, who had composed the Irish national anthem and the haunting 'Down by the Glenside', a spirited commemorative song that was recorded by the Dubliners and widely sung for four decades afterwards.

Behan used a traditional tune called 'Musselburgh Fair' in Scotland, and drew on the tradition of a famous ballad about the nineteenth-century greyhound which won the Waterloo Cup three times for Ireland, Master McGrath. McGrath's exploits were commemorated by a ballad still popular in Arkle's time, published in the folk song collections of Walton's and played on the Saturday afternoon Irish songs programme presented by Leo Maguire. Though there are two statues of the greyhound still extant, his deeds are lesser known nowadays, particularly as coursing slips out of fashion.

Behan noted in his 1973 collection *Ireland Sings* that Arkles's victory over Mill House was the 'second battle of any significance the Irish won on English soil'. His comment on Master McGrath which is also in

Ireland Sings is 'the first battle of any importance the Irish won on English soil', hence his comment on Arkle.

At the start of the Dubliners' recording Ronnie Drew said, 'This is a song about probably the only victory we've ever had on English soil.'

It happened in the springtime of the year of sixty-four,
When Englishmen were making pounds and fivers by the score
He beat them in the hollow and he beat them on the bumps
A pair of fancy fetlocks he showed them o'er the jumps.

He's English! He's English! As English as you've seen
A little bit of Arab stock and more from Stephen's Green
Take a look at Mill House and throw out your chest with pride
He's the greatest steeplechaser on the English countryside.

Then a quiet man called Dreaper living in the Emerald Isle
Said, 'That horse of yours called Mill House surely shows a bit of style,
But I've a little fellow and Arkle is his name,
Put your money where you put your mouth and then we'll play the game.'

Well the English racing gentleman laughed till fit to burst,
'You tried before Tom Dreaper and then you came off worst,
If you think your horse could beat us you're running short on brains
It's Mill House that you want to fight and not those beastly Danes.'

Arkle now is five to two Mill House is money on,
They're off! And dear believe I do the Champion has it won,
There are other horses in this race to test the great chap's might
But deary me it's plain to see the rest are out of sight.

There are three more fences now to go he leads by twenty lengths
Brave Arkle's putting in a show, poor chap he's all but spent
Mill House sweeps on majestically great glory in each stride
He's the greatest horse undoubtedly within the whole world wide.

Two to go still Arkle comes he's cutting down the lead,
But he's beaten bar the shouting for he hasn't got the speed,
They're up on one up to the last my God can he hold out,
Look behind you Willie Robinson man what are you about.'

They're at the last and over Pat Taaffe has more in hand,
He's passing England's Mill House the finest in the land.
My God he has us beaten! What can the English say?
The ground was wrong. The distance long. 'Too early in the day.'

Mill House was a great horse until his heart was broken. Then from
1964 to 1966 his mighty conqueror bestrode the steeplechasing world
like a colossus, reducing not only the Cheltenham Gold Cup but also
the big handicaps to mockeries, so few being prepared to take him on.
Until his tragic accident at Kempton Park, Arkle only tasted defeat
twice, first by Flying Wild and Buona Notte in the Massey-Ferguson
Gold Cup and then when he narrowly failed to give Stalbridge
Colonist two and a half stone in the 1966 Hennessy Gold Cup. Since
then what have we seen to equal him? His stable companion,
Flyingbolt, eventually broke down. Captain Christy is unquestion-
ably the only horse of great class to have taken the Blue Riband of
steeplechasing in the past eleven years. Bula was a star over fences as
well as over hurdles, but he did not stay the Gold Cup distance

MICHAEL SEELY, *London Times*, 23 December 1977

Behan was wrong. Walwyn did not make any excuses for the defeat of
his big horse. 'Arkle made the most fantastic improvement between
November and March' was what he said. But years later Willie
Robinson, Mill House's jockey, was not so sure. He felt Mill House had
suffered from back problems which affected his performance.

Robinson told Bob Harman of *Sporting Life* that Mill house had leg
problems after the Hennessy win in November 1963, but he seemed to
get over them. He said he was a horse that took a fair bit of getting
ready and his last run prior to Cheltenham had been at Sandown in
mid-February. 'We needed more time,' Robinson said. 'He didn't give
me anything like the same feel against Arkle in the Gold Cup. They
were two great horses, but there would never have been much more
than necks and heads between them in a race.'

Much later in his career Mill House took a heavy fall at Ludlow in 1968. When he was taken to Newmarket's equine research station he was found to have fused vertebrae in two different places. Harman concluded that the fused vertebrae could have remained undetected for many years: 'Superior jumping skills had long been one of Mill House's strengths, and any underlying problem with his back could have caused this strength to become a weakness.'

He is a terrific horse to ride. When you start to canter him don't take hold of his head. Let his head be, and he will put it down. I've never found him do anything wrong, bucking, whipping around, anything like that. If the pace is strong he will settle well enough till he feels it is time to go on. If they go too slow at the start he will go on without them and make his own running. I just let him alone. I never give him a kick at all now, a squeeze maybe, but not even that near the start of the race. Otherwise he'd take off too early.

PAT TAAFFE interview, February 1966

From then on Arkle's chief enemy was the handicapper. Even before the Mill House duel, the handicapper for the 1964 Irish Grand National had put him 19 lb ahead of Scottish Memories and 28 lb ahead of Flying Wild.

Even here Arkle continued to win, making nonsense of the old racing adage: 'Weight will stop a train.'

Whole new systems had to be devised to give his rivals some chance against him. For the 1964 Irish Grand National they started issuing two separate handicaps, one for use if Arkle ran, another if he didn't.

Arkle went on to win two more Gold Cups, a King George, a Whitbread and two Hennesseys carrying 12 st 7 lb. Just twice in the next three years the handicapper did get the better of the argument. But the only result was to demonstrate even more clearly Arkle's total supremacy. In December 1964, only seven days after winning the Hennessey Gold Cup with 12 st 7 lb, he was asked to carry 3 lb more in the Massey-Ferguson Gold Cup. Over two miles five furlongs, a distance short of his best, he failed by a single length to give 32 lb to the good mare Flying Wild and 26 lb to Buona Notte, the best young horse in England. It was a defeat worth more than many victories.

All this time Arkle's fame and popularity had been growing. He became endeared to an audience of millions who hitherto thought of horses only as things to bet on. Every day of his life letters and presents used to arrive at Dreaper's stable, some addressed simply 'Arkle, Ireland.'

The scene round the winner's enclosure was barely credible in a place where polite handclapping and a gentlemanly hurrah or two generally greet a winner. It was a race as good as anything those who were there will ever see again. Sensing it, thousands left the course forthwith. They had a lot of people to tell. There will be a repeat next year. But it can't be as good.

DEREK MALCOLM in The Guardian

Cheltenham needed Arkle just as much as Arkle needed Cheltenham. The *London Times* noted in its report of Mill House's 1963 victory that 'the crowd is already beginning to look forward to the meeting next year of Mill House and Arkle'. It is sometimes forgotten how badly Cheltenham needed the revival provided by the rivalry. The winter of the big snow had devastated racing in general and Cheltenham in particular.

The attendance at the meeting had been down £7,000 on the first two days. The press noted that it was only five days before the meeting that there was any certainty the fixture would take place. 'Race meetings usually take time to recover after a long hold-up through the public getting out of the habit of travelling and through losing interest. Watching television in doubtful winter weather is always a temptation.' The *London Times* noted: 'Irish trained horses won four out of a total of nineteen races in the three days, a result more favourable to the home trained runners than generally was expected.'

'Car parks in which hard core was embedded a few years ago have again become holding, causing long struggles and hard words in the mud.' The same paper noted in February that 'another winter like the last would finish off many racecourses. Anyone attending recent meetings could not have failed to notice that, even in open weather, the size of the crowds was reduced to something like those of the slump days in the early 1930s. For this the ready money betting offices must take much of the responsibility.'

He often jumps unnecessarily big and then puts his head on one side as if to say—that will show them.

PAT TAAFFE, 1966 interview

Arkle's profile lifted the entire sport. 'He is quiet as a lamb and when children scramble on and off his back he enjoys it as much as the children do,' Jack Leach wrote in a typical profile in *The Observer* in 1966.

'In fact he likes company in general. Like most horses he loves sweet things such as sugar, chocolate and especially fig rolls. Carrots, apples, eggs and Guinness are also part of his diet. He does condescend to eat oats and hay, of course.

'This extraordinary horse is also a music lover. He will stand like a statue listening to a transistor. This is very useful when he is being photographed, although I suspect he likes being photographed anyway. He really does play to the gallery and looks round him before a race to see if everybody is watching him. Of course, everybody is.

'Arkle is very good looking. Unlike his stablemate Flyingbolt, who is also a great chaser, but who looks lonely without a cart behind him.

'After a race and when he gets home, after morning walks he likes to roll—ten rolls is his record in one go—and then he sits up on his behind like a dog, shakes his legs and licks the inside of his forelegs.'

There never has been a flat horse that generated those warm, folksy profiles. Desert Orchid in the 1980s generated almost as much warmth, but not as much success.

I'd like to ride him in the Grand National, but the duchess . . .
PAT TAAFFE interview, February 1966

Arkle's absence from the Aintree Grand National confirmed, if confirmation was needed, that Cheltenham had outpaced the older race in terms of prestige.

Arkle was too good to be risked, his owner reasoned, all the time pointing out that he was certain to win. 'So what's the point in running?'

Aintree supporters pleaded with her to let him run. After the fatalities of the 1950s, the build of the fences at Aintree was altered before the Grand National of 1961, reducing the number of falls by two and a half times. It was still not enough to persuade Anne Grosvenor to enter Arkle for the race. The modified fences were still too extreme a test of a horse's jumping ability. Such was her devotion to the horse that she refused to run him over the hazardous Aintree obstacles.

I get the feeling that he'd never fall. He's too clever. The only way he
would fall is through over-confidence.

PAT TAAFFE, interview with IVOR HERBERT, February 1966

Pat Taaffe confidently opined that Arkle would never fall, in an
interview with the *Daily Mail* a month before winning his third Gold
Cup. He didn't, but it was close, because Arkle galloped straight
through the eleventh fence en route to victory by the unprecedented
distance of 30 lengths and at the unprecedented odds of 100/8 on in
1966, the shortest odds the race has known.

When Arkle went straight through the last fence on the first circuit,
the thump that reverberated around the stands was followed
immediately by the sharp and shocked intake of 20,000 breaths. He
galloped straight ahead and level and struck the fence full on with his
chest. Birch flew in all directions, dust and twigs exploded in a brown
cloud. But the shamrock pinned on his brow band, for it was St
Patrick's Day, barely moved. Pat Taaffe thought afterwards he was
distracted by a group of people standing in on the left of the fence and
just beyond it. Taaffe felt he was not going to fall, even then. Peter
O'Sullevan's BBC race commentary conveys the sense of shock: 'Another
complete circuit. Oooh. And he barely took off at that one. He just
looked at it and ignored it. And how he got to the other side? Well, you
should have heard the gasp from the crowd here. It looked as if he
wasn't going to jump at all. He just ignored the fence completely, and
how he got to the other side is a mystery.'

It was the only incident of note in a race in which Arkle's four
opponents fought out second place. As Arkle and Pat Taaffe returned to
a hero's welcome, shamrock was sprinkled on racegoers from a light
aircraft.

Arkle was then put away for the season. The plan was to return for
the Hennessy Gold Cup in November, where he was caught by a useful
grey, Stalbridge Colonist, to whom he gave two and a half stone. A cut
picked up in training had curtailed his preparations. He won at Ascot
in November, a race in which Pat Taaffe retrospectively felt 'he could
have given that foot a tap' and had noticed he was jumping left over the
last three fences, causing an over-reach.

No injury showed up, so he travelled across to the King George VI at
Kempton. Rival trainer Ivor Herbert, an Arkle admirer, declared: 'We

couldn't beat Arkle if we started five minutes earlier.' Sadly he was
wrong. It was the race that ended Arkle's career.

> We have decided to retire him. Not even Arkle, with his immense
> courage, could be expected to reproduce the old brilliance.
> ANNE GROSVENOR, Duchess of Westminster's statement on retiring
> Arkle, 9 October 1968

Kempton was experimenting with a rudimentary Pay TV arrangement
on St Stephen's Day in 1966. Frost, however, caused the race to be put
back a day. That and the fact that television coverage was restricted
pushed the crowd slightly up to 16,000, four times the attendance of the
previous year and back towards the levels of twelve years earlier. Arkle
had six opponents, had 21 lb to carry and seized the lead from the start.

Pat Taaffe felt something was wrong at the second fence when Arkle
jumped to the left 'which was very strange. After that he seemed okay,
at least till the seventh from home, but he was never jumping brilliantly. He went right through the first fence along the back.' Spectators
noticed the alarm signal too. He was not jumping with the usual
fluency and made a mistake at the open ditch on the second circuit.

'He could always find a fifth leg,' recalled Taaffe, 'but not on this
occasion. Going to the last he started changing his legs. I knew then
something was wrong. But he was not pulling up. Even then he was not
pulling up. We came to the last and he still jumped it and made for the
line and it was only in the last 50 yards that he started to stop. It
happened at the second last. I think he galloped all those three miles in
pain. He was hanging all the time, never really going well. His jumping
wasn't the same.'

Dreaper was told in Leopardstown by broadcaster Micheál O'Hehir
that Arkle finished lame. For the next few weeks, with his leg in plaster,
Arkle was the most famous invalid in Ireland.

Veterinary bulletins were carried on the front pages of newspapers
on the two islands. Arkle had cracked his pedal bone and might never
race again. One-third of the pedal bone, the outside third of the off-
fore, had broken away. The crack was two and a quarter inches long. He
had run three miles in mounting pain and almost won. It took delicate
surgery, and he recovered well enough to give some hope of a
comeback.

Several comeback dates were announced for Arkle before his official retirement in October 1968, when his owner and trainer wisely decided not to risk the horror of seeing him a subject where once he had been king.

So Arkle retired to Anne Grosvenor's farm at Bryanstown, near Taghadoe, in Maynooth. He never won a Grand National because he was never given the chance. And he won only three Cheltenham Gold Cups to Golden Miller's five. But no horse ever crossed a steeplechase fence faster or more safely. No horse ever produced a more deadly turn of speed at the finish of a gruelling three mile chase. No horse ever conceded bigger weights, and no horse ever had a bigger heart. Perhaps there will be another like him one day, but those who knew Arkle in his prime will believe that only when they see it.

There is little doubt that a fit Arkle would have won three more Gold Cups, breaking Golden Miller's record.

Woodland Venture, who was being beaten by the injured Arkle at Kempton, won the 1967 Gold Cup in the absence of Arkle's highly rated stablemate Flyingbolt. Flyingbolt was the nearest thing to an Arkle contender. The Irish handicapper put him within 2 lb of Arkle. In *My Life and Arkle's* Pat Taaffe reckoned the difference was more like a stone. 'Over two miles it would have been a closer thing, but Arkle would still have won.' Flyingbolt won the Champion Chase by an astonishing fifteen lengths in 1966 before finishing third in the Champion Hurdle the following day and going on to win the Irish Grand National. A rare viral infection that affected his limbs meant he never contested a Gold Cup.

Another Arkle stablemate, Fort Leney, rated three stone inferior to Arkle by the Irish handicapper, won in 1968, trained by Dreaper and ridden by Pat Taaffe. The 1969 Gold Cup was won by a contemporary of Arkle called What a Myth, then 12 years old and a horse that could not be rated anywhere near the champion.

As this should have been Tom Dreaper's Gold Cup anyway had Arkle been fit and well, no one now begrudges him the race with Arkle's deputy.

RICHARD BAERLEIN, *The Guardian*, 22 March 1968

Fort Leney's 1968 Gold Cup victory deserves to be more than a mere footnote in the Arkle story.

Owned by a London banker, John Thomson, Fort Leney was rated 25 lb behind Arkle. At one stage his reputation was second only to Arkle's. Pat Taaffe said he had never ridden a horse that battled harder at a finish. But he was diagnosed early in his career as suffering from intermittent heart trouble. He made an amazing recovery and started favourite for the Gold Cup in 1967. Taaffe was injured for the race and with Peter McLoughlin on board, Fort Leney crashed out of the race at the second and never entered the fray. The trainer thought the going was too firm, and firm ground was useless to Fort Leney.

His victory the following year came in a bad season for national hunt racing. Foot and mouth was reported in November 1967 and all racing in England was cancelled until Christmas. The ground at Cheltenham was a bit hard for Fort Leney's liking. He was taken out of the ante-post market ten days before the race. But enough overnight rain came to change Dreaper's mind. With What a Myth withdrawn from the race because of the going, there were just five runners. He flew Fort Leney over the day before the race and stationed him on a farm owned by Maurice Tollit. 'It isn't that Fort Leney is a bad traveller,' Tom Dreaper said, 'but he does get excited and if he spent yesterday with all the noise of the crowd and loudspeakers he would not have slept a wink and not have run so well. Down on the farm he slept peacefully.'

Arkle's old adversary, Mill House, now 11 and the favourite, set the pace until he crashed into the open ditch at the far side of the water. Pat Taaffe was reluctant to take over and left the pace instead to The Laird.

Three horses fought out the finish, Fort Leney winning by a neck at 11/2. Taaffe confirmed his status as a top jockey because of his efforts at the finish, traditionally not the strongest part of his ride. 'Two tired horses came over the last, but mine was gamer,' Taaffe said. 'There have been great but few more courageous winners of the Gold Cup', Michael O'Farrell wrote in *The Irish Times*.

The Cheltenham Gold Cup was his first win in England. He won fourteen of his 27 races but broke down in Fairyhouse in November and was retired to his owner's Oxfordshire stud where he survived to the ripe old age of 26. He was that rarity in a sport where geldings prevail, the son of a Cheltenham Gold Cup winner, Fortina, in 1947.

Asked to compare him with Arkle, Dreaper said, 'Let's say they always work in different lots at home.'

At the same festival L'Escargot won a division in the Gloucestershire

Hurdle, ushering in the era of the snail. Ireland had four winners when Taaffe rode another Dreaper-trained horse, Muir, to the Cathcart Chase.

> If you term me as successful in training horses I don't know how badly off financially the poor fellows who have been unsuccessful are.
>
> TOM DREAPER interview, 19 December 1971

One would expect the greatest jump trainer of his era to have made a fortune out of his career as the trainer of Arkle. Not so.

Unlike his great colleague Vincent O'Brien and later practitioners like Mick O'Toole, who instigated famous raids on the largesse of the bookmakers, Dreaper did not bet. It meant he was above suspicion when Arkle beat his stablemate Kerforo that famous day in Navan in January 1962. But it also meant he always felt he would be better off keeping cattle and sheep rather than racehorses.

'I think I could have made a million out of the cattle trade all right, but not from racing,' Tom Dreaper told Seamus Counihan of the *Sunday Independent* in an interview published on 19 December 1971. 'However, the enjoyment wouldn't have been as good. A national hunt trainer nowadays only gets a living out of his profession. I have never heard of any trainer either here or in England becoming a millionaire out of the game. I don't think there is money in training horses anyway.

'There are a certain number of trainers who have rich owners. At one time I had the chairmen of five major English banks. They are just doing it for the sport. Stables that bet to make money last a few years and then they go. Any fellow nowadays who buys horses and sends them to a trainer is very lucky to get out even. To begin with, it will cost him £1,000 a year in training fees. And if you go through the figures, how many of them in training make that sort of money? How many of them in fact even win a race in a year?

'At the moment it doesn't pay me to send a horse over to England without making sure it has a chance of being either first or second. It costs so much in travelling expenses that you have to go for a £1,000 race minimum. If you are only placed second you have lost a lot of money.

'I don't bet. Our stable is not a betting stable. It never has been. In fact, I don't even know the bookmakers to speak to or even to meet in the street.'

It was a familiar refrain from all those trainers who did not supplement their earnings from betting. A prime example was Pat Rooney from Oldtown, in north Dublin, who provided Ireland with its only Cheltenham success with Arctic Stream in the post-Arkle year, 1967, who only ever kept a few horses and concentrated on tillage. The winner of the Cotswold Steeplechase was owned by a neighbour, another tillage farmer, Johnny Duffy. He had saddled his first winner at Down Royal in 1955 and had suffered a break-in to his hotel room the night before his only Cheltenham success.

The few horses he kept enjoyed disproportionate success. What he and others could have achieved in a better funded industry is a matter of speculation.

We'd much rather see Arkle in happy retirement than coming in third somewhere, a tired, dispirited horse.

BETTY DREAPER

Rheumatism set in on the leg that had been operated on and Arkle found it more and more difficult to stand. He made a celebrity appearance at the 1969 Horse of the Year Show at Wembley Stadium in London. As he was led in to a rapturous welcome he cocked his ears and put his head up, like he did when he was racing. He would give a little jump as he was being led in by Johnny Kelly from Bryanstown. One afternoon he ate the contents of a fruit seller's cart of apples and pears. Another night standing in front of the parade with David Broome's showjumper, he set about the show's hydrangeas and munched them all up.

But the arthritis was getting worse. One day Pat Taaffe called over from nearby Straffan with his daughter Olive to see Arkle in Bryanstown and saw that he was having a lot of difficulty moving. Taaffe called Anne Grosvenor. She flew over from Cheshire to say goodbye.

On Sunday afternoon of 31 May 1970 veterinarians Maxi Cosgrave and James Kavanagh came by. Arkle trusted them completely as they administered their injections. James Kavanagh gave the last injection. The great horse went down in his box and went to sleep for ever. He was 13.

They buried him beside the garden at Bryanstown, with a single word on his headstone, Arkle. Beside him, his companion, who did not long outlive him, was buried with the epithet 'Meg, a Good Hunter'. Anne Grosvenor and the Mooney family, who purchased Bryanstown in 1976, agreed to have his skeleton exhumed and put on display in the National Stud in Kildare.

The centrepiece at Newmarket is the skeleton of Eclipse, the champion on the flat who was daddy to all of England's thoroughbred race horses. The centrepiece at Tully is the skeleton of Arkle, Ireland's greatest steeplechaser. It sums up the difference between the two racing cultures.

Chapter 7 ~

GREAT SNAIL IN PARTY TOWN

L'Escargot may not be the best in the world but he is one of them.

RAYMOND GUEST

As the nation mourned the demise of its greatest ever equine hero, another one was emerging. L'Escargot was a very different kind of horse from Arkle. He won the equivalent of the Supreme Novices Hurdle in 1968, then known as the Gloucestershire Hurdle. He had plenty of speed and he was still showing his turn of pace eight festivals later, running a highly creditable fifth in the two mile Champion Chase, a preparation race for Aintree, in 1975.

The chestnut gelding L'Escargot had been bred by Mrs Betty O'Neill at Mullingar and bought for 3,000 guineas at Ballsbridge by Tom Cooper of the British Bloodstock Agency (Ireland) on behalf of Raymond Guest. Guest was one of those larger than life characters who seemed to find an affinity with national hunt racing. He was a grandson of Henry Phipps, who was a partner of Andrew Carnegie in the early days of the steel business, and a son of Frederick Guest, an Air Minister and promoter of military aviation in Britain. He graduated from Yale in 1931, then served as an assistant to Ambassador John Gilbert Winant in London in 1945, and finally as US President Lyndon B. Johnson's Ambassador to Ireland from 1965 to 1968.

Guest was a keen sportsman and he modelled his owning career on the redoubtable Dorothy Paget. Larkspur had won him the 1962 Derby. Sir Ivor followed up with the 1968 Derby. Both had been trained by Vincent O'Brien. He brought Sir Ivor from Ireland to take part in the Washington International at Laurel Racecourse.

Like Paget, he wanted to win all three majors, and he turned to Dan Moore to deliver him the Cheltenham Gold Cup.

Ever since I went as a spectator to watch the tremendous race between Golden Miller and Thomond II, Cheltenham has been my ideal racecourse. I have always had wonderful luck there which has continued down the years.

DAN MOORE in the *Irish Horseman*

Dan Moore had begun his career as an amateur rider in 1932, and turned professional in 1937. He went within a whisker of winning the Grand National himself as a jockey. In 1938 he had ridden Royal Danieli, trained at Athboy by Reggie Walker, when he narrowly lost out to a young Bruce Hobbs on Battleship, the first American-owned horse to win the National.

Remarkably, all three placed jockeys in that Grand National were teenagers (Jimmy Brogan from Trim was third on Workman). Cheltenham was a favourite course of his and he once rode four winners there on the same day. He had worked with Dorothy Paget during the war years when Ireland was neutral. He took out his trainer's licence in 1948, operating out of Old Fairyhouse.

A review of his stock in 1950 concluded that 'naturally his team consists of jumpers, made or in the making' with his eclectic list of owners, all name checked: Mrs G. F. Annesley, Mrs H. Boyd-Rochfort, Major T. H. Bevan, G. A. Barry, Lt Col Dan Corry, Mrs J. P. McAuley, Mrs D. Mack, T. V. Murphy, John McCann, P. McCann, G. V. Malcolmson, Peter McCarthy, A. J. Dinan, Mrs D. Vard, J. R. Magee, R. Kelly, T. McD Kelly and P. Shevgdar. It was impressive, but in twenty years Moore had had only one Cheltenham winner, Bahrain, in the County Handicap Hurdle in 1963.

The 1970 Gold Cup was a bit of a retrieval mission for Moore, as well as satisfying Raymond Guest's ambition to emulate Paget by capturing both the Grand National and the Gold Cup. L'Escargot won them both, the first horse since Golden Miller to do so, though not in the same year.

I thought two and a half miles was his distance. I wanted to run him in the Champion Chase, but Mr Guest was anxious to go for the Gold Cup.

DAN MOORE after L'Escargot's first Gold Cup victory, 1970

Tommy Carberry had rejoined Moore's yard in 1961. It was Carberry who would partner L'Escargot in most of his races over ten seasons. Moore's stable jockey at the time was Willie Robinson, but he was soon to leave to join Fulke Walwyn and become famous for that ride on Mill House against Arkle in 1964.

Carberry was only 21 but he was to become Moore's stable jockey at the yard where he had first wandered in as a schoolboy, leaving to become twice champion apprentice jockey before his return. In time he would become the trainer's son-in-law, marrying daughter Pamela and starting the Carberry dynasty that would yield the famous 1999 Aintree Grand National victory on Bobby Joe when Tommy trained the 10/1 winner, ridden by his son Paul, the most famous family team to win the great race since Reynoldstown in 1935.

L'Escargot was broken in and prepared for a bumper in Navan in 1967 when he was 4. His first rider was Ben Hanbury, who later went on to great success. After that bumper he moved to hurdles, and L'Escargot's partnership with Carberry began to grow. It culminated in the Gloucestershire Hurdle in Cheltenham, but there were signs of breathing problems. They were to cause L'Escargot to miss the entire 1968 season.

He returned to Cheltenham to contest the 1969 Champion Hurdle. The 17 hands high bundle of energy with his *Fág a Bealach* style of running caught the eye of many punters. He was the only horse reckoned by the punters to have any chance of beating Persian War but finished a distant sixth behind the champion.

Three weeks later he switched to fences and began to compete against more experienced horses. He was beaten by Kinloch Brae, the impressive Cathcar Chase winner at Cheltenham.

L'Escargot followed up with two wins in two weeks before Raymond Guest decided he should travel to America and attempt to win two races a fortnight apart over there. He won the first but was lame the night before the race and failed to make the second. The Carberry family used to recall the difficulty in explaining the situation to Guest for many years afterwards.

L'Escargot tried again in Belmont Park in the autumn, finishing third, before returning to Ireland to continue novice chasing. The tour earned L'Escargot a 'Jumper of the Year' award in America and a rare transatlantic profile for a steeplechaser. Tabloids warmed to the 'globe-trotting L'Escargot' description.

Guest now had a sense that this horse was his chance of winning the Gold Cup. Although Dan Moore, suspecting he wouldn't last the distance, would have preferred the two and a half mile Champion Chase instead, and many wise horsemen thought he might have waited for another year, L'Escargot's record in the Wills Premier Chase finals at Haydock tempted Guest to go for the big one.

He started in the 1970 race as a 33/1 outsider. Kinloch Brae, owned by Anne Grosvenor, Duchess of Westminster, was a more likely Irish challenger for the Gold Cup. Trained by Edward O'Grady's father Willie, he had won the Gainsborough Chase at Sandown, giving a 5 lb and ten-length drubbing to the fancied horse, The Laird.

England's challenge was led by the 7-year-old Spanish Steps, owned and trained by a wheelchair bound Edward Courage, which had run away with the novices gold cup. The Dikler, an ex-point-to-pointer bequeathed to Miss Peggy August in her uncle's estate, was also fancied. The Dikler went on to compete in a record seven Gold Cups, but 1970 was going to be L'Escargot's day.

He wasn't jumping brilliantly, just fiddling his fences nicely.
TOMMY CARBERRY after L'Escargot's first Gold Cup victory, 1970

The big Irish challenger for the 1970 Gold Cup was Willie O'Grady's 15/8 favourite Kinloch Brae, but there were also high hopes for Kelso Stewart's strapping 8-year-old French Tan. He had won three races, including an inspired Ascot success over the former Tom Dreaper star Flyingbob (now trained by Ken Oliver at Haywick). He was ridden by Pat Taaffe in his tenth and final Gold Cup, his remarkable career in the saddle shortly to come to an end.

Titus Oates, the King George winner, led for over a circuit with Timmy Hyde tracking him on board Kinloch Brae, who was jumping well and looked like he was enjoying himself.

As they went down the far side for the final time, Pat Taaffe took up the pace at the third last. Kinloch Brae was feeling the pressure and fell at the third last. French Tan landed marginally in front, but L'Escargot got away at the last, held on to the stand side and ran away to win by a length and complete an Irish one-two for the first time in Gold Cup history. But for the fall of Kinloch Brae, Ireland would have filled the first three places.

As he won, the horse threw his head nonchalantly in the air, a habit that would stay with him throughout his career.

Kinloch Brae developed leg trouble afterwards and after being sent to Toby Balding in England, he missed the 1971 Gold Cup, as did French Tan.

Spanish Steps was missing too as a result of a bizarre mistake at the declaration stage. The Courage family mixed up his name with another horse. The champion had his own troubles. L'Escargot had a season of falls and disappointments until showing some of his old pace at Leopardstown in February. With The Dikler and Herring Gull he was back at Cheltenham to face a new field. He was backed to 7/2 alongside Tom Dreaper's new hope, Leap Frog, winner of the Embassy Chase Final at Haydock.

A third Irish challenger was backed to 7/1. Francis Flood's tough and talented little mare Glencaraig Lady, just 16 hands high, had chipped a bone in her knee in only her second start in a bumper in Dundalk and was to have an unlucky career. The floating bone was never operated on and necessitated hours of walking during training.

She had been bought cheaply by Flood for only 800 guineas. Flood, who had been Irish amateur champion on numerous occasions, had started in training as assistant to Paddy Sleator, trainer of 1960 Champion Hurdle winner Another Flat. A depleted field of eight faced the starter.

Glencaraig Lady, ridden by Bobby Coonan, surprised the field, took the initiative and still looked full of running when she fell at the notorious third last, a fence that has decided the outcome of so many Gold Cups. 'She would have won,' Coonan said afterwards. 'She was jumping perfectly at every fence and she jumped the third last just as well but she keeled over on landing. I cannot understand it.'

That left two horses clear, much as the fall of Kinloch Brae had at the same fence a year earlier. This time L'Escargot was ahead of Leap Frog, ridden by Val O'Brien. L'Escargot's jumping was not great. He had a tendency to stray to the right, but Tommy Carberry pushed him on to a ten-length victory with The Dikler a further fifteen lengths behind.

'The second Gold Cup was much easier than the first. He won it quite smoothly,' Carberry recalled later. He reminisced that L'Escargot was the best horse without doubt he had ever ridden. He won every chase he could when he went to England. Everyone's sights were on the three in a row that had been won by the mighty Arkle.

No war is merrier than Ireland's three-day war with the Cheltenham bookmakers and the song we were singing at the end of it was not at all sad.

HUGH McILVANNEY, 19 March 1972

After holding out against the tide of commercialism for over a decade, sponsorship came to the Cheltenham Gold Cup in 1972 with Piper Heidsieck as the first incumbents.

Leap Frog was back in business and was the 3/1 ante-post favourite at one stage during the winter. By the time they reached the post it was Crisp, trained by Fred Winter, who had most money on his nose at 3/1 with Leap Frog and treble-seeking L'Escargot, arriving without a win for the season, both at 4/1.

Glencaraig Lady, so unlucky to fall when leading a year earlier, was back too at 6/1, and the mare went on to win by three-quarters of a length, with Royal Toss gaining second, a head in front of The Dikler. Crisp, according to some accounts, was held up on Winter's instructions and sulked, finishing fifth.

Glencaraig Lady was a daughter of Fortina. She broke down yards from the line and never ran again. The jockey Frank Berry, just 20 years old, was on his first visit to Cheltenham, having shot to fame giving the Irish President victory in the Irish St Leger on Giolla Mear. Weight necessitated a shift from flat racing to the jumps, where he gave Glencaraig Lady a memorable ride and showed great coolness under pressure. She survived a steward's inquiry and an objection to the winner by Nigel Wakely. Glencaraig Lady was declared winner all right.

She passed straight to the paddocks, but none of her progeny showed any sign of inheriting her talent and she suffered many barren years.

Limerick-born Barry Brogan might have won the Gold Cup for The Dikler if he had not gone so early for home. Brogan had to return to Ireland and the horse was back to win the race the following year with a new jockey, Ron Barry, beating Arkle's record time for the course in the process. L'Escargot was Ireland's hope once more.

Eight runners went to post with Pendil a very warm favourite at 4/6, and indeed sailed over the second last a couple of lengths clear. His jockey chose to steady him instead of going for home, a decision that probably cost him the race. He cleared the last three lengths clear but had lost momentum. The Dikler, responding to Brogan's urgings behind, cleared the last with a fantastic leap and began to come back at the leader, took the lead with twenty yards to go and won in a victory of bobbing heads. For Barry it was a sweet victory, particularly as an injury meant he would never be allowed to ride the race nowadays.

Some said afterwards that the hard-pulling The Dikler would not have won but for Barry's injury. He was forced to let the horse have his head from the start of the race. The horse settled to the task and proved to be one of the great Cheltenham rides.

L'Escargot finished well beaten in his fourth consecutive Gold Cup but had found another forum. He reverted back to the two mile Champion Chase in 1975, and went on to famously beat Red Rum in the Aintree Grand National.

He was immediately retired by a proud Raymond Guest. Following a misunderstanding over whether the horse should ever race again— L'Escargot was narrowly beaten in the Kerry National at Listowel later that year—Guest took the horse back to the US and retired him to the family estate, Powhatan Plantation, in Virginia.

He enjoyed a happy old age there until he died suddenly in his paddock in June 1984 at the age of 21.

If I have one dream, it is that I shall school and train an Arkle of my own.

PAT TAAFFE, *My Life and Arkle's*

Pat Taaffe retired in 1970 after the victory of Gay Trip, a horse bred at nearby Piper's Hill, between Naas and Kilcullen, in the Aintree Grand National. He returned to his farm of 125 acres, Alasty, Ardclough, near Straffan in Co. Kildare. 'A few cattle and sheep, I do a little tillage, and what I hope to do eventually is start a little stud,' he told Arkle's equographer. He discovered, as Dreaper and all others before him, that being Ireland's best-known jockey, the first celebrity of the new era when jockeys could become celebrities, was not enough. He now had to attract owners who would place with him national hunt horses of a high enough quality to start winning races in Ireland and, importantly, in England.

Captain Christy was his breakthrough, the first novice to win the Gold Cup since Mont Tremblant 22 years earlier, a horse that had a terrific record over hurdles which might have won the famous double. It was a victory memorable also as it was achieved in glorious sunshine.

An unruly individual in his early days, Captain Christy was ridden in an early hurdle race by his eccentric owner Joe Pidcock. Pidcock won only once in six attempts, and was run out on one occasion in Limerick. Pat Taaffe purchased him for £10,000. His performances were variable (one writer dubbed him a 'Jekyll and Hyde' character). Captain Christy hospitalised three of Taaffe's workers during one of his mad spells. 'Captain Christy always took a fence with him somewhere along the line, but on his day he was a serious horse,' Taaffe's son Tom says. Taaffe himself struggled to keep him together. In the end he turned to reformed alcoholic Bobby Beasley, and the headstrong gelding was brought under control.

By the age of 26, Beasley had won a Cheltenham Gold Cup, a Champion Hurdle and a Grand National. He did not take his first drink until he was 24, but alcohol soon took control of his life. He lost his position as stable jockey to Fred Winter, one of the biggest jobs in the sport, and his marriage collapsed. His weight soared to fourteen stone. Eventually he was persuaded to attend Alcoholics Anonymous. He was 38 and had been sober for five years when Pat Taaffe gave him the ride on Captain Christy at Cheltenham.

They struck up an instant rapport and it gave Beasley hope he could achieve another Gold Cup success fifteen years after his first. Captain Christy might have been the first horse to win the Champion Hurdle-Gold Cup double, but in 1973 Beasley got involved in the hurdle much too late and the Captain finished third, three lengths behind Comedy of Errors. Beasley was not going to let that happen again.

The jockey knew instinctively where to be in a race, reducing the risks. He also knew to expect the unexpected from his own mount. Both instincts were to prove crucial in the 1974 Cheltenham Gold Cup, a strange race which revolved around the dramatic fall of 100/1 outsider High Ken at the notorious third last downhill fence. Pendil was cantering at the time and was brought down. The two jockeys who went on to fight out the finish, Beasley and his opponent, both said they were fearful of tracking High Ken. Captain Christy looked a winner from then on, and would have won by more only for a huge blunder at the last. But Beasley was prepared for that too. He sat tight and powered past The Dikler up the hill to win by five lengths.

Beasley retired from the saddle for good in 1975 and trained for a time at Lewes and Marlborough. As if to prove that he had beaten his addiction, for eight years he ran a pub.

At Kempton in 1974, Pendil was odds-on to gain his third consecutive win in the race, but Captain Christy ran right away from him. The following year saw one of the most devastating performances ever produced at the highest level on a British racecourse. Captain Christy set off fast and went up through the gears leaving Bula 30 lengths behind.

In a poetic turn of justice, Gerald Newman rode Captain Christy to victory in that race. Gerald was the son of Eddie Newman, whose injury in 1950 had given Pat Taaffe the chance to ride regularly for Tom Dreaper.

Captain Christy returned as a strong favourite for the 1975 Gold Cup in an attempt to emulate L'Escargot. Some of his supporters thought he might even be the new Arkle. Pat Taaffe was among them. 'Captain Christy was as good as Arkle, but only for his head.'

Guts won the day. I am certain the horse was never the same afterwards.

JIM DREAPER after Ten Up's victory in the 1975 Gold Cup

Jim Dreaper had taken over the stables at Greenogues. His big hope for 1975 was Ten Up, an 8-year-old bay gelding who had won the previous year's SunAlliance Novices Chase on good ground.

Ten Up had been bought as a 3-year old by Tom Dreaper for 5,500 guineas at Goff's for Anne Grosvenor, Duchess of Westminster. Jim rode him to victory on his racecourse debut. The horse was a slow learner when switched to fences as a 6-year old. Dreaper was dismayed at the horse's inability to clear the fences but schooled him to the SunAlliance victory that marked him as a potential Gold Cup candidate. He had already won at Ascot in February in atrocious conditions. It was a good marker for what was to come, because if the 1974 Gold Cup was run in glorious sunshine, 1975 was a mud bath.

Killiney had been quoted as low as 7/1 for the Gold Cup in 1975 after he had routed the opposition in the Tote Novices Champion Chase, his eighth win in a row over fences. But he fell fatally at Ascot in April. Bobby Beasley had retired from the saddle and the Irish champion jockey Bobby Coonan was now riding Captain Christy. The Captain was sent off the 7/4 favourite ahead of Ten Up at 10/1 with Bula next in the betting at 5/1. Captain Christy had indicated he would struggle on heavy ground, having been beaten into fourth in the Leopardstown Chase, and indeed pulled up.

In the heavy ground Tommy Carberry had no choice but to give Ten Up his head from the start, knowing there was no point trying to fight the hard-pulling bay. Only Bula and Soothsayer were still with him as he approached the second last. Ten Up made a mistake and let Bula take a narrow lead. At the last Bula and Soothsayer could not get high enough through sheer exhaustion. Ten Up took the last formidably and powered up the hill to win by six lengths ahead of Soothsayer.

Anne Grosvenor, Duchess of Westminster, became only the second person after Dorothy Paget to win the Gold Cup with a second horse, and Jim Dreaper became the first second-generation trainer to win the trophy. It was a great festival for him. His three winners brought him the title of top trainer at the age of 24. Poignantly, his father Tom was there to see the victory. Tom Dreaper died the following month.

Captain Christy ended his career on a high later that year, winning the King George VI at Kempton on St Stephen's Day in record time by 30 lengths from Bula. Tendon trouble meant he would never race again.

Between hard ground and accidents, Brown Lad's attempts to win the Gold Cup have never quite materialised, and he stands out, with the possible exception of Crisp, as the best chaser never to have won a Gold Cup.

RICHARD BAERLEIN, *The Guardian*, 15 March 1979

The 1976 Gold Cup should have been a great race for the ever-swelling Irish support, but Captain Christy was forced out through injury and then Jim Dreaper was forced to withdraw the best of his three Gold Cup hopefuls, the ante-post favourite Ten Up, on the morning of the race.

Ten Up had begun to break blood vessels. He was allowed to run in Ireland, having been injected with a coagulant, but at Cheltenham the stewards informed him that if he administered the medication prior to the race, then the horse would be disqualified. Dreaper had used similar injections on 1975 Champion Chase winner Lough Inagh and also on 1972 Gold Cup runner Leap Frog. Amid what was described as 'much shaking of heads', Ten Up was withdrawn and, to rub salt in the wound, Dreaper was fined £125 for pulling the horse out.

Dreaper still had a say in the proceedings, though most people felt his chance of winning the race was gone. Brown Lad began his racing career late in life and was 7 when he became champion novice hurdler (then called the Lloyds Bank Hurdle) in 1975. Dreaper famously told the press: 'If Brown Lad is alive he will run' in the SunAlliance the following day. Then as champion novice chaser he won the first of his three Irish Grand Nationals, and was to be placed second in the Gold Cup twice. He had stuck to handicaps all season and was backed down to 13/8. Dreaper's second string and former Irish National winner Colebridge, ridden by Frank Berry, was regarded as a 12/1 chance, but punters felt the fast ground was against both horses. England's big hope, Fred Winter's 6/4 favourite Bula, had lost some of his confidence after the Stephen's Day annihilation by Captain Christy.

Tommy Carberry produced a storming run-in on Brown Lad, having ridden with great care in conditions that the gelding did not like. Colebridge challenged for the lead six from home. Bula made a mistake at the third last. Fred Rimmell's Royal Frolic kept up the pace to win by five lengths with Dreaper's horses second and third. Ireland had to wait twelve months to win back the Gold Cup.

> There would be something wrong if St Patrick's Day passed without at least one Irish winner. This year there were four and the celebrations were still going on late into the night.
>
> MICHAEL PHILLIPS, *London Times*, 18 March 1977

The 1977 Cheltenham Gold Cup, staged on St Patrick's Day, started at a blistering pace, considering the atrocious conditions and the fact that none of the thirteen runners had ever contested the race before. Among the new names to note was Anthony Robinson's Tied Cottage, who showed with Tommy Carberry a soon-to-become characteristic by setting the early pace.

Lanzarote, who had been running well in his quest to become the first horse to win the Champion Hurdle and the Gold Cup, tragically slipped as he landed at the ninth fence and had to be put down as his near hind leg was broken. In the process he brought down the 11/4 Irish fancy Bannow Rambler, whose strong support was due to the fact that he had come into the race after three straight wins including the Leopardstown Chase. Michael Furlong remounted Bannow Rambler but never caught the field and eventually pulled up.

Meanwhile, Tommy Carberry hared along in front on Tied Cottage, unaware that the first and second favourites were already out of the race with the third, Fort Devon, soon to follow. Seven fences out Tied Cottage made a mistake, handing the lead to Somerville, who in turn began to tire between the last two fences. Dessie Hughes seemed to be struggling to get Davy Lad into the race and put pressure on the leader between the second last and last jumps, going on to win by five lengths from Tied Cottage. The photogenic Ann Marie McGowan had won the Gold Cup with the first horse she had ever owned.

Mick O'Toole had moved to national hunt from greyhound racing (he won the Oaks in Haringey in 1965). He bought Davy Lad as an unbroken 3-year old for 5,000 guineas on impulse at Goff's one day because he had always wanted a horse by David Jack, as he was a friend of the two brothers the sire was named after. Davy Lad had won in the mud at the 1975 festival. O'Toole had at least one festival winner every year for the next six years. He was fond of a speculative punt and put £500 on Davy Lad at 50/1 before Christmas, winning £25,000. He had only decided to go for the Gold Cup ten days before the race, when he heard that Brown Lad and Border Incident would not be running.

When O'Toole offered Davy Lad to his first prospective owner, he declined to take it. Instead O'Toole persuaded Joe McGowan, owner of one of the biggest house-building companies in Ireland and master of the Galway Blazers at the age of 31, to buy the horse as a present for his wife. The McGowans achieved three festival wins from four horses, gambling a fortune on Hartstown.

Davy Lad suffered from injuries and broke down the following season before retiring to the McGowan Stud near Fairyhouse. He suffered from arthritis and was put down in 1984.

Ireland had won ten Gold Cups in fifteen years, but would wait nine years to win another, thanks to the intervention of an allegedly aphrodisiac alkaloid found in chocolate.

In his time jockey Dessie Hughes won three Arkles, the SunAlliance Hurdle twice and a Champion Chase before becoming a trainer and passing the stable on to his son Richard. His win on Monksfield in the second of the brave horse's Champion Hurdle victories two years later would remind punters of how he won the race on Davy Lad.

> This Champion Hurdle went beyond simple excitement into that area of experience where sports events become mysteriously moving.
>
> HUGH McILVANNEY, 22 March 1979

Irish eyes had been turned back to the Champion Hurdle by a remarkable horse. Des McDonogh from Moynalty paid just 740 guineas for Monksfield as a yearling for the Newfoundland-based Dr Michael Mangan, from Dunmore, Co. Galway.

He won five times on the flat to add to his hurdling triumphs and won four times in his first season hurdling, as well as finishing second in the Triumph Hurdle at Cheltenham.

His first attempt at the Champion Hurdle resulted in a second place behind Night Nurse, but he returned to bring Night Nurse's quest for three in a row to a halt in the Champion Hurdle of 1978, taking up the running two flights out from the defending champion and holding off a late challenge from a horse that was to initiate another of the great Anglo-Irish rivalries in Cheltenham history.

Monksfield was an out and out galloper. His great rival, Sea Pigeon, son of the 1965 Epsom Derby winner Sea Bird, had finished seventh in the Derby as a 3-year old and was the archetypal one-shot speed horse.

Monksfield's victory was Ireland's first in the Champion Hurdle for fifteen years, at a time when Ireland was dominating the Gold Cup and in the midst of what was regarded as a glorious era for hurdling. A tremendous gamble on the morning of the race had brought his price back to 9/4.

Des McDonogh used the Erin Foods Champion Hurdle at Leopardstown as his preparation race for the 1979 Champion Hurdle. McDonogh instructed jockey Tommy Kinane to hold up the horse as long as possible. But as the race was run at a slow pace, Monksfield's renowned stamina could not be brought to bear, and the horse trailed in a disappointing sixth as Sea Pigeon sprinted away up the hill to avenge his defeat.

McDonogh blamed Tommy Kinane, telling him he should have used his initiative instead of sticking to instructions. Kinane felt the instructions were part of a conspiracy to get rid of him. The result was that the 45-year-old Kinane was jocked off on the orders of McCann, according to *Irish Independent* journalist Raymond Smith, but more likely by the trainer. McDonogh found a new jockey for Monksfield's second Champion Hurdle victory, Davy Lad's rider Dessie Hughes.

Despite rumours concerning the horse's health, Monksfield went on to win the second round of what was being dubbed the Streetfighter v the Pigeon. Dessie Hughes took up the running two flights from the end and held off a late challenge to win by three-quarters of a length in one of the great Champion Hurdles.

It was a famous ride. 'Monksfield stuck out his head so low in his determination it would be no surprise to find mud on his tongue when he was pulled up beyond the winning post', Hugh McIlvanney wrote. A lasting impression, according to Michael Clower, was 'the rider's style and determination'. Despite being tall for a jump jockey at 5 foot 10 inches, 'Hughes rode finish after finish on this horse as if defeat did not exist.' Raymond Smith wrote that Hughes was 'lean, like a gunfighter, and deadly'.

Sea Pigeon's trainer Peter Easterby said afterwards that it was owner Pat Muldoon who cost Sea Pigeon the race when he told Jonjo O'Neill in the paddock beforehand not to come too late. 'It put Jonjo in the wrong frame of mind—it wasn't his fault.'

Monksfield went for three in a row in 1980, but his stamina was beginning to wane and he was left for dead as Jonjo delayed his challenge and Sea Pigeon sprinted away up the hill to avenge his defeat. Sea Pigeon won the race for a second time twelve months later under John Francome, who delayed his challenge even longer.

Monksfield was that rarity in jump racing, an entire horse. McDonogh claimed he was once asked about rumours that the horse found ways to masturbate in the box. 'Some people can't accept that a stallion like him can perform as he does on the racecourse and yet be so mild at home that a small child can get up on his back as if he were a seaside donkey.' When he died in 1989 after nine years at stud, his winning progeny included Lakendara, Garrylough and It's a Snip.

Timeform rated The Night Nurse (182) ahead of Monksfield (180) and Sea Pigeon (175). In more recent times Istabraq (180) is the only one to rate alongside them. Dawn Run was rated 173. Another horse of the era was rated 176, higher than Sea Pigeon, but sadly Golden Cygnet never got to race in the Champion Hurdle.

Being so young, I fully expected that another every bit as good would come along and I simply didn't realise that a horse of his ability would prove quite so rare.

EDWARD O'GRADY, interviewed by MICHAEL CLOWER in Kings of the Turf: Ireland's Top Racehorse Trainers (2007)

The 1979 race had been diluted by the absence of what many felt was one of the greatest hurdlers of all time. One of Monksfield's potential major Irish challengers had been removed by a fatal fall at the Scottish Grand National the previous April.

Golden Cygnet, owned by Galway insurance agent Ray Rooney and trained by Edward O'Grady, had been turned into a potential champion with a set of leather covers for his knees to prevent him racing with his head dropped low between his legs. He won the 1978 Supreme Novices at a prohibitive 5/4 on.

To this day Golden Cygnet is regarded as one of the greatest horses never to have run in a Champion Hurdle. The intelligent face and the unusual markings, a white blaze in the form of an inverted V under the star on his forehead, are fondly recalled by racegoers.

O'Grady still mourns the loss of his challenger, an 'extraordinary horse' who started strongly and finished as fresh as his starts, the best he had ever handled.

Golden Cygnet's jockey, Niall 'Boots' Madden, still rates him as the best hurdler ever. 'He was a freak. Early in the race he would be pushing along, yet when you said it was time to go, he would rev up underneath you, and he had some gears for a national hunt horse.'

He started his fatal race as joint favourite with Sea Pigeon and initially survived the fall at the last. O'Grady recalls how, in the race-course stables, the horse rubbed, first the left side of his head, then the right side, against O'Grady's shoulder as if to say, 'There is something wrong with me.' The following day the horse had a brain haemorrhage at the Royal Dick veterinary hospital in Edinburgh and was put down.

Arguments raged afterwards what might have happened if Tied Cottage had stood up. In my opinion, Alverton, with his flat racing ability, would have taken command on the run-in for Tied Cottage must have tired after setting such a strong gallop over the three and a quarter miles.

RICHARD BAERLEIN, The Guardian, 16 March 1979

The 1978 Gold Cup was postponed until April because of snow, with Davy Lad unavailable because of an injured foot and the previous year's favourite Bannow Rambler also missing from the original field. Jim Dreaper's Brown Lad ('Surely one of the best horses not to win a Gold Cup,' Michael O'Farrell pondered in *The Irish Times*) would have preferred softer going and finished seven lengths behind Midnight Court. The winner was bred at the Airlie Stud near Lucan and had been trained by Tom Costello before moving to Fred Winter.

In 1979 the Dan Moore-trained Tied Cottage was Ireland's best hope for the Gold Cup in the absence of Davy Lad and J. P. McManus's Jack of Trumps, trained by Edward O'Grady, a late withdrawal which cost its owner a potential £250,000 in winning bets.

The race was an ordeal for jockeys and spectators alike. It began to snow as the runners were at the post for the first race, and it continued for the rest of the afternoon with a driving wind. 'I doubt if riders have ever experienced a more uncomfortable time,' Richard Baerlein wrote in *The Guardian*, 'and this may have accounted for some of the more fancied runners never getting in the race.' Run in a mixture of snow and driving rain on very soft ground, the sleet was at its worst as the riders were mounting.

By the last turn Tied Cottage had burned off all challengers except Alverton, a highly rated winner of seven flat races in 1976. Tied Cottage was a fraction ahead but caught a glimpse of Alverton out of the corner of his eye, and knuckled on landing. 'I wanted him to put in a short one to get over,' Tommy Carberry said afterwards. 'He was very tired.'

The race was over, and the question of what might have been for Tied Cottage has lingered ever since, especially in the light of what happened twelve months later.

'A big horse who likes to get out in front and did' was how Kevin O'Connor described Tied Cottage in *The Irish Times*. 'Stayed out there in the hail, thundering over ditches and fences. Appearing out of the hail at odd spots, seen clearly as they passed within view of the stands, then out to the country again. Three miles of it. Leading the field of fields and coming up to the final fence, stubbed his hind legs on the brush and on landing lost his balance and splayed out, neck stretched out, to settle down on the ground. Stopped. Passed by Jonjo O'Neill, guiding Alverton past him. Less money on the poker tables tonight. An English win with a Cork jockey.'

Bob Harman of the *Sporting Life* recalled: 'He wasn't exhausted.' He may not even have been distracted, despite Alverton's Cork-born jockey Jonjo O'Neill's suspicions.

O'Neill's after-race comment was simply 'I was glad to see the other lad go.' Later in his biography he recalled how he had pulled Alverton to the right in search of better ground and he made sure at the same time he was not in Tied Cottage's tracks in case Tied Cottage fell.

The great horse's reputation perished in the blizzard of history.

As for Alverton, he met a dramatic end. He was within sight of the Gold Cup-Grand National double a few weeks later when he suffered a heart attack approaching Becher's for the second time and ploughed straight into the fence.

> If ever a horse deserved to win a Gold Cup it was yesterday's hero, Tied Cottage, a runner-up to Davy lad in 1977, a faller at the last fence 12 months ago when contesting the lead and now, at 12 years of age, third time lucky, having made every yard of the running.
>
> MICHAEL O'FARRELL, *The Irish Times*, 14 March 1980

If 1979 was the Gold Cup Tied Cottage should have won, 1980 was the Gold Cup he won and then lost in the testing laboratory.

Tied Cottage had a reasonable King George VI at Kempton on St Stephen's Day, where he finished a distant fourth behind Silver Buck and Jack of Trumps on unsuitably fast ground.

On heavy ground in February in Sandown, he was second to Diamond Edge. Dan Moore ran Tied Cottage at Naas a fortnight before the Gold Cup in yielding ground over two miles. He ran poorly. This was a glorified gallop.

The 1980 race was a catalogue of disasters for fancied horses. Tommy Carberry on Tied Cottage took the lead from the beginning and stayed there to the winning post. Border Incident had proved difficult to get right because of injuries, but was cruising until the fourth last. He fell. Jonjo O'Neil laughed as he went by on Jack of Trumps, only to fall at the third last.

Tommy Carberry meanwhile left Tied Cottage to run his own race and never once attempted to hustle him in any way. Looking relaxed and finding the right rhythm, he pounded his rivals into the ground, beating the previous year's SunAlliance Chase winner Master Smudge by eight lengths and was greeted by what Michael O'Farrell called 'a mighty roar that would have done Arkle proud'. Joan Moore was the trainer on the day; her husband Dan was at home watching on television. 'He settled well and while he got close to a couple of fences he never made a mistake,' Tommy Carberry said. 'I was always happy. A great ride. When he heard a horse pull up behind him at the third last, he immediately pulled away again.'

'It seemed that the crowd had held its collective breath,' best-selling novelist Maeve Binchy wrote in *The Irish Times*. 'When he came to the last fence, the one where he fell last year, the sigh was like a great breeze rippling through the people as he did the last bit up to the post.'

> In all cases the disciplinary committee of the Jockey Club found that the dope had come from contaminated foodstuffs and were unwittingly administered.
>
> Jockey Club statement, 21 May 1980

The relief was premature. Traces of the myocardial stimulant theobromine were found in Tied Cottage's post-race urine sample at the Equine Research Station at Newmarket.

Theobromine was one of the main focus additives of the rudimentary testing process which had been introduced in 1963. A year earlier theobromine had caused the disqualification of a Worcester winner, No Bombs, when the horse, trained by Peter Easterby, had famously snatched a Mars bar from the stable lad on the way to the races on 21 April 1979.

The Moores were informed of the positive test a fortnight after the Gold Cup when they were at Aintree. Subsequent investigation showed that the banned substance had infiltrated soya beans in his feed that had travelled in a cargo hold which previously held cocoa beans, the source of the contamination. Not only was Tied Cottage disqualified and the cup taken from him on 22 May, but also Mick O'Toole's horses at the festival, whose feed came from the same supplier. They included Chinrullah who had won the Champion Chase and finished fifth in the Gold Cup the following day. No blame was attached to either trainer. Master Smudge was officially declared the new Gold Cup winner on 21 May. The Gold Cup was officially transferred at Warwick a few days later.

Tied Cottage's victory in the Irish National weeks after the Gold Cup was a poignant one. He was amateur ridden by his owner Anthony Robinson, who had already been diagnosed with cancer. Within months of the race both he and Tied Cottage's trainer Dan Moore were dead, Joan taking over the training of Tied Cottage and Arthur many of the other horses in the stable.

> Soon after I first started I had two horses capable of winning the Gold Cup, Chorelli and Bright Highway, but neither of them ever got there. I would still love to win that race.
>
> MICHAEL O'BRIEN, interviewed by MICHAEL CLOWER in *Kings of the Turf: Ireland's Top Racehorse Trainers* (2007)

In 1981, the year of the disabled, there were high Gold Cup hopes for Bright Highway, trained in Co. Kildare by Michael O'Brien, the Newcastle, Co. Dublin-born trainer, who had been confined to a wheel-chair as a result of a fall when riding for Raymond Guest in America in 1974.

Bright Highway was bred by the Taaffe family, who helped O'Brien establish a small training operation in Rathbride, with almost immediate success. Bright Highway delivered O'Brien's first Cheltenham win in 1980, won both the Macheson and Hennessy Gold Cups and was installed as ante-post favourite for the 1981 Gold Cup. But he picked up an injury in January which forced him out of the reckoning. Sadly, another injury prevented him running in 1982, and in 1983 he was retired, placing him alongside Flyingbolt among the greatest horses never to have contested the Gold Cup.

Tied Cottage, Jack of Trumps and Royal Bond were the leading Irish challengers in the absence of another promising newcomer, Daletta. Tied Cottage fell early in the race at the sixth fence. Jack of Trumps was beaten into sixth place, depriving J. P. McManus of the fruits of a gamble to win £25,000.

Little Owl, the eventual winner, had been bred in Ireland and purchased by Peter Easterby as an unbroken 3-year old at Doncaster for 2,200 guineas. His original owner Bobby Gundry had left the horse to her nephews, the Wilson brothers, Jim and Robin. So Jim Wilson, born in Leighlinbridge, Co. Carlow, became the first amateur jockey to ride a Gold Cup winner for 35 years. His father Captain Jack Wilson had been a renowned huntsman with the Carlow hounds.

The veteran Tied Cottage, his Gold Cup victory excised from the records, set a frenetic pace in heavy ground in 1982, his final Gold Cup appearance at the age of 14, only to tire after the fourth last. Three times winner Tommy Carberry was to have no better luck in his last Gold Cup, riding Royal Bond, a horse trained by his brother-in-law Arthur Moore. Royal Bond started as 4/1 second favourite, having won at Leopardstown in February, but trailed the field from the off, never looked like getting into the action and finished eighth, a place ahead of Tied Cottage.

Instead the race went to an abrasive 10-year old bred in Co. Antrim by Edith Booth, Silver Buck, at 8/1. Bought at Goff's in 1975 by the O'Connors from Cashel who wanted a suitable horse for their son to break in and ride, they sold him when they found Silver Buck totally unmanageable. When another buyer ducked out of the deal, Silver Buck went instead to Jack Doyle's base in Shankill. Attempts were made to calm him down for racing purposes with some success. He went to Paul Doyle's stables on the Curragh and began to make an impression at point-to-points, winning two, and an outing at Clonmel in a bumper race before legendary punter Barney Curley offered £7,000 for him with the predictable ambition of battering the bookies with him.

Curley made his inevitable killing on Silver Buck at a race for amateurs in Catterick. He sent the horse to be trained by Tony Dickenson at Gisburn. And thus it came to pass that Silver Buck, having passed through a series of Irish stables, came to win the 1982 Gold Cup for England.

There was no Irish challenger in 1983 when Michael Dickinson trained the first five horses past the line. The winner Bregawn had been trained in Ireland in the latter stages of his career by Paddy Mullins when he won a two mile bumper ridden by Willie Mullins, later to take over his father's stables and become king of the Champion Bumper himself as a trainer.

The Irish challenger for the 1984 Gold Cup, Dromlargan, struggled to keep tabs on the leaders and the race was won by Jenny Pitman's Burrough Hill Lad.

Barney Curley had a hand in the career of a second Gold Cup winner, having contacted Tipperary-born trainer Jimmy Fitzgerald with a view to selling Forgive n Forget. Both Curley and the trainer, who backed him at 33/1, made a killing when he won the 1985 Gold

Cup after a disappointment in the 1984 SunAlliance Chase. Mark Dwyer brought home Forgive n Forget for an English victory for an Irish-bred horse, an Irish-born trainer and an Irish-born owner, Roscommon-born Tim Kilroe, by then based in Manchester.

It was nine years since Ireland had won the Gold Cup. A new 'Dawn' was due.

Chapter 8 ~

| LADY AND THE CHAMP

Even Dawn Run's belligerent appearance after the race takes some believing. It was the combination of O'Neill's refusing to give up and the brave mare's incredible will to win. O'Neill and Dawn Run working in total unison began a surge of power that devoured the ground ahead of them.

BOB HARMAN of the *Sporting Life*

On 27 June 1986, four years after Charmian Hill had ridden the mare to her first success, Dawn Run broke her neck attempting her second French National Hurdle. It was a crushing blow to national hunt racing.

The effect that her brief career had on the sport was magical. The tri-national champion transformed perceptions of the sport in all three countries where racing over jumps is practised. When the Irish gather for Cheltenham, her name is discussed with reverence and there is always someone whose party piece is to recite the commentary of how she returned from near certain defeat to win the Gold Cup in 1986.

Dawn Run was 17 hands high, nimble and quick. She trained on the small all-weather oval to the side of the field of Paddy Mullins's stables in Doninga on the outskirts of Goresbridge, Co. Kilkenny. That little uphill run made her something of a Cheltenham specialist.

Mullins has trained over 1,500 winners on the flat and over jumps. They include Irish National winners Vuline and Herring Gull, as well as 1973 Champion Stakes winner in Newmarket, Hurry Harriet. But Dawn Run is the one for which he will always be remembered.

During her career she swelled attendances in Ireland. Racecourse executives fought over staging races to get Dawn Run. She was a crowd pleaser and we could do with another one.

Mullins saw her potential from the start. Dawn Run's dam was an Arctic Slave brood mare. 'There is no doubt they were brilliant brood mares,' he said in an interview. 'Deep Run was a great sire. His legs were twisted and he was small for a national hunt stallion, but that did not stop him. A good national hunt family can be ruined in a couple of generations by mating with the wrong stallions. You need class and you need speed.'

This is even more so with hurdlers, who flick rather than jump over fences. They best win their races by a combination of stamina and speed allied to fast, clean jumping. If they can flick over the hurdles with minimum effort, they will gain priceless lengths.

It is one of the great anomalies of the code that the most truly brilliant hurdlers have failed when put over fences. They try to hurdle the big fences instead of standing off and arching their backs to jump like steeplechasers.

But Dawn Run proved she could do both. She is the only horse to have won the championship over both hurdles and jumps.

> They came to a muddy patch that would have slowed up most horses, but Dawn Run never changed her stride or altered her rhythm. Mrs Hill's hopes began to run high. Could this gentle mare turn out to be the one, the stuff that dreams are made of. When she rang her trainer Paddy Mullins the only doubt she expressed was that she's so placid that I am afraid she may never make a racehorse.
>
> ANNE HOLLAND, *Dawn Run* (1986)

Paddy Mullins used to say that the horse always sensed when her owner was coming, and would recoil at the far side of the stable. Because if Dawn Run was one formidable dame, her owner was another.

Charmian Hill was the first Irish lady to ride in a mixed race at Fairyhouse in 1973 when she was already 54 years old. With no horsey background behind her, she rode her first races at an age when most people have given up riding, not only winning them but, aided by her supportive and enthusiastic husband who died a year before the Gold Cup triumph, bringing on and schooling young stock. She survived a terrible fall after which her life was in danger, only to be back in the saddle again when well over 60. At 63 her licence was withdrawn because of old age, and she never forgave the authorities for the indignity.

Charmian Hill bought the 16.2 hand high mare at the November Sales in Ballsbridge on 7 November 1981 for 5,800 guineas and gave it the name because her daughter Penny had taken up jogging and was settling to the routine of a dawn run herself.

'Look at that long line right from her withers down over her quarters,' Mrs Hill said on her first glance at the horse. 'That's what makes a jumper with speed.'

Mrs Hill took over Dawn Run's early education herself, riding her in a bumper at Tralee.

After Dawn Run went on to win the Champion Hurdle and the French equivalent in 1984, she had a year off with a pastern injury. After winning a two mile chase in Navan, beating Mouse Morris's Buck House in the process, Mrs Hill decided that Dawn Run should be schooled for the Gold Cup.

'It looked a very tall order after just one win,' Mullins recalled. Dawn Run had two more wins in Punchestown and Leopardstown in December and went to practise the Cheltenham fences in January, where she threw Tony Mullins. He managed to remount and finish fourth. But it cost him the ride in the Gold Cup.

> I still regard that Gold Cup victory as a bit of a disappointment. She was a super mare, but to be asked to prepare a horse like her to win the race and be treated the way I was, sickened me.
>
> PADDY MULLINS, interviewed by MICHAEL CLOWER in *Kings of the Turf: Ireland's Top Racehorse Trainers* (2007)

Why did she do it? Paddy Mullins says that Charmian Hill resented having her licence taken away at the same time that Tony Mullins became professional. He rode Dawn Run to thirteen of her 21 wins, but never at Cheltenham where Ms Hill kept jocking him off.

Both Ron Barry and Tony Mullins had ridden Dawn Run at Cheltenham and failed. Jonjo O'Neill had won. He knew just how far he could go with the mare, how much coercion she would need. He also understood how tough it was on Tony Mullins. It is Mrs Hill who made the decision to switch from hurdles to fences, and it is she who will stand over them.

'She had the final say and she knew it,' Paddy Mullins said. 'If Charmian Hill wanted to do something she usually had her reasons. As an owner I had no complaints about her. But I did hear that the mare's trip to France had become a necessity from a financial point of view.

You feel very vulnerable as a trainer. I wasn't always fully in control of Dawn Run. There was nothing I could do about it if I wanted to continue as her trainer.'

To this day every time I drive down Cleeve Hill into Cheltenham, I get a buzz. The hairs on the back of my neck stand up.

JONJO O'NEILL

Gold Cup day arrived and Dawn Run was backed down to 15/8 favourite. The Hills felt that the 2/1 ante-post favourite status was false. 'She's only a novice,' Penny Hill said. 'She really needs another race before the Gold Cup.' But privately they were happy with what they heard from Dawn Run's workout at Punchestown the week before Cheltenham.

She had ten rivals, all of them more experienced. Forgive n Forget had suffered mishaps and disappointments but was back to defend his title. Wayward Lad had gained a third win in the King George VI Chase.

Dawn Run had only four steeplechase races behind her and some intensive schooling. Jonjo O'Neill concentrated on setting a domin-ating, draining pace while coping patiently with the wearing company of Run and Skip, the Welsh National winner, whose rider Steve Smith Eccles was determined to profit from what McIlvanney called 'the blunders that might be expected from an 8-year old with only four previous outings over fences'.

Smith Eccles had the right idea. Jonjo planned to give her a breather before the final push, but had to disregard the plan when she dropped a hoof in the water, and then made a serious blunder and hit the fifth last. She came out from that a length or two adrift of Run and Skip.

She now had to sit tight to survive. O'Neill got after her to retrieve the lost ground and get back the rail position that Run and Skip now occupied.

Dawn Run took over again two fences from home. She jumped the third last strongly on Run and Skip's inside. Jonjo then used the mare's long stride to gain ground and seize the all-important rail position as they turned for home.

The previous year's winner Forgive n Forget and prolific winner Wayward Lad (on whom O'Neill had been third in the 1983 Gold Cup) were closing in on the two leaders and were full of running. Jonjo was running out of options. He kicked the mare into the second last fence and she gained another length in the air on Run and Skip.

Wayward Lad and Forgive n Forget came back at her and jumped the last side by side. Dawn Run looked set for third place behind the front two. On the run-in Wayward Lad quickly went three lengths clear.

'If ever a horse looked beaten at the last fence it was her,' Richard Baerlein wrote in *The Guardian*. 'She seemed to drop out of the race before the final fence.' Even Jonjo said afterwards that when she approached the final jump he thought she would be lucky to be placed.

Halfway up the run-in, O'Neill switched Dawn Run over towards the stand side. She needed to gain three lengths in 150 yards, all the time uphill into the killing slope. Wayward Lad was drifting violently to the left almost diagonally up the run for the post. Mark O'Dwyer had lost vital momentum just as he needed to sustain the challenge, and Dawn Run gradually gained on Wayward Lad, lifted by a deafening roar from her supporters.

Her 5 lb sex allowance and Jonjo O'Neill's strong right arm began to tell. 'She picked up after flying the last,' O'Neill said, 'and I knew we had it won as the others were stopping in front. I let her get her own feet and she jumped it well. So we both got stuck in together.'

'No horse in Gold Cup history has ever looked so beaten only to get up and win', Cheltenham historian Stewart Peters wrote.

Willie Mullins, the son of Paddy who was to take over the stables at Doninga, was among those who thought she was beaten. He turned away under the archway thinking to himself, she is young, there is always next year. He then heard a huge roar, a humungous roar, and thought: that isn't for an English winner.

'She wasn't absolutely knackered,' Jonjo said. 'She was taking a breather saying: I'm going fast enough here. After Wayward Lad went two or three lengths up, he began to hang across in front of me towards the rails. I realised he was tired and stopping, and so did she. I thought we were beaten when we came to the last, but she is as game as a pebble.'

'At the line Jonjo went crackers,' Hugh McIlvanney wrote, 'which left him twice as sane as the reception party that nearly made him the first rider to have a leg broken in the winner's enclosure.'

Her win had the unsurprising additional distinction of running the fastest ever Gold Cup, her six minutes 35.3 seconds was 1.9 seconds faster than The Dikler in 1973.

Twenty yards from the line, Jonjo O'Neill punched the air as he crossed the line and the crowd erupted. His moment.

There have been many memorable outpourings of Irish emotion on the acres of Prestbury Park, prompted in recent years by such iconic horses as Istabraq and Moscow Flyer. But nothing, to my mind, can quite match the reaction in 1986 to the greatest Gold Cup I have seen, won against all odds by the Irish mare Dawn Run and her talismanic jockey Jonjo O'Neill

ALAN LEE, *London Times*, 11 March 2006

The Irish cheers echoed round the course over and over again as the finish was replayed several times on closed circuit television in the stands and the hospitality rooms high above the course with their geranium-lined balconies and tables laden with food and drink.

The crowds chanted 'Here we go.' Charmian Hill was in the AIB suite with *London Times* editor Charles Wilson, Henry Kelly, Seamus Mallon of the SDLP and Danno Heaslip of the PDS in Galway. J. P. MacManus and Alex Higgins were in nearby suites.

The stampede into the winner's enclosure could have been dangerous, but good nature just held the line against hysteria.

The winning entourage with Charmian Hill, trainer Paddy Mullins and jockey Jonjo O'Neill, who understandably looked most concerned, made their way precariously towards the number one berth, and once inside were followed by the crowd who swept policemen and officials aside, as Michael O'Farrell said in *The Irish Times*, 'like a pack of cards'.

Charmian Hill was cheered; Jonjo O'Neill was cheered. When he dismounted, Jonjo hoisted Dawn Run's former jockey Tony Mullins on to his shoulders and carried him round the ring into the presentation ceremony.

'The Queen Mother was not cheered,' Michael O'Farrell wrote in *The Irish Times*, 'but it might have been a near thing. There were unprecedented scenes of sheer exuberance that would have done Arkle proud.'

'If you didn't celebrate that day there would be something wrong with you,' Jonjo O'Neill recalled.

'The explosion of euphoria was such that some of the hats sent spiralling into the air might have had heads in them for all the owners cared', McIlvanney wrote.

There is no doubt that the new 5 lb weight allowance which is claimed by mares helped Dawn Run to become only the second of her sex to capture the hurdler's crown.

MICHAEL SEELY, *London Times*, 14 March 1984

Did the mare's allowance turn the battle between Dawn Run and Wayward Lad into an unequal battle? In the north of England they still think so.

The 5 lb mare's allowance was introduced in 1984, the year of Dawn Run's Champion Hurdle victory. Victories for mares such as Stormy Dell were the first indication that things had changed for fillies. The previews of the 1984 Champion Hurdle noted the absence of Gaye Brief and the 5 lb weight allowances would be influential. Even without it the pundits felt her form was superior to anything else in the field. She became the first mare to win the Gold Cup since African Sister, bred in Tipperary by Allen Baker, was adjudged lucky to win the race in 1939.

Mares took many years to benefit from the advantage. They were still dispatched to stud, something that was not an option for geldings. The traditional view has been that jump-bred mares, who represent the only purpose-produced breeding stock in the sphere, should be retired at the earliest opportunity and let the boys in the family get on with upgrading the pedigree.

The 1993 meeting was the best Cheltenham for mares with Shawiya, Gaelstrom and Shuil Ar Aghaidh all successful in grade 1s.

We were privileged to see the ride of a lifetime, a monument to patience, nerve, courage and technical brilliance, the mature masterwork of a great jockey.

HUGH McILVANNEY, *The Observer*, March 1986

Jonjo O'Neill said after the race that he owed everything to Tony Mullins for telling him what to do. 'She's a moody old devil,' Jonjo said in his post-race television interview, 'and neither me nor anyone else could get her to do something if she didn't want to.'

He had a specific incident in mind when he said that. When he was schooling Dawn Run at Gowran Park the previous January, she had backed off from some fences, dived to the left at others and generally conducted herself badly. O'Neill endured two circuits of this, after which he was less than impressed. 'At the end of that I didn't think she should be running in the Gold Cup, let alone be favourite to win it. She did jump the last fence of that schooling run well, but one out of fourteen is not exactly encouraging.'

On the Thursday before Cheltenham he went over to school her again at Punchestown, and this time Tony Mullins on another horse accompanied Dawn Run. This time she did everything Jonjo asked her to do.

'When people say that they could see I was a lot more nervous than usual before the Gold Cup,' he told Hugh McIlvanney after Dawn Run's victory, 'that I was obviously feeling the extra pressure a bit, I think I have got to correct them a bit. I had to be aware how important Thursday was for me and everybody connected with the mare, but the responsibility that brought is not the kind to weigh me down.

'I love the game. It's my flippin' hobby as well as my living, and above all I love riding really good horses. Going out there with something exceptional underneath you and getting the job right together is the greatest satisfaction. It is far better to be on a good horse than a moderate one and the responsibility involved can never reduce the thrill of that for me.

'Whether it is a favourite or a 100/1 shot I go out to try to get the job right. I am riding to try to fit the horse as much as I want the horse to fit me.'

We can ill afford to lose such magnificent chasers as Dawn Run and Buck House.

MICHAEL O'FARRELL, *The Irish Times*, 28 June 1986

Dawn Run was back in action within weeks, unaccountably failing to take off at the first fence in the Whitbread Gold Cup at Aintree, then jousted with Buck House in Punchestown. On 27 June 1986 Dawn Run broke her neck in a fall four fences from home attempting another French Champion Hurdle at Auteuil. The death was front page news and led the main TV bulletins. There was some speculation that she had suffered a heart attack in the heat. She was 8 and the highest earning national hunt horse until then with winnings of £250,000.

Another why did she do it? The prize money in France was equal to that in the Gold cup. Finance may have been a lure, but adventure more so. Some horses die young even without their shoes on. Her great rival, Buck House, was found dead within a few days of Dawn Run's demise.

Princess Anne (Windsor), eldest daughter of Queen Elizabeth, unveiled a half-sized bronze of Dawn Run before the 1987 festival with O'Neill in the saddle, looking across at the statue of Arkle as he surveys the winner's enclosure.

O'Neill spent six months fighting lymphatic cancer just when he was setting up as a trainer. 'I felt I had to go out and prove myself all over again.'

Tim Clarke, who had looked after Dawn Run, couldn't bear the thought of life without her and left Paddy Mullins's yard to work in a credit betting office.

> The excuse that the going was good is facile. Rather the English jumpers were too fast for ours—on perfect jumping ground. All too many Irish races, especially hurdle events, are contested at a poor gallop, frequently developing into five furlong sprints.
>
> MICHAEL O'FARRELL, *The Irish Times*, 24 March 1987

After the 'Dawn' came the darkness. In 1987 and 1988 Ireland had just one winner in each year, John Mulhern's Galmoy, a facile winner in the Stayers Hurdle. In 1987 at least there were nine placed horses and the excuse of two deaths in the family, Dawn Run and Buck House. But in 1989 things got even worse, with no Irish winner for the first time since 1947.

The 1947 festival was postponed because of bad weather and all the key races run off in a single day with just three Irish contestants, Cool Customer, Distel and Happy Home. Before that you have to go back to 1945, when there were no Irish contestants at all at the first post-war festival: eight races run off on a single day with the Champion Hurdle following a fortnight later.

It was little consolation that half the winners in these festival meetings were Irish bred, more a reflection that the days had returned when the best horses were being exported out of the country. More depressing again was the fact that eight of the 1987 winners had been trained in Ireland at one stage or another. The industry, in common with the economy, was facing penury.

'The traditional Anglo-Irish battle for the Gold Cup was in danger of becoming a thing of the past,' Bob Harman of the *Sporting Life* wrote. 'The economy of Ireland was such that exporting their best talent to cheque waving Britain had become a way of life which was undoubtedly eating into their own challenge at Cheltenham. Things would be very different towards the end of the 1990s with the Irish economy going through the roof and trainers able to find wealthy businessmen at home willing and in a position to stave off the attention of their English counterparts.'

Dawn Run had provided a welcome oasis in a barren period for Irish horses in the Gold Cup, and at the festival in general. She had broken a losing run going back to Davy Lad in 1977 and one that would continue until Imperial Call in 1996, when Ireland was back up to seven winners.

The introduction of the Champion Bumper in 1992 was a barely concealed attempt to bring back some Irish success to the festival. It helped. The winning numbers improved, two each in 1990, 1991 and 1992 and six in 1993 to restore normal service. Three winners in each of the years 1994, 1997 and 2000 were regarded as a new low base level as consistent trade surpluses from 1987 on began to wash through the Irish economy. In 2006 Ireland had a record ten winners.

Every so often, probably too often, a monster is created by the press. In this case a true behemoth, the ultimate Job Horse by the name of Carvill's Hill.

BOB HARMAN of the *Sporting Life, The Ultimate Dream, the History of the Cheltenham Gold Cup*

The blank in 1989 does not tell the full story, of course, as Ireland had a new folk hero. Bought as a 3-year old at the Derby Sales at Ballsbridge, Jim Dreaper's novice Carvill's Hill, one of the most fancied Irish horses of this or any era, was looking very good in 1989 until he came a cropper at the tenth. Ten Plus also fell in that race.

Desert Orchid got a heroic welcome in victory, England matching Ireland in enthusiasm, as Dawn Run had a few years previously.

Carvill's Hill was never to win the Gold Cup. In 1990 he was backed into third favourite in a race surprisingly won by Norton's Coin, Wales's first Gold Cup. The horse returned to Weathercock House. Celtic Shot, a Champion Hurdler in 1988, was another Irish hope of the age.

Carvill's Hill went off favourite again in 1991 ahead of the new veteran Desert Orchid. He led four out, but a blunder put paid to his chances and the race was won by Garrison Savannah for Jenny Pitman's stable.

After Carvill's Hill found a new owner and was moved to Martin Pipe's stables in England, he was beaten again in 1992, this time by the Toby Balding-trained Cool Ground with the new Meath cult jockey Adrian Maguire on board. There were suggestions that Golden Frieze was entered in the race specifically as a spoiler to unsettle Carvill's Hill.

Ireland continued to send hopefuls. Charles Haughey's John Mulhern-trained Flashing Steel was the big hope in 1994 in a race won by French-trained The Fellow. In 1995 Jim Dreaper believed Merry Gale, a 7-year old, was good enough to win a Gold Cup, but lost out to Kim Bailey's Master Oats. Fergie Sutherland eventually took the Gold Cup back to Ireland in 1996 with Imperial Call.

> Every day of the festival featured game old stayers plugging away up the notorious hill. The Queen Mother was one, and Fergie Sutherland, the wooden-legged trainer of the Gold Cup winner Imperial Call, another.
>
> ANDREW BAKER, *Independent*, 17 March 1996

Fergie Sutherland was an unlikely Irish hero. He had attended Eton, reserved for the top strand of England's antiquated class system, and at Sandhurst, the engine room of the country's imperial killing machine. After he lost a leg to a landmine in Korea, he always travelled with three false legs, one for walking, one for riding and one for dancing.

He returned to the hunting fields and to the racehorses he loved as he rode out with trainer and friend Dick Hern when he went back to Newmarket to become assistant to Geoffrey Brooke and then Joe Lawson. He took out a licence of his own in 1958 in Newmarket and moved to train on his mother's estate in Carrigadrohid in Cork in 1967, saddling his first winner at Limerick the following year. 'Sutherland is a figure from another age,' Andrew Baker wrote, 'stone-faced, patrician, snorting like one of his equine charges.'

Nearly forty years into his chosen career, Fergie produced a surprise Gold Cup. Imperial Call's mother Menelik III (there was Arctic Slave blood there) was sent by her breeder Tom O'Donnell to visit Callernish at Garryrichard Stud. It was a lucky choice: there two classy national hunt sires (the other was Over The River) managed to sire three Gold Cup winners between them, Cool Ground (1992), Imperial Call (1996) and Cool Dawn (1998).

Sutherland paid £20,000 for the foal after seeing him jump just one fence at Tom Costello's indoor arena in 1992. He put the money down at the second fence, buying on behalf of David Blackmore, who runs a car business in the Channel Islands and owned the Henry Ford ancestral homestead in Lisselan Estate in Clonakilty.

His first victory was in the Shannon Maiden Hurdle in 1993. After several more runs up Mad Woman's Hill at Aghinagh, Sutherland began to think of the horse as a Gold Cup prospect when he was only 5. He improved every day through the 1995–96 season and Sutherland returned to Cheltenham after a 30 year absence.

> In the end the horse people and the hoarse people of Ireland had their hat-flinging, tricolour waving, raucous day of ecstasy.
>
> PAUL WEAVER, *The Guardian*, 15 March 1996

Imperial Call made his intentions known less than five weeks before the Gold Cup when he broke an English stranglehold on the Hennessy Cognac Gold Cup in Leopardstown. He trounced a high-class field, beating Master Oats and Monsieur Le Curé and was slashed in price from 33/1 to 8/1 and eventually 9/2 to become the new second favourite behind the flying grey, One Man.

The Wexford-born Conor O'Dwyer was a young and inexperienced jockey. 'Imperial Call can be a bit odd at times,' he said. He took over as the last minute substitute for the Hennessy from both Richard Dunwoody and Charlie Swan who opted for other horses, and kept the ride for the Gold Cup.

The Gold Cup was the first time the horse had run over two and a half miles. Owners Lisselan Farms had already turned down some hefty bids for him as his reputation for an impressive combination of speed and stamina grew. Sutherland told O'Dwyer to hang on to him for the first mile, stick third or fourth, take him a bit wide to get a bit of daylight ('don't forget he's only a second-season chaser') and to get him jumping and enjoying himself, bowling along in touch with the leader to keep him jumping, and kick on when he could. They worried a little about the firm ground. The horse, evidently, did not.

The race unravelled quickly and not without some tragedy. Monsieur Le Curé crashed into the sixth fence and was dead before he touched the ground. The Tim Forster-trained third favourite Dublin Flyer took the field along at a good pace, but blundered at the thirteenth. The chasing pack closed in on him and three fences later he had been swallowed up by the chasing bunch.

Conor O'Dwyer had been biding his time on Imperial Call and took up the running with Couldn't Be Better and the Gordon Richards-trained One Man with Rough Quest in behind. As One Man began to show signs of distress, Imperial Call turned on the engine, measured the last and pulled clear of Rough Quest up the hill to win quite comfortably, prompting an Irish roar of Dawn Run proportions. 'I didn't have just money on him, I had my religion as well,' one punter told Brian O'Connor of *The Irish Times*.

'When it works it looks good, doesn't it?' Sutherland said. 'He did it very stylishly. He jumped like a buck and enjoyed the afternoon.'

One Man, who had been tipped to be the next Desert Orchid, was beaten into a bedraggled sixth place with Richard Dunwoody mourning, 'He emptied very quickly on me.'

'When you are travelling so well it is easy,' O'Dwyer said. 'He was going very smoothly at the top of the hill and coming to the last I was still expecting Richard on One Man to challenge. When I looked around, I went and looked the wrong way, but I could see Rough Quest behind. My lad was probably idling a bit up the hill and I am sure there would have been a bit more.'

Imperial Call felt ready to lick creation and he did.

FERGIE SUTHERLAND, quoted by BOB HARMAN

What followed was pandemonium. A section of the crowd, of whom 1,000 had come from Cork, started singing a tuneless 'Banks of My Own Lovely Lee'. A large Imperial Call banner appeared from nowhere and was unfurled. Paul Weaver in *The Guardian* described the scene: 'The horse people and the hoarse people of Ireland had their hat-flinging, tricolour waving, raucous day of ecstasy.' Sutherland's distinctive voice could be heard calling, 'Let me get to my horse. I want to get to my horse.' An almighty scrummage was ensuing in the winner's enclosure. Senator John Dardis later recalled in a speech to the Seanad how he was almost trampled by 10,000 people. Conor O'Dwyer thought he was going to get dragged off the horse as he made his way back to the enclosure.

'The post race celebration made the mad cap twenty minutes following Dawn Run's triumph in 1986 appear positively tame by comparison,' Bob Harman of the *Racing Post* recalled. 'How no one got injured is a mystery known only to those watching as those actually involved were as ever, totally oblivious to the danger. Nevertheless it was a colourful sight to be sure, a sea of waving tricolour flags. O'Dwyer joined in by waving one as he sat astride the new Gold Cup winner, the pride of Ireland.'

'The scenes of celebration would have done Arkle and Dawn Run proud,' Michael O'Farrell wrote in *The Irish Times*.

Edward Gillespie recalls it was the first time that the safety of the post-race arrangements at Cheltenham attracted 'outside attention', something that had not happened even after Dawn Run's success in 1986.

Imperial Call was the first Cork-trained Gold Cup winner since Cottage Rake in 1948, as well as the first festival winner for jockey, trainer and owner. Dan O'Donoghue composed a twelve-verse ballad of Imperial Call to the air of 'The Boys of Kilmichael':

When the tape was released they all started,
And half way from home he smelled luck,
He raced up the hill on the outside,
And he jumped o'er the last like a buck.

He was instantly installed at 7/2 for the following year's Gold Cup, but preparations for his attempt to retain the cup in 1997 were interrupted by injuries, and the prevailing fast ground did not suit.

Fergie Sutherland retired in 1998 after 30 years training in Killinardrish.

His assistant Raymond Hurley took over the responsibility for training Imperial Call, although apart from a brief return to form against Florida Pearl in April 1999, his appearances were few and far between.

Conor O'Dwyer was approached by Kim Bailey to come to England and ride for his stable, just as had happened when he went to ride for Geoff Hubbard before the Imperial Call success. It did not work out and he returned to Ireland, establishing a successful partnership with Arthur Moore and with Michael O'Leary's Gigginstown Stud. At an age when most jump jockeys have long since retired, he rode War of Attrition to win the 2006 Gold Cup and the Dessie Hughes-trained Hardy Eustace to capture the Champion Hurdle in 2004 and 2005.

The Cheltenham management set about implementing a new security system for the following year.

'They must have breathed a collective sigh of relief when Imperial Call or any other Irish horse failed to win the Gold Cup', Bob Harman of the *Racing Post* wrote. He was referring to the big Irish prospect, the latest in a line of 'people's champions' extending back to the 1940s, the novice Danoli.

But there was a new Irish winner in one of the lesser events the following year, one who was going to create an unexpected stir once more in the winner's enclosure and who was going to capture public affection beyond what even Imperial Call had done.

His name was Istabraq.

Chapter 9

ISTABRAQ: THE SILKEN TRAUMAS

This one's for John.
Istabraq jockey CHARLIE SWAN to Channel 4's Lesley
Graham after his 1998 Champion Hurdle win

Should the story begin with the man or the steed? And if so which man? J. P. McManus had created his own legend first before Istabraq arrived to carry his colours into legend.

But should it be Sheikh Hamdan bin Rashid Al Maktoum, who bred Istabraq for the flat and abandoned him to the netherworld of national hunt after seeing him as a one-year old. Or John Durkan who was to have trained Istabraq but died of leukaemia before the horse he was inspired by had eventually run. Or Aidan O'Brien, the trainer who took charge of Istabraq temporarily until Durkan's return.

When they were galloping around the paddocks, Istabraq never looked any faster or better than the others, but what was different about him was the way he showed himself off. It was almost as if he knew he was worth a fortune.

TOM DEANE, stud groom at Derrinstown, quoted in
MICHAEL CLOWER's *Legend of Istabraq*

The tradition of flat horses turning to jumps is more usual in England that Ireland. In England many jumpers are recruited from the flat, then graduate to fences after a year or two of hurdling. Good flat horses could not guarantee hurdling success. Interestingly, moderate flat horses sometimes made great hurdlers.

The crowning example of this was Persian War, whose two flat wins in modest company gave no clue as to his hurdling potential. He went on to win three Champion Hurdles in succession at Cheltenham from 1968 and finished second in the fourth.

There is a pattern. Since the 1960s, a higher breed of flat racer was being recruited to hurdling. Aurelius, winner of the 1961 St Leger, was put to hurdling after an unsuccessful first year at stud, finishing second at Cheltenham in the 1967 Champion Hurdle, only to be disqualified for failing to keep a straight line at the run-in.

While other flat horses have also succeeded over hurdles, the majority of champion steeplechasers are bred for the jumps. Not running them on the flat gives them valuable time to grow their true strength.

An occasional flat horse ended up hurdling in the 1950s and 60s and trainers such as Vincent O'Brien often did both simultaneously to confuse the bookie and the handicapper as much as anything else. But the supply of champion flat horses was not as great in those days. It had increased substantially after Finance Minister Charles Haughey introduced tax exemption on stallion profits in 1969, transforming the Irish horse breeding industry.

Ireland became the third largest producer of thoroughbreds in the world, behind the US and Australia. By 2000 Ireland was producing about 12,000 thoroughbred foals each year, more than France and Britain combined. By the time the tax relief ended in 2008, Ireland was home to 70 per cent of the world's top stallions, while the country accounts for 42 per cent of total thoroughbred output in the European Union.

Most of the country's top stallions were found in a handful of studs: Kildangan Stud owned by Dubai's ruling Maktoum family, the Aga Khan's Gilltown Stud and John Magnier's Coolmore Stud in Co. Tipperary.

Even today Ireland's national hunt champions are more likely to come from small farms, from specialist breeders and spotters such as Tom Costello in Clare, than big studs. Istabraq was the exception. His owner, Hamdan bin Rashid Al Maktoum, Minister for Finance for Dubai, was one of the wealthiest and most ambitious owners in the world, with 300 horses training with twenty trainers in England, Ireland, Dubai and the US.

Istabraq was of noble stock, by Sadler's Wells, one of the greatest flat racing stallions of all time. The racing success of Sadler's Wells, the 1984 Irish 2000 Guineas, Coral-Eclipse Stakes and Phoenix Champion Stakes, was surpassed by his success as a stallion, repeated champion sire in Europe and responsible for more group 1 successes than any other stallion.

A Sadler's Wells covering fee was 150,000 guineas, and he sometimes produced more than a hundred foals a year.

Istabraq's dam, Betty's Secret, was sired by Secretariat, one of the few horses to win America's triple crown. She never raced but her half-brother, Caracolero, won the French Derby and her grandma produced Majestic Prince, who won the first two legs of the Triple Crown in 1969. She was owned by Eddie Taylor, the legendary Canadian breeder who stood Northern Dancer and bred Nijinsky, and had her first foal by Northern Dancer. He was Secreto, winner of the 1984 Epsom Derby and trained by Vincent O'Brien's son David, at 27 the youngest ever trainer of a Derby winner. Secreto beat his dad's horse, the supposedly unbeatable El Gran Senor, in the race.

Betty's Secret produced twelve foals, but none matched Secreto's achievements, although they were sold as yearlings for huge sums. In 1987 she was sent to visit Sadler's Wells and boarded in Ballysheehan Stud. When Taylor died in 1989, she was sold for $6 m to Hamdan Al Maktoum, second eldest of the four wealthy Maktoum brothers.

He sent her to Derrinstown and that is where Istabraq was born on 23 May 1992 after a four-hour labour. The Sheikh gives all his horses Arab names. Istabraq means silk in modern Arabic, but the Sheikh cited an earlier meaning, lightning, or lightning fast.

On the flat I put him down as a slow maturing type and a slow learner. He lacked speed and was not at home on fast ground.

WILLIE CARSON, Istabraq's jockey on the flat racing circuit

A horse with Northern Dancer, Sadler's Wells and Secretariat blood isn't bred for Cheltenham. Istabraq was destined to be pounding the firm ground of the great flat racing venues in high summer. In flat racing you get one shot at this—your winning has to be done as a 3 or 4-year old. A flat race horse's career is over before they have got all their teeth.

Istabraq won two of his eleven races on the flat for John Gosden, including one spectacular victory in the Gordon Carter Handicap in Ascot in 1995. Sprinklers had been used on the course to soften the ground which had been subjected to the best summer in decades. A patch of ground near the far rails had not been reached by the sprinklers because of overhanging trees. Carson brought Istabraq down the hard ground and came home six lengths clear.

Carson, who rode him throughout most of his flat career, told Istabraq's equographer Michael Clower he thought the horse was one-paced. 'National hunt horses are not as good as those on the flat where everything happens much quicker, particularly on firm ground. It is also a matter of adapting and maturing. A lot of horses improve if they are given the time. I remember Dick Hern having a similar animal called Persian War. He wasn't that good on the flat and trained on to win three Champion Hurdles.'

In 1996 Istabraq developed problems with his forefeet. Sheikh Hamdan sent instructions down to Gosden that he didn't want to keep a 4-year old unless he could be guaranteed to win group races. Istabraq was barely inside the top 90 horses on the flat and would have to go.

Gosden reflected later: 'The sadness of flat racing is that so many horses go wrong. Too much is asked of them too soon in life when they are not mature enough to take it. The list of horses who could have gone on to be something special, but who got destroyed at 2 or 3, is very long.'

Istabraq's options were to retire to stud, to be sold abroad where racing continues for 5 and 6-year olds, or to go to the winter code.

Gosden's assistant, John Durkan, had decided to embark on his own training career. He persuaded J. P. McManus to buy the horse and send him hurdling.

> We didn't know exactly what he was going to make, although Timmy thought it could be 100,000 guineas, possibly a bit more. I left the exact limit to him, but I said we ought not to pay much more than that. He got him for 38,000.
>
> J. P. McMANUS

The man who discovered Istabraq's talent over jumps never saw his greatest triumph. John Durkan grew up in Stepaside where his father, a builder who had made some money in London, set up training stables and trained his brother's horse Anaglog's Daughter to win the Arkle Trophy by twenty lengths in 1980 after star novice Beacon Light fell two lengths from the finish.

The victory raised the biggest roar of the 1980 festival as the family and friends of the 'boys from Bohola', who had poured into Cheltenham for the occasion, swamped the winner's enclosure and staged a memorable party in the Hilton in Stratford. Young John was hooked. Instead of joining the family building business as his father had hoped, his ambition was to train horses for the flat.

When John left school in St Benildus in Kilmacud, he did a course in the National Stud and went to Lambourn in England to work with Charlie Brooks's racing stable and ride as an amateur. He spent two and a half years there before going on to work with another Lambourn trainer, Oliver Sherwood. He rode over a hundred winners in his time at Lambourn. One of those winners was trained by John Gosden, and in 1994 he moved to Newmarket to become assistant trainer at Stanley House.

Two months later he married Carol Hyde, a jockey in her own right with eleven successes to her name and a spell on the Irish three-day event team. She was the daughter of a successful trainer and the granddaughter of the man who had ridden Tom Dreaper's Prince Regent to Cheltenham Gold Cup success in 1946.

Durkan was convinced Istabraq was no soft flat horse. He told Timmy Hyde this is 'the sort that does not get going until he is in a battle. He has more guts than class and that is what you need. He will win next year's SunAlliance hurdle.' It was a tall order for a horse that had never run over hurdles.

His father–in-law was a good friend of J. P. McManus. J. P. was reluctant to buy Istabraq and put him with Durkan, but Durkan tore a page out of a sales catalogue and wrote down the relevant details for McManus:

Won two of his seven starts last season. One mile six for maiden at Salisbury on good-firm ground. Was second in next three starts before winning competitive two mile h/cap at Ayr, soft ground. Favourite for Cesarewitch. Went over the top and didn't run.

Feet: Flat footed and wears bar shoes and when feet give trouble. Quarter crack in first week of April. Walking and trotting for three weeks. Back for strong work after that rest and feet have been no problem since. Rain at Haydock three weeks ago. Finished second giving the winner two and a half stone.

Apart from feet which are no major problem, he has a floating chip in OF joint which he had since a yearling and gives him no trouble at all. Touch wood he has always been a very sound horse, who in my opinion, goes in any ground except firm.

The floating chip in the near fore (rather than the off-fore claimed by Durkan) may have scared other bidders off. 'A one pace galloper who had problems with his feet and who did not have a turn of foot' is how the Sheikh's racing manager Angus Gold described him.

J. P. says he had heard this sort of thing many times before, but he was happy to have a horse with John and was impressed at how bullish he was. Carol Hyde's father Timmy did the bidding and secured Istabraq for 38,000 guineas. Istabraq was on his way to the Hyde stables in Camas Park, between Cashel and Dundrum in Tipperary, to be gelded.

Even as the excitement of his new career mounted, John Durkan was not feeling well. When the autumn sales were held in Newmarket in October 1996, he thought he had a bad cold. He returned to Dublin for the Goff's yearling sales where a doctor prescribed some antibiotics and he missed the last day of the Goff's sales. The following day he was sent to St Vincent's for blood tests.

His mother noticed he was perspiring a lot and she had to keep changing the sheets. She assumed the sweating was normal.

When the word came back from Vincent's that the blood count was extremely low, she thought he might have leukaemia. She had never known anyone with leukaemia before, but that was as much as she had picked up about the condition. Three days later John began a course of chemotherapy. He was 30.

Durkan arranged for his horses to be sent to other trainers. McManus sent Istabraq to Aidan O'Brien, on condition that he would return to John as soon as the treatment was successful.

Aidan O'Brien is the worst kept secret in Irish racing.
    JOHN MAGNIER, announcing VINCENT O'BRIEN'S successor in 1994

Many racing people were surprised that someone so young and un-assuming had been invited to take over the multimillion euro training establishment at Ballydoyle in succession to Vincent O'Brien in 1994. The word was that the centre was going to be turned over to several trainers. The 24-year-old O'Brien was the only one invited to the party.

Aidan O'Brien was born on 16 October 1969, third in a family of six to Denis O'Brien, a farmer from Killegny near Clonroche and Stella. Denis had trained some point-to-pointers and rode as an amateur, winning 140 races, mostly on horses trained by himself.

After a disastrous start to his career looking after his father's six point-to-pointers, Aidan worked in a mill at Clonroche for eight months before he left to work for P. J. Finn, a brother-in-law of Charlie Swan. Two months later he moved to work for Jim Bolger in Gowran. He stayed with Bolger for three and a half years and made his name as an amateur rider. Aidan rode his first winner in a bumper in Galway, the day he met the woman who was to become his wife.

Anne Marie Crowley had taken over her father's stable at Owning, near Piltown, and was in the process of becoming Ireland's first female champion jumps trainer. Aidan got on with both father and daughter. 'I would have done anything to keep Aidan bar marry him,' his father-in-law Jimmy Crowley said. At the end of the 1992–93 season she handed over her licence to her future husband.

Aidan O'Brien swept all before him as a trainer, schooling his horses on an uphill gallop on Pilltown Hill, modelled on Jim Bolger's famous Doninga gallop, enabling him to run his horses more frequently and successfully on national hunt courses than his rivals. It was also peculiarly suited to preparing for Cheltenham, where he had his first success in 1996 with Urubande. In 1998, before his 27th birthday, he was champion national hunt trainer for the fifth and final time. In 1999 he became Ireland's champion flat trainer for the first of many times. Soon he was to move all his attention to the flat, but in the meantime he had Istabraq to mind.

For John Durkan's sake.

Istabraq is the sort to do well over hurdles.
    CHARLIE SWAN to J. P. McMANUS after his debut at Punchestown,
                                        16 November 1996

Even after Aidan O'Brien was asked to take over Coolmore, he retained Owning, and was Irish champion trainer over jumps and on the flat for three successive years.

Forty years after Vincent O'Brien had switched codes to the more lucrative flat racing circuit, Aidan did not even have a set of hurdles at

Ballydoyle, so Istabraq was sent off to the Curragh, 70 miles away, and was put over five of the eight hurdles on the schooling ground.

Charlie Swan, his jockey, couldn't believe how good he was. Convinced, O'Brien erected six baby hurdles alongside the main gallop and six bigger ones on the other side of it. Istabraq came second to the Paddy Mullins-trained Noble Thyne on his first outing, the Locks Restaurant Novice Hurdle in Punchestown on 16 November 1996, throwing away a winning opportunity with a last-flight blunder. Swan followed O'Brien's instructions not to use the whip, but privately felt if he had used it he might have won. 'I was as kind to the horse as I could,' he said in an evening telephone call to McManus.

He started favourite on his next outing, a £25,000 grade 1 race at Fairyhouse fifteen days later, and finished ahead of English raider Lake Kariba and twenty lengths ahead of Noble Thyne.

There were still problems with Istabraq's feet. Enter Ken McLoughlin, from a family of seven generations of blacksmiths and whose grandfather once had five forges dotted throughout Dublin. He identified Istabraq's problems: he had flat feet and he was heavy for his build. He decided to use stick-on shoes, enabling him to pare back the hooves much more than Gosden's farrier had done.

John Durkan flew home from his treatment in Manhattan for Christmas 1996 and went to see Istabraq win at Leopardstown at 100/30 on. He won the Deloitte and Touche Novice Hurdle, a recognised Cheltenham trial, at Leopardstown in February by a short head from his stablemate Finnegan's Hollow, who finished looking like he had more to offer.

This was in direct contrast to Vincent O'Brien's policy of not running stablemates in the same race and raised questions about both Istabraq's ability and O'Brien's pre-race strategy. O'Brien told a pre-Cheltenham forum in Cork a few weeks later that his instructions to Finnegan's Hollow's jockey Conor O'Dwyer were 'to track Istabraq and arrive at the last, but I didn't say anything about what he was to do then'. He brought the house down.

O'Brien felt Istabraq could go further even than Durkan's audacious ambition for him, that he would thrive in a race where there was a strong pace throughout. He considered racing Istabraq in the Supreme Novices Hurdle, five furlongs longer than the SunAlliance. But with ten days to go to the 1996 Cheltenham meeting, he said he would leave the final decision to his owner.

Owner J. P. McManus, typically, consulted both trainer and jockeys before making a decision. Christy Roche, who had ridden Istabraq in training, reckoned he was better suited to the short race, a two mile race over hurdles, contradicting Durkan's prediction. O'Brien was prepared to do the unconventional, to run both horses in the same race.

J. P. never decided. He just commented: 'Well, Aidan, if you think Finnegan's Hollow is right for the Supreme Novices, and if Charlie thinks so too, perhaps we should run Istabraq in the SunAlliance.'

The going is the most important thing. Set out to make a point or two over the odds and go in with two fists. And above all, beware of certainties.

JOHN P. McMANUS

John Patrick McManus was born in Dublin during the week of the 1951 Cheltenham Festival. He was 23 when he went to the Cotswolds festival for the first time and was hooked. Since then Cheltenham has been top of his agenda.

His father Johnny McManus had grown up in Arigna in Co. Leitrim where two of his brothers worked in the coal-mine. Johnny went to work in Dublin and then in Ballygar, Co. Galway, before settling in Limerick where he became a dairy farmer and also ran a small plant hire business. That is where J. P. grew up. He still wears his allegiance to Limerick hurling on his sleeve and his racing colours are based on the local hurling club. He named some of his racehorses after members of the 1973 Limerick hurling team.

He watched Merryman II win the 1960 Grand National and the following year backed O'Malley Point who was third at 100-6. McManus discovered at the age of 12 that all the world is a betting ring, and all the men and women are merely punters.

In 1963, young John invested half a crown at 15/2 on Owen Sedge in the Leopardstown Chase. He bet for the heck of it rather than the funds, because it offered an escape from the drudgery and penury of work on the family farm.

Because single bets were taxed and multiples were not, he learned about accumulators in Alf Hogan's betting shop in Limerick. Here was the key to success: with accumulators, losses were small and gains were great, and he could avoid losing the tenner a week he earned on the farm with no return.

He fancied a horse that was running in Limerick Racecourse on the same day as his Leaving Cert history exam at Sexton St Christian Brothers School. Department of Education regulations prevented any student leaving the room for the first twenty minutes, until any late candidates were admitted. That left J. P. with a tight schedule, about 45 minutes, between the start of the exam and the race. He made his escape as soon as he could and cycled to the racecourse, just in time to see the horse he would have backed win the race. Needless to say, he also failed the exam.

He began working for his father, driving a bulldozer. One of the sites that he worked on became a nine-bedroomed house and 400 acre farm, Martinstown Stud, which later became his Irish base. He never dreamed he would own it one day.

When the time came for the next brother, Kevin, to leave school, J. P. asked his father if the business would be big enough for all three of them. 'All five,' said the father. That convinced him he had to look outside the family business for work.

In 1971 at the age of 20 and against his father's wishes, McManus became a bookmaker, betting on the racetrack during the day and at the dogs in the evening. He says that, at first, he was still more of a punter than a bookmaker, 'but the numbers had to add up'. He ran out of money twice, but his mother bailed him out on the sly and put him back in business. 'Because it had my mother's blessing, I suppose I had more respect for it than any money I've had before or since,' he told Raymond Smith.

Unusually, he found he earned less as a bookie than by taking money from other bookmakers. McManus concluded from watching his colleagues that most bookmakers were glorified punters who were apt to panic when they were running out of money. His immense aptitude for figures, later to be seen to full effect in his currency dealings, gave him an advantage over his colleagues. He worked out that jump racing offered better value for the punter, because a horse can commit an error and recover, something that is almost impossible to do on the flat.

Other bookies would reduce their margins to try to recover their losses. J. P. decided that the advantage would then lie with the punter.

He also learned the value of not trying to recoup losses too quickly. He became both punter and bookmaker.

He also became an owner in the most spectacular fashion, buying the 1975 Irish Cesarewitch winner Cill Dara at the age of 24. The horse was trained by Con Collins, who then prepared her to win the same race the following year.

> J. P. goes for quality. He's looking for potential Cheltenham winners, and the whole Irish nation is involved in Cheltenham.
>
> RAYMOND SMITH, *Irish Independent*

Cheltenham bookmakers first took notice of McManus in 1975 when he left the Queen's Hotel at the top of the promenade in Cheltenham with a satchel full of cash, walked into a bookmaker's and put it all on an Irish-trained Gold Cup contestant. It lost.

The Observer sportswriter Hugh McIlvanney named him the Sundance Kid after the 1979 Cheltenham Festival, and the phrase became a favourite reference point for colour writers. Like many Irish owners, McManus backed his horses heavily when they were going for races he thought they might win, not always successfully. He once wrote to the English bookmaking firms saying that if they extended any more credit to him, they did so at their peril.

He picked the National Hunt Chase in Cheltenham as his first big target at the festival, reckoning it was the weakest in the festival in terms of class and therefore the easiest to win, but Jack of Trumps (1978) and Deep Gale (1979) both fell. McManus had gambled £50,000 on Deep Gale. His Eddie O'Grady-trained Jack of Trumps fell at the seventeenth in the 1978 National Hunt Chase because, in the words of jockey Niall Boots Madden, 'The others weren't good enough. He settled to a certain degree but they just couldn't go quick enough to allow him to settle completely.' A year later he gambled £50,000 on Deep Gale to win the same race. Again it fell. When the Edward O'Grady-trained Bit of a Skite eventually won the same race in 1983, McManus hadn't backed him.

Among punters he acquired mythic status after he took £250,000 off the Cheltenham bookmakers by backing his own horse, Mister Donovan, again trained by Edward O'Grady, from 6/1 to 9/2 to win the 1982 SunAlliance Chase. He described it as 'a nice little touch'.

The annual McManus punts at Cheltenham, the identity of the

horse who will carry his cash, the crafty men who train and ride them, and the jubilant scenes when the winners return to unsaddle, became the currency of Cheltenham in the nineties and noughties.

Not all of them succeeded. Another horse trained by Eddie O'Grady, Gimme Five, was backed from 10/1 to 4/1 in the Gold Card Handicap in 1994 but finished 20th. 'He almost ran away with me down to the start,' Charlie Swan recalled. 'He was wearing blinkers for the first time and at no stage did I think he was going to win.'

J. P.'s racing colours are based on the Treaty hurling club. He named some of his racehorses after members of the 1973 Limerick hurling team, including Joe Mac, named for Joe McKenna, which was backed to 6/4 in the 1998 Champion Bumper, but was second to Alexander Banquet, saving bookmakers about £2 m in winnings. 'He was too green,' jockey Conor O'Dwyer recalled, 'but he was beaten by a good horse.'

Even at Cheltenham, the strongest market on the calendar, he began to experience difficulty getting his bets on. Many refused to take his money. McManus was limited to a small number of brave bookmakers. In 1994 when Time for a Run won the Coral Cup at 11/1, the bookies would offer no better than 8/1. He had instructed one of his brothers to put the money on if the bet was 10/1 or better. His brother arrived back to the box just in time to see the horse win and told him there was no bet.

Bath-based bookmaker Stephen Little took a bet of £30,000 to win £250,000 on McManus's horse Gimme Five in the 1994 festival. It finished down the field. The following day McManus returned to Little to bet £80,000 to win £155,000 on Danoli in his old stomping ground, the Novices Hurdle, and more than recouped the previous day's losses. The phrase he used after the bet has become part of Cheltenham folklore: 'That put the wheels back on the bike.'

Unusually for a rich owner, McManus's runners attract widespread popular support. The sight of his emerald green and orange hooped colours causes a ripple of excitement through the crowds at race meetings throughout the two islands. He is apt to declare, as he did with Istabraq: 'The public own the horse now.'

He gets it about national hunt racing.

Not all owners do.

J. P.'s arrival is one of the rituals of the festival. His appearances are a bit special, which is why he is never taken for granted.

EDWARD GILLESPIE, Cheltenham's managing director

J. P. moved to another type of accumulator. He accumulated horses, friends and a reputation for finding the best odds and knowing when to strike. He accumulated and accumulated until he became the richest man in racing, apart from the sheikhs and Robert Sangster. His strategy was so successful that within five years he was terrorising bookmakers across Ireland, England and France.

From 1992, shortly after he gave up his bookmaker's licence, his attention turned to another kind of punt. McManus's mate and partner in many of his new business dealings was Dermot Desmond, whose northside Dublin accent and absence of a university education betrays an incisive business mind and whose political advice was sought by governments and proved the foundation of the 1995–2008 boom years.

Together they indulged that other national passion, the one that you can discover at Cheltenham by reading the sponsors' names—bricks and mortar.

The brash Sandy Lane Hotel in Barbados, purchased by McManus and Desmond, became a symbol of their wealth and of the new generation of Irish bookie-whisperers.

Desmond showed him how to team up with Michael Smurfit and others to make serious money from stocks and property deals in Ireland and beyond. They also entered the world of cross-channel soccer. Desmond had become the largest shareholder in Glasgow Celtic after Fergus McCann. McManus too became a big investor in Manchester United.

The most inspirational of these new alliances was between McManus, Magnier and Lewis. McManus turned to taking a punt on currency, and saw his fortune rise from £80 m to £120 m in the five years 1994–99, playing what he calls the money wheel of currencies and bonds.

His address in Switzerland, where he moved from his home at Martinstown in Co. Limerick to Geneva for tax purposes, gives us a clue that most of what happens in the real world of J. P. takes place far from the bookmaker's ring.

But all the time he kept up his interest in horses and maintained 100 in training in Ireland. He is a generous benefactor and contributed

£50 m towards the new national sports campus at Abbotstown, which was only partially completed. McManus organises the charity pro-am that has brought the best golfing field to Ireland outside the AmEx in Mount Juliet in September 2002 and 2004 or the Canada Cup at Portmarnock in 1960, including Tiger Woods.

He shrugs off his wealth as the accumulation of horseflesh and luck, cautions people to beware of the certainty, and carries a naive gait, framed by his west of Ireland shoulders. 'His success is no accident,' an anonymous private bookmaker claimed in one newspaper profile. 'He has a tremendous mathematical brain and he puts in a lot of effort.'

He has very simple advice for the gambler: to follow the going and compare it with the horse's form over similar ground.

This is the key to J. P.'s 'public profile'. He is the realisation of every punter's dream. He personifies the ambition of everyone who lays an each-way bet on a maidens' race on a wet Wednesday evening in Ballinrobe.

The reality is that punters don't end up as multimillionaires. Not then. Not now. Some of the most heavily backed failures in Cheltenham history have been McManus horses. For every Istabraq, there was a Joe Mac or Deep Gale.

He shows how much success really means to him. In any other sport people would run the successful man down. But if J. P. does well at Cheltenham, all the Irish do well with him. Of all the horses he has run, Istabraq was the favourite.

Yes I would put my last £40,000 on Istabraq. I would also mortgage my house and put out another £40,000.

TED WALSH to JOHN McCRIRICK on Channel 4's *Morning Line* programme before Istabraq's run in the SunAlliance Chase at Cheltenham, 1997

Istabraq danced up the hill to win the Royal & SunAlliance Novice Hurdle, offering salvation for Irish punters embarrassed by a first day at the 1997 festival without a single success.

What one observer described as 'a sense of desperation in the marketplace' had forced his price down to 6/5 and showed the level of expectation that had accumulated around the horse. The Cheltenham stewards, fearing the sort of scenes that had followed Imperial Call's victory a year earlier, had new security plans in place should Danoli win the Gold Cup. They had to implement them a day early.

There was a scare in the paddock, Aidan O'Brien professing afterwards that he did not think the horse would win. Charlie Swan dropped the horse back to last and then came through to win, the horse surviving a bump at the second last. The trainer survived the indignity of being rugby tackled by Edward Gillespie in the winner's enclosure, only to have Ted Walsh save the day, and the owner survived a loss of £100,000 the previous day to recover his money. 'I had a few quid on Finnegan's Hollow but downed tools after his fall,' McManus said. 'I chased my losses with this horse and now show a small profit.' McManus rang John Durkan in New York to tell him of the victory.

Sadly, Durkan lost his battle with cancer and died the following January. Istabraq ran one more time that season, a nine-length victory at Punchestown.

I had to make it a test of stamina. I was under the impression that the others were queuing up behind me, waiting to challenge. Sixty yards after the final flight I looked to my right. I couldn't believe I was so far in front. The crowds were making such a fuss I thought there had to be something coming. I looked again, this time to the left. There was nothing there.

CHARLIE SWAN after Istabraq's first Champion Hurdle in 1998

Istabraq went into the 1998 Champion Hurdle with nine successive victories behind him. McManus laid on £30,000 at 3/1 with bookmaker Victor Chandler. The race was predicted to be an Anglo-Irish battle in the great Cheltenham tradition between Istabraq and Malcolm Jefferson's Dato Star. Istabraq surprised even his jockey with the manner in which he won by twelve lengths, the widest margin for 66 years.

Theatreworld, Istabraq's stablemate who had raced on the flat during the previous summer, came in second with the 6/1 Dato Star nowhere to be seen.

Istabraq was unexpectedly beaten at Aintree in his next race due to the desperately heavy ground, but he went undefeated through the next season and was brought almost casually through the field by Charlie Swan and caught the long-time leader French Holly at the last to win his second Champion Hurdle by three and a half lengths.

His supporters did not doubt he would win the treble, although the novice race at Cheltenham that year was won by Hors La Loi III in a time two seconds faster than the Champion Hurdle, and was turned over by Limestone Lad (another 'people's champion', this time from humble origins) on unsuitably soft ground at Fairyhouse in November. He was showing an increasing distaste for heavy ground.

When he arrived in Cheltenham he was bleeding from a nostril, but he made his third victory look ridiculously easy. The day before the 2000 Champion Hurdle, Paddy Power and Liam Cashman both announced that they would be paying out on ante-post betting on Istabraq, his victory was such a formality.

Charlie Swan played the now customary Istabraq tactics, cruising around the inside and bringing him carefully through the field before sending him powerfully clear at the final fence and bursting up the hill to win by four lengths from Hors La Loi III and Blue Royal. His time of 3 minutes 48.1 seconds beat the previous Champion Hurdle record time set by Make A Stand in 1997 of 3 minutes 48.4 seconds.

He was put away for another season, for unlike great hurdlers of the past, Istabraq's races were carefully chosen. At only 8 years old there seemed little to stop him becoming the only horse ever to win four Champion Hurdles.

> The three-times champion found the years howling all around him yesterday, but he leaves not as a loser but the great monarch of this Gloucestershire realm for so many years.
>
> RICHARD EDMONDSON, *Independent*

Even before that 2001 Cheltenham meeting was cancelled there were signs of trouble for Istabraq. He looked slightly heavier than usual. Shockingly, he fell for the first time ever when looking tired at the final flight. It was probably a combination of the extra weight and dire ground, but nevertheless rumours that the champion may have been on his way out were rife. He won his next race, although the winner of the race in which he fell, Moscow Flyer, had this time fallen himself. He again fell at the final flight in the next race with Moscow Flyer again taking the race.

When he reappeared the following season, he defeated Bust Out by just a head in December, a surprisingly small margin considering he was rated 25 lb superior. He looked edgy and uneasy in the parade ring before his attempt to win a fourth Champion Hurdle and his jockey was never happy with him. Charlie Swan had been instructed by Aidan O'Brien not to take any chances with the horse. After clearing the second, Istabraq gradually dropped back through the field, from eighth to last.

To the astonishment of the packed stands, he was then eased to the outside, where he was brought to a standstill before the race had even taken shape, 'the Festival equivalent of a great boxing champion's corner throwing in the towel halfway through the first round', J. A. McGrath wrote in the *Daily Telegraph*. The Cheltenham crowd gave him a standing ovation as he bowed out. He was later found to have pulled muscles in his back. Hors La Loi iii won. The unlucky Valiramix was simply cruising throughout before fatally falling after clipping his hooves.

Istabraq won 23 of his 29 races over hurdles in all and made over £1 m in prize money. Timeform rated him the equal of Monksfield in 1979 and 2 lb behind Night Nurse in 1977, joint second greatest hurdler of modern times.

'He wasn't the old Istabraq. He has been very stiff this year, and Charlie said he hit his back at the first flight,' Aidan O'Brien said. He called it a privilege to have had Istabraq under his care and said he would probably never have a national hunt horse so talented again.

Chapter 10 ~

| CAPTAINS, KINGS AND WAR

*I think he's a bit special. Terry and I adored him when we
saw him in a point-to-point in Ireland and we were
determined to have him.*

HENRIETTA KNIGHT, November 1999

Tom Costello is the king of horse dealers. From his base not far
from Spancilhill, as the ballad might go, he buys foals and rears
them until they are 3 or 4 years of age. He then sells them on.

He knows the breeders and small farmers who don't like going to big
sales. He knows their stallion masters and pedigrees and what their
foals have done. He speaks their language and they trust him.

He enjoys closing a deal. He will write a cheque for a small amount.
Then he will engage in conversation and write a cheque for a larger
amount. Eventually the price will be agreed. Tom is happy, the seller is
happy, and an ancient ritual has been re-enacted.

When the time comes they get a run and they are sold off, generally
after winning at a point-to-point. Now Tom is the salesman. He will be
asked if he has a special horse. 'I do,' he will say. 'But I don't want to sell
it.' The price is already rising.

There are hundreds of farmers who make a living spotting potential
national hunt winners. Tom is the best. He has put half a dozen
Cheltenham Gold Cup winners through his hands: The Thinker, Cool
Dawn, Cool Ground, Imperial Call, Midnight Court and Best Mate.

Best Mate is his most famous. Tom knew his sire, Un Desperado, a
French bred standing at Declan Weld's Old Meadow Stud in Donadea
in north Kildare. The horse was bred in Meath by a Dutch breeder,
Jacques Van't Hart, so Tom had him spotted and bought him for 2,500
guineas as a foal at a Fairyhouse sale in 1995. He was entered in a point-
to-point in Lismore in February 1999. Best Mate ran poorly and was
pulled up before three out on the desperately heavy ground, but his
stately gait caught the eye of two celebrity visitors.

Henrietta Knight, a former schoolteacher who had taken out a full training licence late in life on the family farm in Oxfordshire, and her husband Terry Biddlecombe, an ex-jockey who rode against Arkle in the 1960s, were picking their way through the Lismore mud when they first saw him. It was love at first sight. 'We bought him virtually on the day because there were about five people queuing up behind us trying to do the same.'

'It was pissing down with rain, a right miserable day, and we had owners with us looking at another horse we'd come to see,' Biddlecombe recalled later. 'But I couldn't take my eyes off this other fella in the parade ring. There was something about his outlook. It reminded me a bit of Arkle. I said to Hen: I've seen a lovely horse. This is one we've got to have.'

'Terry and I have just seen the horse of our dreams,' Henrietta wrote to her most supportive owners, Jim and Valerie Lewis. 'He is the perfect racehorse.'

On 29 March 1999 Tom met Henrietta Knight and the Lewises at Shannon Airport from the 11.15 flight from Heathrow. Within half an hour he had them at Fenloe to show them the prospect.

'He looked superb and once more he stood up against the wall for a thorough examination', Henrietta recalled in her book about Best Mate.

Tom then led him through the doors of the huge indoor school behind the stables. The Lewises followed behind and were told to stand in the middle of this huge covered area. Down the long sides of this rectangular-shaped building were two jumps. One of these comprised various timber poles balanced on large barrels, and on the other side there was a plastic steeplechase fence. The poles were about three feet off the ground and the chase fence was over four foot high.

It looked solid and imposing. Tom Costello and his son picked up a couple of lunge whips and stood at either end. Best Mate was let loose. Off he went, with a buck and a kick. He cantered round and round the outside of the school on the deep sandy surface, jumping the two obstacles every time he reached them. He always met them correctly and in his stride, demonstrating his athleticism. They stopped him with a shout of whoa and he obediently stood still, head held proudly, nostrils barely moving despite the sudden, somewhat violent exercise. He returned to the yard and Jim Lewis took another look at him in the stable. He returned to the house and after twenty minutes of negotiation Lewis bought the horse.

'The only reason I've sold you this horse,' Tom Costello said, 'is because I know Henrietta will train the horse better than anyone else.'

So ended the Clare connection with the first horse to win three Gold Cups since Arkle.

We may not have found Arkle's better, but yesterday we found his equal. This may just have been racing's answer to the Second Coming.

MARCUS ARMYTAGE, Daily Telegraph, March 2003

Another Tom Costello horse that had been tested in a point-to-point in Lismore (and another to be called 'the next Arkle' after winning his debut over fences) was Ireland's big hope for the 2002 Gold Cup. Willie Mullins was training Florida Pearl who won four Hennessy Gold Cups but was never to win the Cheltenham Gold Cup. He finished third in 1999 (as 5/2 favourite), second in 2000, and a notable victim of foot and mouth in 2001 when he was 9 and in his prime. Persuaded by critics that the final two and a half furlongs were too much for Florida Pearl, Mullins ran him in the Queen Mother in 2003, but he was not fast enough over two miles and finished unplaced.

The 2001 Gold Cup had a competitive field with eighteen contestants. The French-bred First Gold had been snapped up by Aidan O'Brien early in the season but was out through injury. The favourite was the defending champion Looks Like Trouble, injured the season before, but a horse that had won his only outing of the season stylishly. Such was the strength of the field that 1999 winner See More Business was considered third outsider.

In the absence of First Gold, there were eight contestants from Ireland, led by Willie Mullins's prospect, the King George winner Florida Pearl, his stablemate Alexander Banquet and Mouse Morris's fast improving Foxchapel King. The very fast ground was likely to favour the former Triumph Hurdle and Irish Grand National winner Commanche Court, trained by TV personality Ted Walsh and ridden by Ted's son Ruby.

Commanche Court arrived to fight out the lead with See More Business at the third last. But Best Mate had been improving from the seventeenth fence. Kerry jockey Jim Culloty took up a position on the inside rail and began to accelerate, taking the lead at the last.

Best Mate powered up the hill to win by a length and three-quarters. Culloty went on to win the Aintree Grand National on Bindaree a few weeks later.

'Anyone not satisfied with this will have to wait a long, long time for it to get any better, unless, of course, you count Best Mate's third Gold Cup win in 12 months' time', Peter Thomas wrote in the *Racing Post*.

The wait was worth it. Henrietta Knight and Terry Biddlecombe claimed in 2002 that Best Mate was a stronger, better horse than a year earlier. He had won two races during the season, including a rattling defeat of Marlborough in the King George. The ground, officially good and soft in places, was in his favour. He started at 13/8, with the big Irish challenger expected to be Michael Hourigan's exciting novice Beef Or Salmon, who had won all four of his races that season but misjudged the third and finished his challenge early. Culloty sent Best Mate clear at the second last and he surged through to win by ten lengths from Truckers Tavern.

The former Lismore point-to-pointer, now 9, returned in 2003 to match Arkle's treble. The 20/1 outsider Harbour Pilot, ridden by Paul Carberry, appeared to hamper Best Mate as he made his move turning into the straight, but Best Mate managed to grab the lead, jumped the final fence clear and held off the late surge of Sir Rembrandt by half a length to become the fourth horse to win a treble.

'Times change and tracks change,' Terry Biddlecombe said. 'The fences are different. But this horse, in a Gold Cup, jumped immaculately, didn't put a foot wrong. Arkle used to gallop through two or three.

'I said to Jim: Be lucky, have a good ride and get round safe, get him switched off early, and he was absolutely brilliant—poetry in motion. Nobody could have executed it better.'

'Just look at him. He thinks he's Arkle,' Knight had said in October 2000.

Best Mate seemed destined to go for a fourth Gold Cup to beat Arkle's record. It was a Taaffe that stopped him.

When this horse won his first race at Leopardstown, my first son, Pat, was born the same day. We jokingly said that now we'd found the new Pat Taaffe, all we had to do was find the next Arkle.

TOM TAAFFE

Tom Taaffe has a policy of buying horses young instead of buying established point-to-pointers. It makes the process cheaper but also much longer and it involves a lot of patience, both on the part of the trainer and the owners. One of those owners was property developer Conor Clarkson.

Conor Clarkson is not from a horsey background but grew up quite close to Leopardstown and says he has had a passion for racing since his grandfather brought him to his first race meeting as a child. 'The very first horse I was involved in never even won a race and I subsequently owned a full brother and a half-brother to him, and neither of them were any good either, but that didn't diminish the enthusiasm.

'Around that time I was in Adare one evening and ran into Michael Hourigan. When you meet Michael anywhere close to his home, you'll be invited to breakfast at the yard the next morning and you don't get out of the yard without owning a leg of something. That happened to me and I've had tremendous luck with him down the years.'

Success in business allowed him to dabble with horses, initially through partnerships and syndicates, and he placed horses with Tom Taaffe, now training at his father's farm in Alasty, Ardclough, in the mid-1990s. Tom Taaffe barely remembers Arkle, the name that dominates his every introduction into racing circles, even if he was the first horse he ever sat on, but he had inherited his father's terrific attention to detail and was building up a winning reputation of his own. He was also proving adept at spotting future winners.

'Through direct ownership and partnerships I had a number of horses with Tom and I got reasonably close to him. He's very good in that when you go down there, he gives you the full tour, and while in the early days I might just have been another owner, he was always very good to spend time with you. And if you walk the fields around his place, you'll always notice the number of young stock he has about the place.

'One of the things we decided to do early on was to buy young stock through Tom as foals and because of that we've been lucky enough to come across a few good horses—King's Advocate, Baker's Bridge and other good horses that have won for us.'

There was one particular animal he saw grow from a foal into a yearling and then into a 2-year old. 'It was an Old Vic horse out of Fairy Blaze and one day I decided to ask about it. Because of the cost of owning horses I was usually involved in partnerships, but I did buy the odd one on my own and this particular day I just spurted out that I'd like to buy the Old Vic 2-year old.'

His daughter Katie was learning the Letterland alphabet system at the time and although she wanted to call the horse after herself ('not too good an idea for a male horse' Clarkson told the *Irish Examiner*), her father asked her to come up with a name beginning with the letter K and she picked Kicking King.

Kicking King won his first 4-year-old bumper at Leopardstown in January 2002, on the same day Tom Taaffe's son was born. Mick O'Toole, trainer of Davy Lad, came to Clarkson in the winner's enclosure and said: 'You're one lucky man. You've got something special there.'

'I'm a fairly patient owner,' Clarkson said, 'and I tend to let trainers get on with the job without interfering, but I'm a great believer that I like to see something in a horse first time out.'

Even though Taaffe was under pressure to get to the maternity hospital, he insisted on being there for the celebratory photographs, telling the delighted owner, 'I want to be in the picture because I'm telling you that one day that horse will win a Gold Cup.'

He went to the Arkle at Cheltenham in 2004, finishing second at 7/2 by a length to Well Chief (who was in receipt of 5 lb). While the connections were disappointed, they knew they had time on their hands.

> Kicking King will not run in the Gold Cup due to having not scoped well this morning.
>
> Statement by TOM TAAFFE

Victory at Gowran and a second place to Beef Or Salmon in the James Nicholson at Downpatrick convinced Taaffe he had a Gold Cup horse.

Would he stay the three miles? There was one race which would tell. In 2004 the three mile King George VI had been transferred to Sandown from Kempton, its home since the first running in 1937, because of redevelopment at the Sunbury track. It was the scene of Kicking King's greatest victory, when he survived a terrible mistake at the last on the way to his first victory in the race.

He was brought to a stop, got going again and was going away at the line. 'We rode him over an easy three miles to find out if he'd stay,' Taaffe said, 'and if he hadn't made that mistake at the last, he'd have won by ten lengths.' His price for the Gold Cup came down to 7/1.

They planned a racecourse gallop three weeks before the Gold Cup. As Clarkson was driving down a drenched Spanish motorway, Taaffe rang him to tell him the horse had run terribly.

A routine trachea wash, a process in which a tube is stuck down a horse's throat and what is flushed out is minutely inspected, revealed an infection. Treating it with antibiotics would have ruled him out of the race.

'Tom rang me to say the horse would not be able to run,' Clarkson said. 'I pulled over and it was two hours before I was able to manoeuvre the car back on to the road again.'

Best Mate was cut to 5/2 favourite from 3/1. A few clever souls didn't believe he was out, and backed Kicking King on Betfair at 999/1 a few days before the race.

Taaffe was considering giving him antibiotics, but then thought he would just give him some time and let nature take its course. 'A few days later he nearly jumped over a gate in his paddock and I thought, okay, we'll put the wheels back on the wagon.'

Two weeks later Clarkson was out one Sunday morning with his children at the Powerscourt waterfall when the mobile rang and Taaffe was on the other end telling him the horse was jumping out of his skin.

'I was like, what the hell are you telling me here, and he was saying, well, he's only missed a week and a bit and while it's not ideal, it's not the end of the world either.' Taaffe waited until Thursday, a week and a day before the first Gold Cup was due to be run on a Friday, before announcing that Kicking King was back in business. That same day a burst blood vessel on the gallops put Best Mate out of the race. A few days later Farmer Jack, who was supplemented for the race at a cost of £17,500 the previous week, died on Philip Hobbs's gallops after suffering a suspected heart attack. Beef Or Salmon, Strong Flow, Celestial Gold and Kicking King were all left within a point of one another at the top of the market.

Before the Gold Cup, many were asking whether Kicking King would stay the trip. He stayed all right, far better than many racegoers, who set off at three-day pace, only to hit the wall halfway through the fourth afternoon.

EDDIE FREMANTLE, *The Observer*, 20 March 2005

In the parade ring Sir Rembrandt was chomping at the bit. As the jockeys gave their mounts a peep over the first fence before wheeling around and cantering up to the start, Barry Geraghty looked relaxed.

The drying ground was in Kicking King's favour on Gold Cup morning. The taps had been turned on at Prestbury Park overnight and he was installed as the 4/1 favourite.

A natural pacemaker, Grey Abbey took up the running. Barry Geraghty settled his mount in midfield and waited, galloping effortlessly through a series of quick, efficient jumps without the hint of a mistake. His performance was, as Greg Wood commented in *The Guardian*, 'as close to flawless as steeplechasing ever gets.'

Beef Or Salmon made a hash of two fences and Paul Carberry had to ride him vigorously just to maintain contact, before pulling up. Sir Rembrandt and Grey Abbey were four or five lengths clear of Kicking King as they went over the water jump for the second time. The distinctive Grey Abbey still led over the fourth last, stalked closely by Kicking King who landed ahead at the third last, followed by Take The Stand. Questions had been raised before the race about Kicking King's stamina, but once he had cleared the last leading by about a length and a half, the doubts evaporated in the spring sunshine as he galloped five lengths clear of Take The Stand, with Sir Rembrandt another eight away in third. As Offaly-born comedian Barry Glendenning put it, 'He won pulling a cart.'

'The one thing that everyone missed,' Taaffe said, 'was that if you look at him very carefully as he picks himself up, the first thing he does is to prick his ears. That was what told me that he still had plenty left to give.'

'Kicking King cantered regally over the line,' Stephen Bierley wrote in *The Guardian*, 'thereby underlining the old adage that distance, weight and the going become academic when a horse has true class.'

'It was just an amazing sequence of events,' Clarkson said. 'I have to say it was the best sporting day of my life when he won. I was so lucky. My parents were there, a lot of family and friends, and the whole thing was just unbelievable. The thing that really thrilled me the most was the style and the manner in which he won. If he was never to do anything again, I couldn't complain.'

Tom Taaffe said: 'The return of the name Taaffe to the winner's enclosure was always going to get the nostalgia industry going. My father got the recognition he got through his achievements both as a jockey and then as a trainer. I'm sure he is looking down on us now and I'm pretty sure he's not embarrassed by what we're doing.'

At the age of 7, Kicking King was among the very best winners of this race, only the fourth horse to win the King George and the Gold Cup in the same season, after Arkle, Desert Orchid and Best Mate. But he was never to compete in it again.

There is nothing in the Bible that says you can't gamble.

FR SEÁN BREEN

Kicking King, withdrawn through injury and unexpectedly back in the race, had had some spiritual help. He was blessed by Fr Seán Breen, unofficial chaplain to the Irish dimension at Cheltenham.

Fr Breen, parish priest at Ballymore Eustace, first attended the Cheltenham Festival in 1964 to see the first of Arkle's three triumphs in the Gold Cup. For the next 41 years, he said, 'the only thing that's stopped me have been funerals. It's very inconsiderate of people to die just before Cheltenham.'

Seán Breen was born on 9 March 1937 in Co. Cavan, where his father was a schoolmaster. He grew up in a small town in farming country, but he didn't have any particular feeling for horses as a boy, once falling off a neighbour's pony when he tried to ride it, a deterrent to any further efforts in the saddle.

As a boy he was a good tennis player, reaching the semi-finals of the under-18s competition held in Fitzwilliam. He caught the racing bug from his brother Ciaran, a dentist, who was a keen follower of the turf. 'If I didn't see a horse for a week I'd be unwell' was a Breener phrase.

Only later as a young priest in north County Dublin did he become entranced with races, largely through his friendship with such people as Jim Dreaper, Tom Dreaper's son, and Joanna Morgan, a trainer.

After St Patrick's College, Cavan, he studied for the priesthood at Clonliffe College, Dublin, and was ordained by Archbishop John Charles McQuaid in 1962. He served initially as assistant priest in the chaplaincy of Mount Carmel Hospital and later in Rathdrum, Co. Wicklow, and Ballymun. He served in Sandyford, Navan Road and Templeogue between 1972 and 1995. He was then appointed parish priest of Eadestown before moving to Ballymore in 2004.

Towards the end of his life he became the subject of an annual media frenzy in the lead-in to the festival, when TV and print media queued up to meet the punting priest. 'They pick my brain,' he told Bill Barich, 'if I am not being presumptuous about having a brain.'

The tales about him were recycled endlessly. During his annual Mass on St Patrick's Day for racegoers at the Thistle Hotel in Cheltenham (better known by regulars under its previous name), one of his prayers implored that the bookmakers would have enough money to pay out all the successful punters.

In praying for the late bookmaker Jimmy Ryan at another festival, he added: 'I hope he's entertaining God as much as he entertained us.'

And he managed to bring new life to old jokes, like the one about the Protestant vicar who backed the horses he saw a priest blessing until one of them lost. 'Ah that's the problem with you Prods' went the punch-line reply. 'You can't tell the difference between a blessing and the last rites.'

His close friendship with Niall Quinn in 2007 led him to visit Sunderland to bless the Stadium of Light.

'I bought a horse with another priest and we really didn't want the bishops to know about it so we named the animal Nobody Knows,' he said. 'Whenever anyone questioned me about the horse they'd inevitably ask its name. I'd just whisper: Nobody Knows, to which the response was always, Yes, yes, but what's his name really?' Nobody Knows won six races.

He later joined forces with three businessmen, formed what they called the Heavenly Syndicate and bought a horse called One Won One. Trained by Fr Breen's friend Joanna Morgan and ridden by Kieron Fallon, it went on to win twelve races including a group 3 sprint at the Curragh and five Listed races including the President's Cup in Abu Dhabi in 2001, and £500,000 in prize money.

Fr Breen was also co-owner of Portant Fella, which won fifteen races, four of them in three weeks in 2006, and Show Blessed, a winner of several jump races. He wrote a weekly tipping column for the *Kildare Post*, in which he flagged the Grand National winners of 2005 (Hedgehunter) and 2006 (Numbersixvalverde). On one occasion at the Phoenix Park he was riding out for Joanna Morgan when the horse bolted and threw his rider. He suffered a broken leg.

He had his own pundit's spot on the local radio station, Kildare FM, earning the gratitude of one listener who had harvested €180: 'I'm a born-again Christian,' the listener declared. In 2005 he gave parishioners and punters a tip that Cardinal Ratzinger would be a good bet for the next Pope at 13/2, but said he 'did not back him myself out of reverence'. His advice was, 'If you have a bet, stick to your first choice and only gamble what you can afford to lose.' He ministered to a people who always mixed spirituality with horse racing. Eadestown man John Archibald's mare, Irish Lass, with rosary beads and scapulars around her neck—the famous 'Paidrín Mare'—had won a race against Black and All Black, the champion horse of a Protestant landowner Ralph Gore in penal times.

Almost inevitably Fr Breen had a racehorse named after him. The Breener was the first winner sent out by the English trainer Oliver Sherwood and subsequently won the Challow Hurdle before finishing third in the Supreme Novices at Cheltenham. The following season he won his first steeplechase, but next time out broke his neck in a fall at Cheltenham.

Fr Breen died in February 2009, and did not live to see his horse Raise Your Heart, trained by his friend Joanna Morgan, compete in a hurdle race at Cheltenham. The congregation at his funeral included Kieron Fallon and the trainers Dermot Weld and Jim Bolger. The Mass lasted two hours; there were 37 priests concelebrating. Among the 'performers' were the comedian Brendan Grace and the singer Red Hurley. Archbishop Diarmuid Martin said in his tribute: 'He was not a sacristy priest, but one who reached out to all walks of life through his own personality which was larger than life. Seán ministered with his talents and his weaknesses and without self-seeking. The secret of his being well loved was just that.'

> I'm very sorry for Best Mate's connections that he couldn't run, but if anyone was going to stop him it was the Taaffe name, especially to protect Arkle.
>
> TOM TAAFFE, press conference after 2004 Gold Cup

Kicking King went on to win the Irish Gold Cup at Punchestown, but from there on the tide would turn against him.

In the Betfair Chase at Haydock he pulled a shoe in the gluey ground and damaged a hoof. The King George VI returned to Kempton in 2005 and Kicking King emphasised his place in history by retaining his title, but it was here that he sustained the injury that was to end his career when landing at the third last.

Taaffe noticed how his horse shortened his action and 'changed to his left fore' maybe a hundred yards from the line. He hung on under tremendous pressure from Monkerhostin to win. Afterwards vet Jimmy Kelly identified a slow bleed into the tendon.

They pin-fired the injury and slowed the recuperation process. 'It's always worrying when you're handling legs,' Taaffe said. 'You nearly become a vet yourself. You sense things. You can almost smell them coming. That was the low point for me—the worst nightmare. But you've got to move on. No one else is going to run the yard for you. And sometimes it's awful important to remind yourself that you're just talking about a horse. That people are dying all over the world. That if everyone sat down at a table and handed in their problems, you'd be very quick taking back your own when you heard everyone else's.'

His last race was a nineteen-length second of four behind another former Gold Cup winner, War Of Attrition. 'I think he was a great ambassador for racing and for ourselves,' Taaffe said. 'It's great that he retired in one piece.'

Little wonder the British are keeping their best horses at home. Even the non-runners here would be too good for them.

CHRIS McGRATH reporting from Punchestown for the
Independent, 27 April 2006

A successor was on his way. War Of Attrition had been beaten by a neck by Brave Inca in the 2005 Supreme Novices Hurdle. The following October he beat Kicking King, the Cheltenham Gold Cup winner, by three lengths in the Daily Star Chase at Punchestown.

He had not previously won beyond two and three-quarter miles, but he delivered on his promise when he headed an Irish one-two-three in the Gold Cup of 2006 at 15/2.

Conor O'Dwyer, just short of his 40th birthday, and on board his first Gold Cup winner since the exuberant victory of Imperial Call in 1996, settled his horse behind the early pace and moved towards the front with about a mile left to run. Just as Kicking King had a year earlier, he cruised into the lead halfway down the hill and turned on the pace with two to jump, holding off Willie Mullins's former Aintree Grand National winner Hedgehunter (who lost a shoe) up the final climb to win by two and a half lengths, with Michael O'Brien's Forget The Past seven lengths back in third.

'I saw the Hedgehunter colours coming,' O'Dwyer said. 'But the way my horse jumped the second last, nothing was going to go by him. It is easy to ride him. Even the last two fences he stood off. He just loves his racing and loves his jumping.'

'I've always held this horse in the highest regard,' trainer Mouse Morris said. 'He has a high cruising speed and a lot of boot, and when you have that in a horse who stays as well, you've got yourself a real racehorse. I told Conor I didn't mind if he came up the inside or ran on the outside—the only place I didn't want him to be was in the middle as that was where the ground was most cut up.'

War Of Attrition had been purchased by Eddie O'Leary from Mullingar four years beforehand on behalf of his high profile brother, Ryanair CEO Michael O'Leary, the most successful and most iconoclastic of the new Irish entrepreneurs. According to Michael, Eddie always thought he had a chance of a Gold Cup. 'I thought he was dreaming. He's well named, like his owner, always causing trouble.'

The 4/1 favourite Beef Or Salmon trailed away for the fourth time to finish eleventh, convincing his trainer Michael Hourigan that the horse does not like the Cheltenham course. 'There were no excuses. He was off the bridle too early,' said Hourigan. Paul Carberry agreed. 'He was never travelling. The ground did not suit him.'

War Of Attrition's success was the ninth at the meeting for an Irish-trained horse, equalling the record set in 1958 and 2005, and the tenth, Whyso Mayo, came in the next race. 'For as long as the economy is good, people will be prepared to keep the best horses at home in Ireland and not be forced to sell them on,' said Mouse Morris.

I never heard a noise like that in the valley—it was so sustained, so passionate, you knew you were living through one of the great moments in Cheltenham.

MIKE DILLON, the chief oddsmaker of Ladbrokes, after the victory of Moscow Flyer in 2005

The Gold Cup had started as a novelty and turned into an institution. The Champion Hurdle had started similarly, but now the Queen Mother Chase too was growing into an event in its own right, a mile and a quarter shorter than the Gold Cup with a commensurate increase in speed and spills.

More than once it has earned the title of the race of the festival. The horse that confirmed that trend was Jessica Harrington's Moscow Flyer in 2005. It helped that Moscow had a cult following of his own. His wide white star on his forehead and sheepskin noseband made him easy to spot.

Moscow Flyer was bought as an unbroken 4-year old for 17,500 guineas for Brian Kearney, for whom Moscow Flyer was his first horse. During his second season over hurdles he shot to prominence by beating Istabraq twice, the only horse to do so over hurdles.

'The attraction of national hunt racing is the excitement,' Kearney said after that season. 'You can be poised to win and then fall at the final fence. It happened to Istabraq against Moscow Flyer and it happened to Moscow Flyer at the second last against Istabraq.'

He was the archetypal small owner's horse in what was becoming a big money game. 'The fact that you can compete against the likes of J. P. and John Magnier and win is remarkable,' his owner told the *Sunday Business Post* in 2003. 'On the night we won the Arkle, I could have walked home across the Irish Sea.'

The story of Moscow Flyer was that if he stood up, he won (26 wins from 44 races). It meant lots of excitement for his huge following.

Like an Irish king, Moscow flyer had a resident *file*, Bill Barich. 'The tension between them,' he wrote, about the battle between Barry Geraghty (Moscow Flyer) and Ruby Walsh (Azertyuiop) for the 2004 Queen Mother, 'was reflected in the contrasting colours of their silks. No costume designer could have done a better job. Walsh was as bold as a crocus in bright yellow with a red star from the Mao era on his chest, while Geraghty wore black and white chevrons such as an escaped convict might sport, a thief out to rob the race. They were the only two in it, and they knew it.'

Moscow Flyer's steeplechasing career began with a fall at Fairyhouse, but he won the 2002 Arkle Chase at the Cheltenham Festival, was sent off the strongly backed 7/4 favourite for the 2003 Queen Mother to cruise clear in the straight to record an easy seven-length success, blundered at the fourth last fence in 2004 and unseated Barry Geraghty, allowing Azertyuiop to gallop to an impressive nine-length success.

Cheltenham is where Moscow Flyer belongs—he is an amazing horse in that, while he is 11, he pulls out like a 6-year old every morning and, touch wood, has never taken a lame step in his life.

BARRY GERAGHTY after Moscow Flyer's second success in the
Queen Mother

Moscow won the Queen Mother Champion Chase again in 2005. Azertyuiop made a vital jumping error which effectively ended his bid, with Moscow Flyer edging out Well Chief by two lengths.

After his horse's win at the age of 11, Barry Geraghty milked every last drop out of the reception which greeted his horse in the winner's enclosure with a Frankie Dettori-style flying dismount.

He told the press conference afterwards: 'He is the best that I have ridden. People have even claimed that Moscow Flyer is the best horse we have seen since Arkle, and I would not argue with that. You need to experience the lows to really appreciate the highs, and though we were really sad when he tipped up last year, it has made winning that much sweeter.'

'People tend to focus on the falls,' said Harrington, a former Irish Olympian in the three-day event, and therefore one whose opinion about leaping technique should be heeded. 'But they forget about just how good he is the rest of the time. Sure, he fell at Fairyhouse in his first chase, but that was just a typical novice's mistake; he'd been ballooning them extravagantly and discovered that when you get in a bit close to one, you can't do that.'

Moscow was retired after finishing fifth to Newmill in the 2006 Cheltenham Festival, despite a number of his main rivals failing to complete the course.

Appropriately, the new champion was another unsung Irish hero from a small yard, with Cork man Andrew McNamara, an un-known jockey at this level, on board, and with many happy punters also on board at the starting price of 16/1 or the even longer ante-post odds. As Moscow made his exit, there was a reminder of why Cheltenham is so precious to the Irish, and to the horse racing community in general.

He was brought out of retirement to contest the charity race at the 2007 Punchestown Festival with Jessica's daughter Kate in the saddle for a thrilling victory that received one of the biggest receptions of the week.

There he basked in the applause of the *Cosmhuintir* of national hunt, the people who understood and appreciated Moscow's magic and indeed Moscow's mysteries.

Chapter 11 ～

THEY DON'T RUN ANY FASTER BECAUSE YOU'RE THERE

For too long the odds have been too short, and our
pilgrims are not happy about it. Nor are they enamoured
by the hefty admission charge to the course or the
exorbitant price fixed by some hoteliers.
                    JOHN KELLY, *The Irish Times*, 6 March 1989

Many of Cheltenham's most ardent fans have never set foot on the course. Cheltenham is experienced in a bookie's shop, in the comfort of a local pub or a rural homestead. The great exodus to Cheltenham is not for the weak hearted. Airlines, ferry companies, hotels and restaurants and not least the course itself gouge the Cheltenham pilgrim with a ferocity that has not abated over the years.

The bookmakers who head to Cheltenham each year, rubbing their hands at the prospect of that £600 m turnover, are the most visible sign of what is now a billion euro industry. As much again is generated by off-course gambling.

'God knows why we have them in England and Ireland,' Bobby Beasley said about bookmakers in his 1974 biography. 'They suck the blood out of the sport.' Bookies were first asked to pay to keep the horse in oats in the 1930s, at a time when they were allowed to take bets only at the track, and were charged an entrance fee five times higher than the public admission.

After 1961, when off-course gambling was legalised, betting shops were asked to pay a levy which currently stands at about a tenth of their gross profit from horse racing.

Just give them enough to eat.

TOM COSTELLO, horse dealer who has produced seven Gold Cup winners, when asked what his secret was.

As Cheltenham's Gold Cup approaches its centenary, jump racing appears to be in good shape.

Some had feared that the abolition of hunting with dogs in England would jeopardise the supply of horses there and one of jumping's traditional nurseries, the point-to-point; that racing over jumps would share hunting's ignominy and eventually become as distasteful as coursing; and that the Cheltenham Gold Cup won by Arkle would go the way of the Waterloo Cup won by Master McGrath.

This would effectively hand Cheltenham over to the Irish and the French and make the festival unsustainable. It did not happen. Point-to-point racing in England is flourishing despite (or even because of) the hunting ban.

The debate over the hunting ban masked a more serious concern: that old-fashioned jumping stock is fast disappearing in favour of horses bred from flat lines. Stamina, jumping technique and durability have been sacrificed at the altar of speed, resulting in more frequent injury absences, shortened careers and, in the worst case scenario, early death, all too often seen at Cheltenham.

Against all the odds, Aintree and the Grand National survived. Dropping flat racing in 1976, the course now stages a three-day spring meeting which punters say is second in importance only to Cheltenham. In 1992 Aintree's autumn meeting was revived.

Most of the present generation of chasers and hurdlers are lightly raced in comparison with those of Arkle's time, taking in a couple of quiet races prior to their Cheltenham Festival target. Then, if there is fuel left in the tank, a trip to Aintree's restyled Grand National meeting is considered.

A consequence of this selectivity is that many valuable races between November and February are failing to attract fields of the highest quality. In response, the British Horse Racing Board has introduced an Order of Merit scheme, which is effectively a reward scheme for horses that keep busy throughout the season.

The Order of Merit prize is not insignificant, nor is the £1 million on offer to any horse that wins chasing's triple crown: the Betfair Chase, a race run for the first time at Haydock in November 2005, the King George VI Chase, run at Kempton each Boxing Day, and the Cheltenham Gold Cup in March.

Whether the Order of Merit and the Betfair Million will have the same effect as the introduction of the National Hunt Chase did almost a century and a half ago, we will have to wait and see.

Cheltenham is the be all and end all of the jumps. The winner's enclosure is like an amphitheatre. You don't have hundreds of spectators; you have thousands, and they're the most appreciative on earth, that mixture of the Irish and the English. When you head for the enclosure, the crowd parts like the Red Sea.

TED WALSH

The popularity that jump racing now enjoys owes much to two inter-related developments of the mid-twentieth century: television and sponsorship. Racecourse attendances were initially hit by TV coverage, but advertisers soon recognised the potential for relatively cheap air-time by sponsoring televised races.

It was a godsend for jump racing, still coping with its 1920s repu-tation among the noblemen of the Jockey Club as the equine equivalent of dog racing and the preserve of 'the needy and the greedy'.

Steeplechasing proved to be a better medium for advertisers than flat racing. The races last for seven and eight minutes and were staged during the winter when audience figures were higher. Products would be mentioned many times during the course of a broadcast, but strategically placed advertising boards around the course provided further coverage.

Having resisted TV in the beginning, the sport decided it could not live without it. The decision to switch the Arkle v Mill House battle in 1964 to Saturday meant a bigger TV audience and it also meant that Cheltenham's reputation was secure for ever. But as the 1990s brought more televised sport on to the screens, racing was effectively sidelined. Cheltenham's midweek audiences on both BBC and RTÉ left it bringing up the rear. Arkle's 1964 victory over Mill House was the third most viewed event of the year on RTÉ television that year. Nowadays Cheltenham doesn't make the top 100, while only the Grand Nationals at Aintree and Fairyhouse, with around 250,000 viewers each, can hope to compete with the triumvirate of GAA championship, international, Premiership and Champions League soccer, and Six Nations, World Cup or Heineken Cup rugby.

Digital and pay per view offered a lucrative, if low-profile alternative. In England the level of the crisis deepened until June 2005, when the sport effectively agreed to pay Channel 4 to televise racing.

Everyone was delighted with the move. John McCririck, normally a man who is viscerally opposed to subsidies, threw a garden party to celebrate. The style of Channel 4's coverage was criticised as outdated (in comparison with RTÉ's, a trefoil format developed by RTÉ's head of sport Tim O'Connor, starring Tracy Piggott, Robert Hall and the loquacious Ted Walsh), but at least it offered a reliable weekly fix for punters with no access to digital TV.

The price of saving televised racing in England was high—too high, some would complain. The agreement made to stump up the cash for coverage of racing on Channel 4 instantly devalued everything else. Events with the prestige of the Derby, Royal Ascot and the Grand National could take the hit, and were still worth paying for. The rest, by and large, were not.

In 2009, the BBC decided to slash its racing coverage by half to just fourteen days. For horse racing, it was not regarded as a good sign.

Under the cavernous awning of Paddington's mainline station, there is no need to enquire which of the dozen platforms is for Cheltenham. A ragged bunch of little men in pork-pie hats, fawn coats and binoculars file on to the Bristol train.

KEVIN O'CONNOR, 8 March 1980

TV is the key to understanding the impact Cheltenham has had on Irish society. Many Irish people who have a strong relationship with Cheltenham have never set foot in the place. The races are watched in the pubs of Dublin, Belfast, Cork and rural Ireland and experienced through the bookmakers.

The off-course bookie, like the game itself, has changed. Small town independent bookmakers sustained the business in Arkle's time. Changes in legislation in the 1990s led to the arrival of chain bookies, with identical layouts, economies of scale and studied efficiency. Many English chain shops opened up in Irish towns.

Paddy Power's, run by the owner and Stuart Kenny, was the Irish chain that responded best to the challenge. They sold off some of their offices to release equity, modernised the offices they kept and added more comfort to the spectacle. 'We are in the entertainment business,' Paddy Power himself said. 'Nobody thought of giving the punter as much as a free cup of coffee in the old days.'

Cheltenham is a brand which gives bookies a chance of winning new business, of attracting first-time punters who want to join the party. Outrageous advertising campaigns and novelty bets became part of the armoury, generating controversy and publicity rather than revenue.

In 2002 one of Power's experts Paul Ryan promised to walk down the main street of Tallaght naked if a fancied horse he disregarded, J. P. McManus's Baracouda, won the Stayers Hurdle at Cheltenham. Paddy Power took bets on the outcome of the prediction as well as the race, then organised the naked run (complete with Paddy Power cap and a discreet cover for the ungelded bits from a horse's head codpiece procured from Ann Summers), achieving massive publicity for the bookie.

Power's other publicity coups included organising a strip poker tournament and persuading the Tongan rugby team to dye their hair green before a World Cup match.

I remember getting up early in the morning to inspect the track to find the same group of fellows still playing cards in the hotel. Some of them never made it to the race track.

DERMOT COX

Bad money was following good. The changes coincided with a recession in Ireland. Just as Cheltenham had proved an efficient place for laundering the largesse of Britain's black economy in the 1940s, attracting the eyes of Vincent O'Brien and others, it was to do so again in the Ireland of the 1980s. As Ireland's budget deficit spiralled out of control, driving the national debt up £3 bn to £7 bn under Liam Cosgrave's Fine Gael-Labour administration of 1973–77, up to £13 bn under the subsequent Fianna Fáil administration and to £30 bn by the time Garret FitzGerald left office in 1987, new taxes, both direct and indirect, were piled on to the population at unprecedented levels to try to meet the bill.

The result of this was a burgeoning black economy. At one stage it was reckoned that a third of commerce never made it to the account books. Cheltenham was a place to spend this underground money, to win it, or even pretend to win it, without any questions being asked.

Until the abolition of currency controls in the 1980s, Irish visitors were supposed to take no more than IR£150 with them out of the country and £1,250 in any other currency. The rule was blatantly disregarded both by the racegoers and the customs officials posted at the ports and airports to monitor them. Shopping bags and suitcases full of cash were transported fore and aft across the channel. A TV documentary which followed a group of Irish punters noted the fact that one of them lost so much money playing poker on the ferry that he returned home without going to Cheltenham at all. Another was anxious that the documentary not be shown in Ireland because he had told his wife he was going to Belfast to buy cattle.

The biggest, boldest and best bookmakers were all at Cheltenham, ready to take hits of £250,000 in a single bet. Cheltenham became a professional gamblers' convention, which occasionally causes the odds to head in odd directions.

This was still not enough to contain the appetite for gambling. Cheltenham attracted a new body of gamblers for whom poker was a specialty and horse racing a secondary interest. The poker games in the hotels of the town were, by their nature, underground and intensely private events, but by the 1970s were being written about as the festival began to attract more press attention.

The betting coup of one of these poker players, Noel Furlong, was one of the best reported in Cheltenham history, a benchmark against which betting strokes are still measured.

When Furlong, a carpet dealer and card shark, backed his own horse, Destriero, to win the opening race of the 1991 Cheltenham Festival, he won about £2 m. Then it emerged Furlong had doubled up Destriero with The Iliad, a 25/1 shot in the Champion Hurdle. Ladbrokes alone were exposed to losses of £10 m. Complete panic ensued at the racecourse. The bookies rained cash on the no-hoper in a hedging fever, forcing it in to 11/2. It lost, but so did the bookmakers.

The rest of the afternoon dragged by for me. I felt depressed, as if I'd fallen myself. I still had some money, but it seemed like chump change after my elaborate fantasies.

BILL BARICH

Cheltenham's gossip circles recoiled when Cork gambler Tony Murphy was arrested when he arrived in Cheltenham in 1975. His crime was not clear either to the man himself or those who were trying to prosecute him.

As important as the battle between Ireland and England is at Cheltenham, a much more important battle ensues each year, between the punter and the bookie.

The history of bookmaking has been distinguished by guerrilla warfare between the two strata of society, the anoraked punters and the trilby-hatted bookies. A century ago a fictitious race called the Trodmore Hunt Steeplechase was invented purely to fleece bookmakers. Today's stings are more sophisticated.

Two of the more famous ambushes in this guerrilla war both involved the same principle, the gamblers taking command of the means of communication at a small country track to confuse the off-course bookmakers into paying out higher odds than they otherwise would have.

Tony Murphy, a building contractor who drove a flamboyant silver Rolls Royce, had chosen an insignificant meeting at the isolated Cumbrian track of Cartmel as the scene of his ambush in August 1974. The track had no telephone link, used by bookies to relay off-course bets back to the track to determine the price. Murphy wanted a horse that was certain to win to act as the third leg of a treble in which the other two horses were withdrawn. All three were listed as trained by Tony Collins, a part-time trainer in Scotland. The third horse was Gay Future, purchased by Edward O'Grady to be passed on to Collins, but in fact kept in Tipperary and prepared for the race.

Collins's other runners Opera Cloak at Southwell and Ankerwyke at Plumpton were both withdrawn from their races. To Murphy's dismay afterwards, they had never left Collins's yard, making the ploy a little too obvious to investigators. Meanwhile all the money in the treble bets placed all over London by Murphy and his cohorts was now riding on Gay Future at Cartmel. All three races were due off between 4.15 and 4.45, with the Gay Future race at 4.20, not giving bookies much time to react to the withdrawals.

Murphy also arranged for other horses in the Cartmel race to be backed to push out Gay Future's starting price at the course.

Soap flakes were rubbed on the horse's neck and flanks before he went into the parade ring to make it look like he was sweating. Timmy

Jones, the amateur jockey who rode Gay Future, fell off the other side attempting to mount, and then went down to the start with his stirrups long so that he would look incompetent.

The bookie-busters won Stg£250,000 when Gay Future won at 8/1. Some of the London bookmakers thought something was afoot and refused to pay out. After an investigation, both Murphy and Collins were fined £1,000 and £500 costs and banned from British racecourses for ten years.

The failed coup was made into the 1979 TV drama, *Murphy's Stroke*. It was a bit of a supreme novices chase of TV filmography; director Frank Cvitanovich was rarely heard of again, although writer Brian Phelan turned out more TV drama. Niall Toibin played the part of Murphy and Pierce Brosnan the part of trainer Edward O'Grady. Memorably, when asked why he had done it by a policeman at the end of the film, Toibín turned to him and said, 'for the crack'. That scene may have introduced the Irish slang word into English popular culture, causing it to be belatedly translated into the Irish *craic* with a spelling it never had beforehand.

In June 1975 another Cheltenham predator, Barney Curley, who was always reminding people he had trained for the priesthood but became a professional gambler instead, used the same principle when he instigated a similar coup at a Wednesday evening meeting in Bellewstown, a hilltop racecourse with one telephone.

A friend of Curley's, Benny O'Hanlon, took over the single phone to enquire about a sick relative and stayed on the phone for the lead-in to the race which was won by Curley's wife's horse, Yellow Sam, at odds of 20/1. Curley had booked the horse to win £300,000 at off-course betting shops. In his 1999 autobiography, Curley reported having earned a further £700,000 in bets on the horse before it was retired.

His success was commemorated by the course in later years, which in 2005 ran the 'Seamus Murphy Yellow Sam 30th Anniversary Hurdle', inviting Barney Curley and Liam Brennan, the horse's trainer, to the event. Curley's other exploits included the purchase and wagering of a Cork mansion in a lottery of doubtful legality.

Curley, Furlong and Murphy were Ireland's first celebrity gamblers astride the stage of 1970s Cheltenham until the arrival of a new breed of gambler, including J. P. McManus. Unlike the famous English gamblers who preceded them, they liked to own their own horses and avoided the 'bet too far' which has brought down many a giant of the ring. 'Better One Day as a Lion' was the title of the vivacious journalist Raymond Smith's account of their lifestyles.

> With stories of drunken parties and all night poker games, I am afraid the three day Cheltenham meeting falls considerably short on style and class of more civilised racing events such as Royal Ascot or the Arc de Triomph. Still, I suppose it does serve some purpose, if only to occupy minor columnists, lost for ideas, poor souls who dream they'll find something new by trotting over to the West Country, but probably end up leading the drunken brawls, losing all their money playing poker and writing about the same names they write about every night here.
>
> ANGELA PHELAN, *Irish Independent*, 22 March 1981

Cheltenham's legend was enhanced by reports at home of the exploits of the card sharks and the bookie-busters. But like many of England's decaying nineteenth-century tourist locations, by the end of the 1970s the place was falling apart.

The propensity of the locals for over-charging did not help. 'Prices? Just double them', one restaurateur was quoted by *The Irish Times* in 1979. It was easily believed. 'Unlike other big sporting occasions, even race week in Galway, the five star prices did not deliver five star service,' travel agent Joe Tully said. 'The Cheltenham hotels charged too much for too little.'

Famously, the owner of the Queen's used to put the good furniture away and put out plastic garden furniture for Cheltenham week. Admission prices to the racecourse rose to £70 in a short period of time in the 1990s. It was becoming a very expensive week.

The late night party of Cheltenham continued unabated and became a magnet for Irish society, bringing the gossip columnists in their wake. The first colour writers from the Irish newspapers arrived to write about L'Escargot in 1970 and 1971. In that decade the Irish presence was paid undue attention by English colour writers as well. 'A great class of person stays on the third night,' a punter told Maeve Binchy in 1980. 'It is only the amateurs that run out of town.'

The arrival of London prostitutes in hotels in the town was also being gleefully reported. 'Ladies of the night were much in evidence again at hotels in the town,' Angela Phelan wrote in 1981. 'Certain potential Irish punters caused a bit of a flap with them when they suggested paying for their services in Irish punts. A quickly convened conference was held among the ladies. But after one whipped out a pocket calculator from her handbag and worked out the rate in sterling, they agreed to accept Irish money.'

Tour operators who send Irish people over in increasing numbers were also grumbling about the way Cheltenham's ageing hotels jacked up race week prices to five star levels without the five star service.

The Irish soon found other options. The growth of Shakespeare-related tourism in Stratford-on-Avon delivered a whole new inventory of hotel beds, and Stratford by the 1980s was as important a party town as Cheltenham itself.

Those who stayed at home saved money and got to taste the camaraderie, the atmosphere and the celebration of horse racing at its purest.

Cheltenham week drives the off-course betting industry and fuels the engine room of Irish racing.

In 2001 the industry and the country got a reminder of just how important Cheltenham was to both when an outbreak of foot and mouth disease on a farm visible from the Cheltenham grandstands caused the meeting to be abandoned. The meeting had barely escaped in 1968. One notable casualty was Istabraq, almost certainly denied a record fourth Champion Hurdle. There were very many others.

Joe Tully, the tour operator from Carlow, had the travel arrangements of 1,500 people paid for when the cancellation came. Many of these had booked when it was clear that Irish horses would not be allowed to travel. He lost a stone in the month he spent sorting out arrangements.

> Not only is it a self-perpetuating club but it is an inept one.
>
> JIM BOLGER comments after Supreme Court case which ruled in his favour against the Turf Club

The scorecard of victories became a gauge of the state of the Irish horse industry. When no Irish horses won in 1989, the first time this had happened since the truncated meeting of 1947, it was regarded as a serious situation both by the Cheltenham management, who instituted the Champion Bumper in 1992, and the Irish industry, for whom Finance Minister Charlie McCreevy and Agricultural Minister Joe Walsh began putting together a rescue plan involving more prize money, upgraded facilities at racecourses, and a more professional approach to administration. The number of race meetings a year rose by 20 per cent to 300. Attendances rose by over 25 per cent to some 1.4 m.

Racing over jumps benefited disproportionately. National hunt racing has always been unprofitable for most of its participants, not least the owners and trainers, who are mainly in it for the love of the sport, not money. Horse owners recoup less than a quarter of their operating costs, far less than in France, Japan or America. About a tenth of the owners and trainers drop out of the sport each year.

Trainers too were in the sport for love, not money. The sport does not have the same lucrative rewards as flat racing. Flat horse owners are wealthier and the horses are sold on to be replaced by new ones every two years. Jump trainers have to balance the intricacies of dealing with the same horse for years and keeping it in one piece, often with bad legs after the wear and tear of the hazards of Aintree, Cheltenham and Punchestown, and appeasing their cranky owners. 'If an owner wants you to go to Thurles and watch his horse finish feckin' ninth, you have no choice but to go,' Ted Walsh said.

McCreevy and Walsh ensured that the gambling community would subsidise the industry. Prize money was increased through a bookmakers' levy, and investment in tracks brought horse racing back as an entertainment option for Irish families.

The Turf Club resisted the push for change at first. Trainers such as Jim Bolger lent their weight to the campaign for change and were ignored. The result was the institution of the Irish Horse Racing Authority (it was initially proposed to be the Irish Racing Authority until someone noticed the acronym IRA), and eventually Racing Ireland.

The new generation of riders and trainers have better facilities and more money than their predecessors. But there are concerns that horse racing is now too dependent on government aid and the betting community.

Ted Walsh told Bill Barich that national hunt racing is in a precarious position, too dependent on government funding. 'Nobody wants to stand around eating bad food and drinking over-priced drinks when their feet are all wet.'

An economic upturn caused more money to flow through the new facilities. Irish owners were keeping horses with Irish trainers.

As a grim reminder of racing's bad times, Ireland's showpiece export business and single biggest foreign high-tech investment, the Intel plant at Leixlip, was built on the site of a bankrupt stud farm.

Cheltenham is like a checklist—if people aren't there, they are either ill or they're dead.

FR SEÁN BREEN

The national health of Ireland's national hunt community, as gauged by the Cheltenham scorecard, improved dramatically. From four winners in 2004, the total climbed to nine in 2005, ten in 2006 before dropping to five in 2007, six in 2008 and eight in 2009.

The scorecard does not reveal the real revolution in Cheltenham's Irish successes. Three trainers, Vincent O'Brien, Tom Dreaper and Dan Moore delivered virtually all the successes of the 1940s, 50s and 60s. In 1958 when there were eight winners, four were trained by Vincent O'Brien and two by Tom Dreaper with Clem Magnier and Joe Osborne providing the others.

In 2009 seven separate Irish trainers were responsible for the eight Irish winners at the festival: Enda Bolger, Tom Cooper, Philip Fenton, Noel Meade, Willie Mullins, Mick Quinlan and Tom Taaffe. Jockeys Paddy Flood and Tom O'Brien had their first wins at the festival. Another star of the show was the second placed Monaghan trainer Oliver Brady, described by Monaghan writer Frank McNally in 2003 as 'a man for whom the description extrovert is not nearly adequate', dying of cancer and full of trademark flamboyant exuberance. Admission to the inner circle, the big breakthrough, was now available to smaller yards and journeyman jocks.

And when the small yard does send out a winner, the phrase 'people's champion' is ready to be applied once more by the cheer-leaders in the gallery.

If Arkle was Achilles and Dawn Run was Ulysses, Danoli is Cinderella, the Cinderella of colts.

Irish Press, 12 March 1994

Cheltenham has changed massively and so has the Irish presence there. Small training stables and farmers have long lost all hope of taking on the wealthy on the flat courses of summer. But this story resonated far beyond the Cotswolds and the Comeraghs.

A small yard produced the great people's champion of the 1990s, Danoli. They have been at work ever since. The honour and glory of the small yard is being sustained, Matt the Thresher style, from a homestead on the Kilkenny-Tipperary border that Charles Kickham, author of the 1879 classic novel of rural Ireland, *Knocknagow*, would have no difficulty in recognising. At Cheltenham they can compete and win.

During his career Danoli penetrated popular culture and became well known to people who did not follow racing, famously decorating the set of the *Late Late Show* in his own particular manner when he became the first racehorse to appear on the show.

Danoli's victory in the 1994 SunAlliance Hurdle was the high point of his 32-race career. After finishing third in the 1995 Champion Hurdle, he fractured a fetlock in winning the Martell Hurdle at Aintree in April 1995 and was never the same horse again. It seemed for a while his life was in danger, but Christopher Riggs of Liverpool University operated, pinning the cannon bone above the fetlock with two metal screws. Danoli returned home in June and raced again in Leopardstown in January 1996, finishing a close third against all expectations.

Interest reached Arkle levels in the horse and his owner Dan O'Neill. The reluctant bonesetter had started fixing horses' injuries and then took a fancy to them. He had a Mass said for Danoli, 'not that he would win, but that he would come back safe'. He had scarcely travelled out of Ireland before going to see his horse race in Cheltenham.

Danoli's trainer Tom Foley ('I sort of make it up as I go along, like') was a local farmer who started dabbling in training seven years before, who had never been on a plane before, and ended up with Danoli because he had called round to have his back fixed by Dan.

The horse was picked up at Goff's like a stray dog at £3,000 below the asking price. In the autumn of 1991 Dan O'Neill from Myshall and his daughter Olivia (hence Dan-Oli) came to Goffs to buy a breeding mare because the wife wanted one. Tom Foley spotted the horse, reporting that there was not one decent filly to be had, but that this one was worth buying. 'Come down and pretend you know something about horses.'

They offered £7,000 for this £10,000 yearling and were refused. A few days later they were contacted by the owner.

'I remember I saw him among a bunch of three or four horses. He was scraggy looking, mange in his tail and that. A Cork man I know asked why I was interested in that lad, because he reckoned he was not a horse at all.'

With Tom Foley, Danoli won his first three races in 1992–93. Dan had seriously considered selling him and doubling his money after only one race. In 1993–94 he won three races over hurdles and a second place in the Irish Champion Hurdle.

A string of victories followed: the Martell Aintree Hurdle at Punchestown, and a race named after his most illustrious predecessor, the Hatton's Grace Hurdle at Fairyhouse. He then disappointed at Fairyhouse and the final pre-Cheltenham mystique was added—secrecy. O'Neill was discomfited by the big money that followed Danoli, contributing to his legendary status.

'There was a lot of pressure and I felt it,' Foley said. 'He was well. He was so fresh he banged me on my forehead, but I was so nervous my heart was banging and my knees were knocking. We thanked God for Danoli.' J. P. McManus, who had watched his own horse, Time for a Run, win the Coral Cup unbacked because the odds were too short, had personally driven down Danoli's odds with a huge gamble to put, in his telling phrase 'the wheels back on the bike'. He was not alone. Fr Sean Breen recalled: 'Danoli got a lot of people out of trouble. We thanked God for Danoli.'

It made us very tense,' O'Neill said. 'I don't mind the fellows who put thousands on a horse. They can afford it. I was worried about the small fellow, maybe who couldn't afford it.'

The winner's enclosure was the scene of what Chris Hawkins of *The Guardian* called 'rampant Irish enthusiasm' when he won the SunAlliance Hurdle. The media gloried in the fact that trainer Tom Foley had never previously set foot outside of Ireland and had chosen to stay in the stable lads' hostel instead of a local hotel. Dan O'Neill was patronised by those who represented Cheltenham as an over-exuberant Hibernic hooley, given to excess of emotion, gambling and various black and amber coloured liquids. 'Foley is something of a rarity, an Irishman who doesn't drink', Hawkins enthused.

Despite the broken fetlock, Danoli returned to win the 1997

Hennessy Gold Cup and even more money followed him to Cheltenham. Course MD Edward Gillespie feared for the scenes in the winner's enclosure should he win and drew up a special Danoli security plan. But it was not to be.

'He changed my life,' Foley told Brian O'Connor of *The Irish Times*. 'He took us to places we have never been like Cheltenham and Liverpool and it was great to see what top-class racing is really like.

'I know in my heart and soul that no one ever saw him even near his best. If he hadn't got hurt, God knows what he would have done. He would definitely have won a Cheltenham Gold Cup or two if he had stayed right.

'He was a lovely horse and a real gent. He was so tough and genuine. He had real courage as he showed at Liverpool when cracking a bone in his leg and still winning.'

Behind the scenes there was some tension between the characters in the fairytale, and it showed when an outburst by Tom Foley was mentioned in the equography, *Danoli—The People's Champion*.

In the book Foley says he told Swan, when informed by the champion jockey that he would not be able to switch from Consharon, an Aidan O'Brien horse, to ride Danoli in his chase debut at Clonmel the previous year, that both he and O'Brien were 'a shower of bollixes. You're not sportsmen at all.'

Foley continues: 'I had been hoping that with the success Danoli had given Charlie over the years, he'd have got off Consharon and ridden Danoli for that reason alone.'

'Two abiding images of the horsey world in 1994 stand out,' the *Irish Press* wrote on 12 March 1994. 'They come from contrasts of the winner's enclosure: Ballinsheen led in by Sheik Muhammad and Danoli led in by Dan O'Neill. In diversity there is life.'

> There was a time when racing was described as the sport of kings, but that is no longer apt, because there are not enough kings to keep it going.
>
> *The Irish Times*, 28 April 1937

It is likely that Danoli's status as the 'people's champion' was partly because the name of the horse played on the name of the owner, Dan O'Neill and his daughter Olivia.

It was a sign of how inventive the naming of racehorses had become. In the old days it was quite simple. They took some of the sire's name (My Prince, Cottage) and gave it to the foal (Prince Regent, Cottage Rake), often with some homage to the dam as well.

The new generation of horse owners decided to have more fun with a horse's nomenclature. Dorans Pride, without a tell-tale apostrophe, was named for the huge family of Dorans who were joint owners of the horse.

Michael Hourigan gave the name Beef Or Salmon to his horse after the limited fare on offer in a Co. Limerick hotel where he stopped off for a meal.

Forpadydeplasterer was named after a political donor to Bertie Ahern's dig-out fund. Aahgowangowan was named after Mrs Doyle's catchphrase in Arthur Matthews and Graham Linehan's TV comedy *Father Ted*.

Numbersixvalverde was named after Bernard Carroll's holiday home on the Algarve, Portugal.

Dawn Run was named after Charmian Hill's daughter's new interest in jogging.

Irish names created no end of confusion. Clive Graham's attempts to pronounce Mill House's sire (Naice na Ree) in the build-up to the 1965 Cheltenham Gold Cup and Peter O'Sulleven's attempts to pronounce Oisín (he tried it in French, waw-san) raised many a smile down the years.

Some of the new names were exotic (Flagship Uberalles, Exotic Dancer, Florida Pearl, Brave Inca, Commanche Court).

Some were simply elongated (Forpadydeplasterer, Numbersixval- verde, Youlneverwalkalone, Areyoutalkingtome, Thisthatantother, Mickmacmagoole, Eversoneversofast, Tatafatatafata, Totheroadyou've- gone, Stormyfairweather).

Some were lyrical (Whyso Mayo, Alexander Banquet).

Some were silly (Speckyfoureyes, Mistermuddypaws, Hellcatmud- wrestler, Forevereyesofblue, Alnasr Alwasheek, It's Mr Blobby, Mrdeegeethegeegee, Lunch Was My Idea. Snooker Table and Spirit Level).

Some were funny (Fr Breen's One Won One, Hoof Hearted, Always Waining, Why the Big Paws and Rooster Booster).

Some were risqué (Billy Ballbreaker, Cute Ass, Smart Ass, Big Tits and Little Knickers). During Transvestite's career there were many predictable comments about how the horse had a great change of gear! The new nomenclature of racing helped make it more accessible to the watcher at home.

This is part-racing, part-pantomime. Fairy tales in which some of the favourites play roles made familiar in the legends, Limestone Lad as Cinderella, each of the seven dwarfs in a saddle.

Evening Herald, Sports on Television column, 3 January 2003

Danoli's successor as 'people's champion', Limestone Lad, the horse bred and trained by its owner on a farm of 300 acres in Gathabawn, Co. Kilkenny, never won at Cheltenham.

But the horse bred by an old age pensioner farmer which once famously beat the horse bred by one of the richest men in racing, Istabraq, by five and a half lengths when he was the 7/1 on favourite at Fairyhouse, served as a metaphor for the dreams of small breeders and owners everywhere and the enduring mythology of Cheltenham.

Limestone Lad also beat Istabraq's stable companion Le Coudray, came to Cheltenham and finished second in 2000 and third in 2003. 'He's a once-in-a-lifetime horse,' declared his owner and breeder Jim Bowe, who had been keeping horses since the 1940s.

The family and the horse were a throw-back to former times. They talked about the handling of their horse as if it had a mystical, metaphysical quality about it. Jim reckoned his horse was the best of an old-style jumping breed because he was all heart. 'He's as strong as a lion,' Jim Bowe said after the victory over Le Coudray, 'a super horse. He could race every day on any ground.'

His son Michael trained him: 'He loves the game and thrives on it. He gets depressed if you don't take him to the races.'

Bowe was knocked unconscious, hospitalised and suffered broken bones as he reeled in Limestone Lad's wayward spirit. 'He calls the shots and thinks I'm his slave,' Michael Bowe told Brian O'Connor of *The Irish Times* in 2003, 'but he is the best thing that has ever happened this family.'

'Limestone Lad is an extremely big personality,' he told Greg Wood of *The Guardian*. 'He's a total boss. He knows he's good and he knows I'm just his servant. As long as I can keep him thinking that, he will perform.'

The Bowes tried to sell him, but he was failed by the auctioneer's vet for having an abnormal heartbeat. 'They didn't say whether it was abnormal in the right or the wrong way,' Bowe said. 'We really didn't think much of him in his 3-year-old days. Limestone's progress was just a gradual thing. Everything you taught him, you had to do it slowly and carefully, but once he picked it up he would die or do it. He was so genuine. All he wanted to do was to please you. He went from being a clumsy no-hoper to being average to above average to quite a good horse to a very good horse and eventually to being a star. If there is one word that can explain why he was as good as he was, it is patience. We always gave him his time.

'The whole key with horses is that they enjoy it, whether it is racing or their work. Stress is a big thing in a racehorse's life. They suffer from it greatly. People don't realise that. It is small things, but you have to listen to the horses and they will tell you if they are not well or they are suffering from stress.

'You have to know how they think. The slightest little things—they might seem trivial or unimportant to you or me—can be huge things in a horse's life.

'It is not so much looking at them that tells you how they are, as rubbing your hands over them to feel them. Then they will tell you themselves. You can tell by the way they feel and the way they react when you touch them.'

We watched him in the parade ring and we thought: Naomi Campbell crossed with Russell Crowe, elegant, volatile, handsome, haughty, and with a look that says: got a problem, sunshine? And a strut that oozes: this ground is not worthy to bear my hooves.'

MARY HANNIGAN, *The Irish Times*, 17 March 2003

The Bowes were successful breeders long before Limestone Lad came along. Jim held his first training permit in 1969 and enjoyed success as an owner, rider and trainer in the 1970s. He sold on the early winners American Eyre, Step On Eyre and Another Eyre to Willie Mullins before deciding to retain the three horses that made the stable's name in the family's red and emerald green colours, Limestone Lad, Solerina and Sweet Kiln.

It took five attempts to get Limestone Lad to win, a £3,000 race at a small Limerick meeting. He won his first handicap over hurdles at Naas in November 1998 off a mark of 99. In twelve months he improved by an amazing 59 lb, winning two bumpers, a Clonmel maiden hurdle and a two mile Naas handicap hurdle.

'Those of us who believed Limestone Lad had all the credentials to go right to the top as a chaser may have to exercise plenty of patience,' Michael Bowe said. 'But he does possess an unbelievable constitution.'

At a time when horses were being run sparingly, Bowe adopted an attacking policy which paid huge dividends. He won more national hunt races in Ireland than any horse for 60 years.

Ridden by Shane McGovern from Beauparc, in 1999 he won at Dundalk, then scored his most famous victory at Fairyhouse over dual Champion Hurdler Istabraq by five and a half lengths. He then defeated Istabraq's stablemate Le Coudray at Navan by twenty lengths (the following day's *Irish Times* name-checked Danoli in declaring Limestone Lad the 'new people's champion'). While Istabraq had started 7/1 on favourite, Le Coudray had started at 9/4 on. The analysis of that defeat continued for a decade afterwards. Istabraq had tired in the heavy ground, Charlie Swan explained on the day, while Aidan O'Brien said Istabraq was a little heavy for that stage of the season (tellingly adding 'as usual'). For the punters it didn't matter. A country farmer had beaten the Arabs and Ballydoyle, not once, but twice. 'I suppose the result is great for racing,' O'Brien said. 'Take nothing away from the winner. He's a very good horse.'

The attacking approach extended to the horse himself. In his victory over Istabraq he had taken a twenty-length lead by halfway. He took to the front early and held it. Which created a problem when he went to Cheltenham to compete in the World Hurdle. Nobody wins the World Hurdle after making most of the running. Limestone Lad is the only front-runner to have even been placed, and it happened twice.

In 2000, Limestone Lad travelled as the winner of seven of his eight previous races, the only defeat coming over the too-short two miles of the Irish Champion Hurdle. He travelled badly on the ferry from Rosslare to Pembroke, landed dehydrated and then refused to eat. There he finished a highly respectable eight lengths behind Istabraq in fourth. The going was bad news for the Bowes—good to firm. Limestone Lad had never encountered fast going and had been beaten in his only two attempts on good. Punters were still unconvinced because one of those efforts on hard ground (third to Istabraq over two miles) was exceptional (his victory over Istabraq was on good to soft). He was sent off at 3/1, burned off most of the field from the front, but Bacchanal proved too persistent and he finished third. 'He has run his heart out and there is not a bother on him,' Jim Bowe said. 'He has done nothing at all wrong and I am very proud of him.' Foot and mouth ruled out revenge in 2001, and Limestone Lad missed all of 2002 because of a freak accident, injuring his back muscles after he got himself trapped under a rail.

He was now 11 and had a new jockey, Paul Carberry, for the World Hurdle of 2003, won by Baracouda for the second time (unusually at a longer price than his first win). It was the last race of his 65-race, 35-win career. He had won three grade 2s, a grade 1 and had been beaten a head in the Irish Champion Hurdle in his last season.

The week of the race had placed him in the heart of popular culture, the subject of broadcast and print profiles that highlighted his penchant for garlic and onions, and his personality. 'An arrogant horse with a street-wise personality,' John Bowe said. 'The equine version of Mike Tyson,' another neighbour declared.

He was sent off joint-favourite, which says more about the way he captured the public imagination than his real prospects. But he still finished third after forcing a strong pace. It was a tragic day for Ireland: Beef Or Salmon's Gold Cup bid came to naught; Limestone Lad finished third and Dorans Pride, now 14, suffered a fatal fall in the Foxhunters at a time when he should have been retired eight years after winning the Stayers Hurdle and five years after being placed in the Gold Cup. 'He died doing what he loved most,' trainer Michael Hourigan said.

Limestone Lad suffered no such risks. There was a plan to send him steeplechasing (he won his first steeplechase in Cork in October 2000 with Barry Cash on board), but his unbelievable constitution did not extend to that.

Incredibly, the Bowes had a second champion in their three-horse stable. Solerina won the Hatton's Grace three times in succession shortly after Limestone Lad had done so, giving the Bowes six successes in the race in seven years. She had 22 successes, including two grade 1 wins. Like Limestone Lad, she had her own personality. 'She was lazy at home but came alive out on the track.' She was due to go to Cheltenham too and was second favourite in the Supreme Novices before injury ruled her out.

Maybe jockeys tend to be so appealing because they learn early (and go on relearning) how to live not only with losing but with losing painfully, sometimes in the intensive care unit.

HUGH McILVANNEY, 1986

On the scorecard of jockeys, Ireland's success was even more marked. Richard Pitman wrote a book titled *Good Horses Make Good Jockeys*. You won't find a jockey to disagree with that. 'If you don't have the horse beneath you,' the sixteen time festival winner Barry Geraghty says, 'it doesn't matter how good you are. You have to be lucky.'

Irish jockeys were luckier than most, commanding the rides from English stables as well as Irish ones from 1945. They dominated the festival long before the trainers did. The charge was led by two remarkable brothers. Racing in Ireland in the 1940s was confined to Wednesdays and Saturdays, and the Molony brothers from Croom took the mailboat to ride weekday meetings in England. In 1950 Martin Molony was champion national hunt jockey in Ireland and runner-up to his brother Tim in England in the same year, a remarkable achievement in pre-motorway days. Martin's brief but brilliant career was brought to a sudden halt by a near fatal fall in Thurles in September 1951. For many he was the greatest of Ireland's national hunt jockeys. Only Ruby Walsh has managed to straddle the channel with anything resembling the same success.

Seven of the ten most successful jockeys in Cheltenham history are Irish, including the top two, Pat Taaffe and Rupert 'Ruby' Walsh, different generations from homesteads a few miles apart in Kill and Ardclough in north Kildare.

Ruby was named after his grandfather, another Ruby, on whose horse, Shurio, Ted Walsh first won as a 20/1 outsider in Wexford in October 1969, a famous day in Irish steeplechasing history when Graeme Walters pulled his horse up, having thought he had won (there was another lap to go). Ted was to have an illustrious amateur career, winning at Cheltenham, and an even more spectacular success as a trainer, winning the 2000 Aintree Grand National with Papillon with Ruby on board and sending Commanche Court to multiple successes. A media favourite as a jockey and trainer for his quick wit, Ted Walsh's career took on another dimension when he was approached by RTÉ head of sport Tim O'Connor in 1983 to front the station's racing coverage. He became a favourite television personality and an ambassador for racing.

Ruby Walsh almost became the first jockey to ride the winner of all four championship races in 2009 when winning the Champion Chase (Master Minded), World Hurdle (Big Bucks) and Gold Cup (Kauto Star), whilst finishing second in the Champion Hurdle (Celestial Halo).

Ruby's emergence helped the jockey scorecard move to another level in the noughties. If it were not for the races confined to amateur jockeys, England would have had just one winner in 2009. Walsh finished with a record seven victories at the festival, and headed the jockeys' list for the fourth time in six years. His great rival Barry Geraghty from Drumcree, Co. Meath, became the fourth jockey to equal the previous record with five winners in 2003. Mick Fitzgerald (born in Cork but raised in Camolin, Co. Wexford) headed it twice with four winners in 1999 and 2000. Tony McCoy from Moneyglass, Co. Antrim, headed it twice with three winners in 1997 and five in 1998. Cloughjordan-born Charlie Swan headed it twice with four winners in 1993 and three in 1994, and Cork-born Norman Williamson headed it with four winners in 1995.

McCoy rode his first winner for Jim Bolger in Thurles on 26 March 1992. A move to England to ride for Toby Balding and Martin Pipe in 1994 raised him to another level. He was to win the English jockey championship for twelve successive seasons and eventually accumulated 3,000 national hunt winners.

Barry Geraghty rode 30 winners as a teenager on the pony circuit before being apprenticed to a family friend, Noel Meade, in Castletown, Co. Meath, and riding his first winner at Down Royal in January 1997.

Tommy Carberry from Meath would have shared with Taaffe the position as most successful Gold Cup jockey, were it not for Tied Cottage's disqualification in 1980. Tim Molony is the most successful Champion Hurdle jockey with Charlie Swan in joint second place. Taaffe is also the most successful Champion Chase jockey with Ruby Walsh in a position to overtake him, two winners behind. Aubrey Brabazon (1949 and 1950) is the only jockey who managed to win the Champion Hurdle and Gold Cup in the same year twice. Tom Cullinan (1930), Ted Leader (1932), Gerry Wilson (1935), Molony (1953) and Tony McCoy (1997) are among the nine others who have done so. Jim Culloty from Killarney was also a three-time Gold Cup winner on Best Mate.

Almost all of these jockeys came along surprisingly similar career paths. They were the sons of trainers, Tom Taaffe, Ticker Geraghty and Ted Walsh; they started on ponies (as did Barry Geraghty) or point-to-points; they spent a year or so waiting for their first winner (nineteen months in the case of Tony McCoy); and they showed the strength of character to step up to a new level when they were sought after by the trainers of the best horses.

Almost without exception they suffered horrific and often life-threatening injuries. Pat Taaffe was back in the saddle five months after surviving a near fatal fall in 1956. Jonjo O'Neill remembers a time when his right leg was so hideously broken it was 'like a sack of gravel' and extensive metal plate and screws had to be inserted to help bind the bones. Barry Geraghty suffered crushed vertebrae on two different occasions and broke his collar-bone and his elbow in his very first year, 2002. Mick Fitzgerald was forced to retire at the age of 38 in 2008 after suffering a serious neck injury in a fall at the Aintree Grand National.

The fall at Fairyhouse in 1997 that left Tipperary-born Shane Broderick, a Cheltenham winner on Dorans Pride, paralysed, the fall of Ballyhooley-born Jim Lombard, 1984 Conyngham Cup-winning jockey in the Coolmore Chase at Punchestown in 1986, from which he died three weeks later, the fatal fall of Carbury-born Kieran Kelly five months after his first Cheltenham Festival success on Hardy Eustace at Kilbeggan in 2003, and the death of Athlone-born Sean Cleary at Galway in November 2003 all serve as reminders that the danger of jumping over obstacles at 40 mph can never be eliminated.

Much more than flat race jockeys, jump jockeys are tacticians, earning their reputation in a game of horseback chess out in the country, then delivering a fresh horse into a key position at race-end.

There are new entry procedures, with an apprentice school in Kildare delivering new jockeys often from an urban background. The demand for Irish jockeys is such in England that many go straight across the water without schooling on Irish racecourses.

Occasionally a jockey performs a feat which is truly astonishing. Barry Geraghty once rode Silver Steel bareback over the last three fences to finish fifth in the gruelling Midlands National at Uttoxeter. It is an achievement in defeat that will be remembered as much as his many great victories.

Famously, trainer Michael Hourigan once said that a jockey needs an old head on a young body. It is a tribute to Ireland's national hunt tradition that so many old Irish heads and young Irish bodies have dominated the Cheltenham Festival.

The peer bets his hundreds, the stock broker his tens, the coster-monger his half crowns. They cannot all bet with one another, for they have other occupations, and their time would be inconveniently consumed in seeking for persons to take or lay them the odds, and who would be good for payment should they lose. The consequence has been the demand for betting agents has created the supply.

CHARLES DICKENS, 1868

Charles Dickens's explanation of the principle of bookmaking held good for 130 years. The spread of the internet changed everything.

Online betting exchanges, effectively upstart bookmakers, allow punters to bet against each other via the internet, rather than against a trilby-hatted bookmaker.

The online gambler is king. Exchanges, the gambling equivalent of online auction sites, have lowered the costs of betting by cutting out bookmakers through matching gamblers offering and accepting bets on just about anything.

More worryingly, online betting exchanges let you 'lay' odds on a horse, in effect, betting on a runner to lose, something that causes no end of discomfort to the people who regulate horse racing.

Gambling is tailor made for cyberspace. The internet's erasure of geography lets people have a flutter without having to leave their living rooms for the racetrack or casino.

The punters embraced it in their millions, especially in America where illegal gambling has long flourished. In 2005, 12 million Americans placed about $6 billion in online bets, half the world's total, before Congress passed a bill that stopped banks making payments to online gambling sites, adding to an already formidable legislative arsenal that outlaws most online gaming.

The internet has also brought a healthy dose of transparency and competition to the industry. State-protected lotteries and horse races generally offer very poor odds for punters, while governments have imposed hefty sin taxes.

The form book is a historical work, useful for predicting what will happen in the past.

Racing adage

The going suddenly got tough. In 2009 came the unthinkable, recession in Cheltenham itself. The corporate hospitality market fell off a cliff. Revenues were down by around 12 per cent. There were still around 35,000 unsold tickets when the gates opened for the four days of racing.

Ryanair scrapped the extra flights it usually puts on and many hotels and guesthouses, normally fully booked months ahead, still had rooms.

'It has put a whole industry of people out of work,' said Joe Tully of Tully's Travel in Carlow, one of the main agencies for Irish racegoers. 'It's back to the 1980s. The committed racing fans are still going, but the corporate clients that used to fill the four and five-star hotels have cut back massively.'

Irish racing too was about to crash land after fifteen years of growth in 2009. Perhaps it was inevitable that owners would suffer, as the growth of the industry was disproportionately built on the construction and banking industries.

The appearance of a former Gold Cup-winning owner in *Stubbs Gazette* just as the 2009 meeting was being run showed the rapid retreat from the sales ring that was about to happen on the part of the owners and sponsors, many of them deeply entrenched in the recessionary fields of property and finance. The going was getting unexpectedly heavy, so to speak.

All through the industry the figures indicated a decline not seen since the 1930s. On-course betting was down 18 per cent, sponsorship was down 5.4 per cent, attendances were down 9 per cent and, crucially, bloodstock sales down 43.6 per cent.

Horse Racing Ireland, which inherited running the industry from the rusty diehards of the Turf Club, blamed the effects of the economic slowdown, coupled with unprecedented bad weather conditions which hit the sector in the second half of the year.

Although the number of horses in training dipped 0.6 per cent to 12,119, the authorities claimed that participation in the sport in 2008 grew to its highest ever level, with record numbers of fixtures, races, runners and owners, and that there was also an increase in total prize money.

There were 1,237 new owners, 5,641 owners in all, and during the year 9,042 horses went to post.

The most worrying trend was in bloodstock sales. The industry employs 16,500 people, a figure that has to be sustained by prize and bloodstock money.

The number of people travelling to Cheltenham was also down. But as nobody is sure how many Irish people travel to Cheltenham in the first place, they weren't sure by how much.

Cheltenham is great as a spectator. But it's hell as a trainer. There's a lot of pressure. You've got to have a winner here, or people will think you haven't done well. They say, 'It's only a horse race.' But it's not a horse race; it's the Olympics.

MICHAEL DICKINSON

Despite the party livery the Cheltenham Festival wears so lavishly and the €600 m betting spree that keeps a smile on bookmakers' faces, steeplechasing is still the poor relation of the horse racing industry.

The question remains how much further the event can evolve and how the high level of Irish interest which established the prestige of Cheltenham in the first place can bring about further change.

When Frank Morgan sent his first horses across the channel, it was the National Hunt Chase, a four mile chase which had been established in 1904, that was the highlight of Cheltenham.

The Irish interest, or to be more precise a small core group of Irish owners, trainers and punters, helped bring about the dramatic changes in the festival since then, and no doubt will continue to do so.

When interest in Cheltenham periodically waned, it was the Irish who sent over the equine saviours: Prince Regent, Cottage Rake and Hatton's Grace in the 1940s, Arkle in 1964, and the string of 1970s champions in both the Champion Hurdle and Gold Cup.

Without the Irish, Cheltenham could have become a local affair, much like the Lancashire Chase that once threatened to rival Aintree but spiralled into decline until it eventually lost its home track in 1964.

The upshot of this is that Cheltenham is a showpiece for Irish horses, an international window on the Irish national hunt scene and a reminder of how important it remains. The breeding and training of horses that race over jumps is a national industry that remains important to the Irish economy. How important will bear further examination over the next decade or so.

Cheltenham provides a TV audience, an accessible venue and can consistently throw up some of the soft ground on which Irish horses love to run. Even an Irish venue like Punchestown, with its gravelly April turf, cannot compete with that.

If Cheltenham did not exist, Irish steeplechasing would have to invent it.

CONCLUSION

So that's the story of the Irish at Cheltenham. Over the years their harvest from the festival has varied from ten winners to no winner at all.

Have they been successful? As measured against the standards of the nineteenth and twentieth-century equine power balance, yes. Yes, too, if you are to consider how Cheltenham helped some Irish rid themselves of the post-colonial hang-up that bewitched so many aspects of Irish culture until the 1960s.

But that was then and this is now. Winning one-third of the races won in a three-nation event does not represent a leadership position in a sport, a status which the Irish sometimes like to accord themselves in national hunt racing.

Maybe the years to come will see a more strident, better-financed and better-prepared set of horses accompany the (grossly overstated) 4,000 or so punters who make the annual pilgrimage to Cheltenham. Maybe Irish horses will begin to dominate in the manner that Irish jockeys already do.

Then we will see if the French, and increasingly the English, respond to their occasional victories with the sort of exuberance that they can produce in special moments, such as when Desert Orchid won the Gold Cup in 1989.

Maybe, someday, scribes of racegoing will write about the English and their relationship with Cheltenham. They might even do so with the sense of whimsical condescension that we frequently saw in English newspapers in the past when they wrote about the Irish and their celebration of victory.

Take this piece from the *Horseman's Year* of 1947–48, and substitute the word 'English' for Irish, and see what you make of it:

Some of the most distinguished Irish steeplechasers have been reared and schooled under conditions that an English stableman might describe as 'not 'alf rough', though the hovels that we might read of in the old books and magazines are a trifle highly coloured.

The Irish farmer who had 'a good harse'—and those fellows always knew—saw that he was as well 'done' as the members of his own family. As a foundation he had the magnificent limestone pastures, and there are plenty of corn and oats grown on those same pastures. If a little rain came through the stable roof, well, it helped to make the horse hardy—well he'll have t' run in the rain sometimes, won't he—and if there was more litter about the yard than the discipline of a good stable allows: Clane that up boy, when y'have toime. If the boy seldom had hygienic time, it did not matter a great deal.

This was what they were writing when Cottage Rake was being loaded on to the plane at Shannon to travel to Cheltenham.

Maybe the next book will be about Cheltenham and the English.

ENDPIECE

Ata dano sechtmonail i corus rig; i domnach do ol chorma,
ar ni flaith techte nad ingella laith as cach ndomnach;
luan do breithemnacht, do choccertad tuath; mairt oic
fidchill; cetain do deicsiu milchoin oic tofunn; taradain do
lanamnas; ain diden do rethaib ech; satharn do brethaib.

Sunday is for drinking ale; Monday for legal business,
for the adjudication between tuath; Tuesday for chess;
Wednesday for seeing greyhounds coursing; Thursday
for marital intercourse; Friday for horse racing; Saturday
for judgments.

Week in the life of an ancient Irish king, as translated by
T. F. BARRINGTON from the *Crith Gablach*, A.D. 700

INDEX